EDUCATIONAL RESOURCE CENTER
COLLEGE OF EDUCATION & HUMAN SERVICES
WRIGHT STATE UNIVERSITY

WRIGHT

UNIVERSITY LIBRARIES

D1470011

A Guide to
Practicum
and Internship
for School Counselors-in-Training

EDUCATIONAL RESOURCE CENTER
COLLEGE OF EDUCATION & HUMAN SERVICES
WRIGHT STATE UNIVERSITY

A Guide to
Practicum
and Internship
for School Counselors-in-Training

JEANNINE R. STUDER
JOEL F. DIAMBRA

EDITORS

Routledge
Taylor & Francis Group
New York   London

Routledge
Taylor & Francis Group
270 Madison Avenue
New York, NY 10016

Routledge
Taylor & Francis Group
27 Church Road
Hove, East Sussex BN3 2FA

© 2010 by Taylor and Francis Group, LLC
Routledge is an imprint of Taylor & Francis Group, an Informa business

Printed in the United States of America on acid-free paper
10 9 8 7 6 5 4 3 2 1

International Standard Book Number: 978-0-415-99747-8 (Paperback)

For permission to photocopy or use material electronically from this work, please access www.copyright.com (http://www.copyright.com/) or contact the Copyright Clearance Center, Inc. (CCC), 222 Rosewood Drive, Danvers, MA 01923, 978-750-8400. CCC is a not-for-profit organization that provides licenses and registration for a variety of users. For organizations that have been granted a photocopy license by the CCC, a separate system of payment has been arranged.

Trademark Notice: Product or corporate names may be trademarks or registered trademarks, and are used only for identification and explanation without intent to infringe.

Library of Congress Cataloging-in-Publication Data

Studer, Jeannine R.
    A guide to practicum and internship for school counselors-in-training / Jeannine R. Studer and Joel F. Diambra.
        p. cm.
    Includes bibliographical references and index.
    ISBN 978-0-415-99747-8 (pbk. : alk. paper)
    1. Educational counseling. 2. Student counselors--Training of. 3. Internship programs. I. Diambra, Joel F. II. Title.

LB1027.5.S85315 2010
371.4071'55--dc22   2009036283

**Visit the Taylor & Francis Web site at
http://www.taylorandfrancis.com**

**and the Routledge Web site at
http://www.routledgementalhealth.com**

This book is dedicated to our former students who trained under us, our graduates who have dedicated their careers to helping school-aged youth, and our future students who will carry on the tradition of the school counseling profession.

Contents

Preface   xv

About the Editors   xix

About the Contributors   xxi

SECTION I   THE PRACTICUM AND INTERNSHIP JOURNEY

1. Getting Started   3

   Jeannine R. Studer
   Joel F. Diambra

   What Is Meant by a Counselor Identity?   3
   What Is Meant by the Clinical Experiences?   4
   What Is the Difference Between Practicum and Internship?   4
   What Are Direct and Indirect Hours?   5
   What Is Meant by Supervision?   6
   What Happens in Supervision?   8
   What Materials Are Needed?   8
      Taping Equipment   8
      Consent Form and Professional Disclosure Statement   10
   How Do I Choose a School Site for Supervision?   10
   How Do I Choose a Site Supervisor?   11
   Conclusion   13
   Web Sites   13
   References   13

2. Understanding the School Culture   15

   Amy Kroninger
   Betty Anne Domm
   Mary L. (Mimi) Webster
   Anne E. Troutman

   The School Counselor's Role in Discipline   16
   Safe School Initiatives: Harassment, Intimidation, and Bullying   16
   No Child Left Behind and Implications for School Counselors   16
   School Improvement Plans   17
   School Counselors' Division of Responsibilities   17

Negotiating Responsibilities, Duties, and Tasks 18
Communication to Stakeholders 18
Testing 19
Special Education 19
Teaching Versus No Teaching Experience 20
Collaborative Relationship Building 20
The School Board 20
School Administrators 21
Teachers 22
Students 23
Parents/Guardians 24
Interaction with Other Counseling Professionals 26
Other School-Related Personnel 26
Conclusion 28
Web Sites 28
References 28

3. Popular Counseling Theories Used by School Counselors 31

   Cynthia Crawford

Contextual Aspects of Schools 31
Person-Centered Counseling 32
Reality Therapy or Choice Theory 33
Cognitive Behavioral Approaches 35
Solution-Focused Brief Counseling 36
Narrative Therapy 37
Creative Counseling Approaches 38
Art Therapy 39
Play Therapy 40
Music in a Counseling Setting 41
Conclusion 41
Web Sites 42
Person-Centered Counseling 42
Reality Therapy 42
Cognitive Behavioral Approaches 42
Solution-Focused Brief Therapy 42
Narrative Therapy 43
Using Art in Counseling 43
Play Therapy 43
Music Therapy 43
References 43

4. Overview of Supervision 47

   Jeannine R. Studer
   Joel F. Diambra

Making the Initial Contact 47
Dress 47
Absences, Tardiness, and Attendance 48
School Policies and Procedures 49

Introducing Yourself to the Students, Staff, and Parents   49
Self-Reflection of Readiness for Supervision   52
    Goal Setting   53
    Personal Safety Plan   56
    Taking Care of Yourself as a Professional   56
The Use of Technology in Counseling and Supervision   58
Conclusion   59
Web Site   59
References   59

5. A Developmental Passage: Models of Supervision   61

    Kristi A. Gibbs
    Virginia A. Magnus

Supervision Roles   61
    Developmental Models   62
    Social Role Models   65
    School Counseling Supervision Models   67
Group Advisement: Planning, Coordination, and Evaluation   67
Supervisory Relationship and Supervision Challenges   68
    Working Alliance   69
    Individual Differences   69
    Evaluation   69
    Other Challenges   70
Conclusion   73
References   73

SECTION II   THE AMERICAN SCHOOL COUNSELOR ASSOCIATION (ASCA)
NATIONAL MODEL AS A STRUCTURE FOR UNDERSTANDING THE ROLE
OF THE PROFESSIONAL SCHOOL COUNSELOR

6. The American School Counselor Association (ASCA) National Model and Components as
   a Supervisory Guide   79

    Jeannine R. Studer
    Joel F. Diambra

A Brief Historical Overview of the Counseling Profession   79
    Summary of a CDSC Program   81
The Professional School Counselor Standards: School Counselor Competencies   83
Recommended Percentage of Time Performing School Counseling Activities   91
Conclusion   93
References   93

7. The Foundation Component   95

    Caroline A. Baker
    Sibyl Camille Cato

Personal and Professional Values   96
Developing a Philosophy of School Counseling   98
What Is a Mission Statement?   100

Standards and Competencies in a CDSC Program   100
Conclusion   105
References   105

8. The Management System Component   107

        Jeannine R. Studer
        Joel F. Diambra
        John R. Gambrell, Jr.

The School Counselor's Office   107
School Organizational Charts   108
Management Agreements, Calendars and Time Management, Data, Needs
Assessments, and Schedules   110
    Management Agreements   110
    Calendars and Time Management   111
    Use of Data and Needs Assessment   112
    Needs Assessments   114
Public Relations   115
    Action Plans   116
Conclusion   117
Web Sites   118
References   118

9. The Delivery System Component   119

        Jeannine R. Studer
        Joel F. Diambra

Guidance Curriculum   119
    Developing a Lesson Plan   119
    Large Group or Classroom Management   120
    Study Skills Strategies   123
Individual Student Planning   125
    Appraisal   125
    Advisement   126
    Placement and Follow-Up   126
Responsive Services   127
    Small Group and Individual Counseling   127
    Crisis Counseling   127
    Peer Facilitation Programs   128
System Support   129
    Professional Development   129
    Consultation and Teamwork   130
Conclusion   131
Web Sites   131
References   131

10. The Accountability Component and the School Counselor-in-Training   133

        Aaron H. Oberman

Types of Data   134
Counseling Assessment Techniques   134

Pre- and Posttest   135
Surveys   136
Retrospective Assessment   137
Experimental Action Research   139
MEASURE   140
Counselor Performance Assessment Techniques   140
Peer Assessment   140
Student Assessment   141
Self-Assessment   141
Portfolio   142
Developing an Assessment Instrument to Measure Effectiveness   143
Conclusion   145
Web Site   145
References   145

11. Applying the American School Counselor Association (ASCA) Ethical Standards   147

    Melinda M. Gibbons
    Shawn L. Spurgeon

Ethical Principles   147
Ethical Decision-Making Models   148
Identify the Problem   149
Apply the ASCA Ethical Standards   149
Determine the Nature and Dimensions of the Dilemma   149
Generate Potential Courses of Action   150
Consider the Potential Consequences of All Options and Determine a Course of Action   150
Evaluate the Selected Course of Action   150
Implement the Course of Action   150
The ASCA Ethical Standards   151
Responsibilities to Students   151
Responsibilities to Parents/Guardians   153
Responsibilities to Colleagues and Professional Associates   154
Responsibilities to School and Community   154
Responsibilities to Self   156
Responsibilities to Profession   156
Conclusion   156
Web Sites   157
References   157

SECTION III   GUIDELINES FOR WORKING WITH SPECIAL POPULATIONS

12. Understanding Differences in the Schools   161

    Jolie Ziomek-Daigle
    Michael Jay Manalo

Introduction   161
Assessment of School Counselor-in-Training Awareness, Knowledge, and Skills   161
Assessment of School Site and Developing a School Profile   165
Culturally and Ethnically Diverse Students   165

Students With Special Needs   167
Students Who Are Gifted   168
Students Who Are Lesbian, Gay, Bisexual, Transgender, and Queer   172
   Legal Implications of Working (or Not Working) With LGBTQ Students   173
Conclusion   175
Web Sites   175
   Multicultural Differences   175
   Students With Special Needs   175
   Students Who Are Gifted   176
   Students Who Are Gay, Lesbian, Bisexual, Transgender, and Queer   176
References   176

13. Developmental Issues of Students   179

       Robin Wilbourn Lee
       Jennifer Jordan
       Lydia Turner Archibald
       Angela Cahill

Developmental Themes and Concepts   179
   Nature Versus Nurture   179
   Continuity Versus Discontinuity   179
   Universal Versus Context Specific   180
   Normative Influences   180
Theories of Development   180
   Psychodynamic Theory   180
   Learning Theory   185
   Cognitive Theories   187
   Systems Theories   188
   Moral Development   190
Basic Forces in Human Development   190
Elementary School-Aged Children and Developmental Issues (Grades K–5)   191
   Biological Development   191
   Childhood Obesity   191
   Asthma   192
   Autism   192
   Attention-Deficit Hyperactivity Disorder (ADHD)   192
   Cognitive Development   193
   Psychosocial Development   194
Adolescents and Developmental Issues (Grades 6–12)   195
   Biological Development   195
   Cognitive Development   196
   Psychosocial Development   199
Conclusion   201
References   201

SECTION IV   COMPLETING THE CLINICAL EXPERIENCES

14. Transitioning Forward   205

    Michael Bundy

    Practicum/Internship Closure   205
        Terminating Relationships With Students   205
        Terminating With Colleagues   208
        Terminating With Administrators   208
    Self-Assessment   209
        Self-Assessment of School Counselor Knowledge   210
        Self-Assessment of School Counselor Skills   212
        Self-Assessment of School Counselor Attitudes and Values   213
    Application Process   214
        Searching and Applying for Job Openings   215
        Preparing for an Interview   217
        The Interview   218
    Professional Credentials   218
        Qualifications Vary by State   219
        The Praxis II   219
        Continuing Education Requirements   219
        National Credentials   219
        Comparison of NCC/NCSC and NBPTS   221
    Membership in Professional Organizations   222
    Conclusion   223
    Web Sites   223
    References   224

Index   225

Preface

Since the inception of the school counseling profession, the role of the school counselor has been a source of confusion among parents, students, teachers, administrators, and even school counselors themselves. Although various school counseling models and role descriptions have been proposed throughout its brief history, it was not until the American School Counselor Association (ASCA) took a vigorous stance by developing the ASCA National Standards and then the ASCA National Model® that school counselors had a template to build a program that harmonized with the philosophy and beliefs of their professional organization. This development served as a catalyst, turning the focus from the school counselor as a service provider in a pupil personnel structure to that of a leader in a comprehensive, developmental school counseling program. In line with this change was an active campaign to standardize the title from that of "guidance counselor" to "professional school counselor." In fact, some states have even mandated that this title modification be used to support these transformations. These endeavors have been instrumental in assisting school counselors provide tasks that are more reflective of our education and training, rather than engaging in quasi-administrative or clerical activities.

As the school counseling profession undergoes a renewal in perspective as it enters a world of change, you as a school counselor-in-training are instrumental in clarifying this new era of school counseling. With your newly acquired skills and knowledge, you will be an influential voice for communicating our role, building on the foundations established by our predecessors, and acting as a change agent who more directly contributes to student growth.

This text is designed for the school counselor-in-training entering the clinical experiences of practicum and internship. These are pivotal field-based opportunities in which you will be supervised under the vigilant eyes of a school site counselor supervisor and program supervisor. We encourage you to take advantage of the supervision you receive, as this will probably be the last opportunity you will have to undertake new activities, self-reflect, and obtain feedback on your skills by members of the school counseling profession. When you transition into the profession, an individual with an administrative background—and with limited understanding of clinical skills such as group and individual counseling—will most likely be performing your evaluation.

This text is divided into four sections designed to help you negotiate your way through the clinical experiences and into the role of a professional school counselor. The chapters contain hypothetical situations, activities, case studies, and worksheets that are designed to facilitate your understanding of the profession and your fit into the profession.

Section I, "The Practicum and Internship Journey," is divided into five chapters. Chapter 1, titled "Getting Started," includes a practical view of the clinical experiences of practicum and internship, professional counseling organizations, what to expect of supervision, materials that will be needed for supervision, factors to consider in working with a site supervisor, and practical activities that are designed for you to think about your personal identity in the profession.

Practicing professional school counselors at various grade levels authored Chapter 2, "Understanding the School Culture." The authors of this chapter include essential topics that helped them gain a basic understanding of how the educational system is structured, first while they were in their clinical experiences, and then later as school counselors. Educational personnel roles, school board structure, federal and state initiatives, grant-based programs, and various divisions of responsibility among school counseling programs are described. After you have had an opportunity to get a basic appreciation for school-related concepts, your attention is then turned to a review of theories most frequently used by school counselors.

Chapter 3, "Popular Counseling Theories Used by School Counselors," provides a summarization of the more widespread approaches for counseling students in schools. Although you have probably already had a class in counseling theories, clinical school counseling students often express a need to review some of the more popular theories that are used in working with children and adolescents. This need becomes particularly relevant when the clinical experiences require application of theory to actual counselees with real concerns. In addition, creative counseling strategies such as art, play, and music that are used to engage students are discussed in this chapter as additional considerations for working with school-aged youth.

Chapter 4, "Overview of Supervision," describes rudimentary initial considerations such as making an initial contact with your school site supervisor, appropriate dress, introducing yourself to stakeholders within the confines of the school policies, and considerations for making a contribution to the school site and the profession. Furthermore, thought to self-care and thoughtfulness toward a personal safety plan are described. As you are apprised of the logistics surrounding supervision, your next step is to have an awareness of how supervision works.

The information in Chapter 5, "A Developmental Passage: Models of Supervision," provides insight into developmental models of supervision with examples of supervisor expectations and expectations of your role as a supervisee. In this chapter you will read about some of the more typical processes, feelings, and stages to which you will be likely able to relate. In addition, supervision does not always go in a smooth progression as there are various challenges that may impair the process. As a student training for the school counseling profession (and later on, when you are an experienced member of the profession), an awareness of these issues can assist in preparation for supervision.

Section II, "The American School Counselor Association (ASCA) National Model as a Structure for Understanding the Role of the Professional School Counselor," contains six chapters that are written to assist you in understanding how the tasks you will be performing at your school site correlate to the essential activities within a comprehensive, developmental program. Five of these chapters are devoted to a specific component of the National Model, with a final chapter on the ASCA Ethical Standards, an integral factor within each of these components.

Chapter 6, "The American School Counselor Association (ASCA) National Model and Components as a Supervisory Guide," summarizes the ASCA National Model and the school counselor's role in leading a comprehensive, developmental program. Although it is likely that you have already been introduced to the ASCA National Model, this chapter will guide you through school counselor tasks with a developmental focus that you may wish to include in your supervision contract.

Chapter 7, "The Foundation Component," provides exercises and activities designed to start you thinking about your beliefs in regard to school counseling as a base for developing a personal philosophy of school counseling, and understanding how your beliefs fit into the vision, mission, goals, and objectives of the school system.

Chapter 8, "The Management System Component," contains practical suggestions for administering school counseling tasks. Considerations such as the school counselor office arrangement and space, sharing data with stakeholders, managing time, charting tasks on calendars, documenting time on tasks, the school organizational structure, and finally publicizing the school counseling program are highlighted in this chapter.

Chapter 9, "The Delivery System Component," reviews the elements of the guidance curriculum, individual student planning, responsive services, and systemic support. Specific techniques and exercises are provided that will be beneficial to you personally, as well as those that you can use with students in grades pre-K–12.

An understanding of accountability is found in Chapter 10, "The Accountability Component and the School Counselor-in-Training." This chapter includes a discussion of program evaluation, specific counseling assessment techniques, a summary of the MEASURE program, and counselor performance assessment strategies.

Central to the components within the ASCA National Model are ethical standards, and Chapter 11, "Applying the American School Counselor Association (ASCA) Ethical Standards," provides a review of the principles of counseling ethics and a model for making ethical decisions. In addition, the ethical responsibilities to various stakeholders with specific scenarios for applying the ethical standards are outlined.

Section III, "Guidelines for Working with Special Populations," includes two chapters that are written to assist with your understanding of unique student needs in the school setting. School counselors have a responsibility to work with *all* students in a school setting, yet too often counselors have not received the training or education to work with students with specific needs.

Therefore, Chapter 12, "Understanding Differences in the Schools," contains information related to working with different groups of school-aged youth. A self-assessment of awareness, knowledge, and skills in relation to working with diverse populations, and suggestions for services in which you can gain experience while in your training program are summarized. Finally, an overview of the knowledge and skills surrounding ethnic and cultural differences, special needs, giftedness, and sexual orientation is included in this chapter.

Chapter 13, "Developmental Issues of Students," provides school counseling students with a summarization of the cognitive, physical, affective, and behavioral issues of students of various grade levels. Furthermore, some of the more prevalent concerns that school-aged youth encounter at various life stages are highlighted for your consideration as you work with youth in schools.

The final section, "Completing the Clinical Experiences," includes the final chapter, "Transitioning Forward." As you terminate your internship experiences, you will no doubt have mixed feelings of sadness and anticipation. Feelings of sorrow are evident when you have connected with students and encouraging mentors while learning the role of the school counselor, and you are leaving these individuals behind as you transition to the next step. Yet, optimism and excitement quickly replace these feelings as you step into your first position as a highly trained professional school counselor. Useful strategies for terminating relationships with the individuals with whom you worked as well as your support system are included in Chapter 14, as are considerations for taking the next step in your professional journey as you apply for a position as a professional school counselor.

The information provided in this text is designed to supplement your practical experiences while you are learning about the role of the professional school counselor in a comprehensive, developmental school counseling program. Knowing the history of this profession enables you to avoid the mistakes of those who paved the path before you and carry on the future of this profession by continuing the work that was begun by our predecessors. This profession has made strides in many areas, is still clarifying issues that have plagued previous generations of school counselors, and continues to predict and adapt to the needs of our society. You are instrumental in continuing these efforts so that the academic, career, and personal needs of our school-aged youth will be realized. Good luck to you on this journey.

About the Editors

Jeannine R. Studer, EdD, was previously a high school counselor in Sandusky, Ohio, as well as an assistant/associate professor at Heidelberg University in Tiffin, Ohio, and California State University, Stanislaus. She is presently a professor of counselor education and the School Counseling Program coordinator at the University of Tennessee. Dr. Studer has made numerous presentations at the regional, state, and national levels. In addition, she has written numerous articles and has two published texts on school counseling issues.

Joel F. Diambra, EdD, LPC-MHSP, NCC, previously coordinated a community counseling program from Virginia Commonwealth University where he worked directly with individuals and families, and consulted with schools and community agencies. He is presently the Counselor Education PhD Program coordinator at the University of Tennessee. Dr. Diambra presents his research at various professional conferences at the local to international level and regularly publishes his scholarly work in professional refereed publications.

About the Contributors

Lydia Turner Archibald, MEd, recently graduated from Middle Tennessee State University with an MEd in school counseling. She previously worked at Coffee County Middle School, Tennessee, as the sixth-grade counselor. She is a member of the American School Counselor Association and Tennessee Counseling Association.

Caroline A. Baker, MS, NCC, earned her MS in school counseling from the University of Tennessee and worked as an elementary school counselor in Knoxville before returning to school for her PhD in counselor education. Her current research interests focus on graduate students' doctoral program experiences, immigrant students' school counseling needs, and spirituality (among other cultural topics) in counseling.

Michael Bundy, PhD, NCC, CPC, is assistant professor in the School Counseling Program at Carson-Newman College where he is responsible for the internship program. Previously, he was an elementary school counselor for more than 20 years in Oak Ridge, Tennessee, where he also served as site supervisor for many interns and practicum students. In addition, he was an adjunct instructor of school counseling practicum and internship at the University of Tennessee. Dr. Bundy has numerous publications and has conducted presentations on a variety of issues related to working with children and young people.

Angela Cahill will receive her master's of education in May 2010. She received her bachelor of arts in psychology with university honors from the University of Memphis in December 2006. She intends to practice as a school counselor in Tullahoma, Tennessee, working with students in ways that bring about positive change in the community in which she grew up.

Sibyl Camille Cato, PhD, earned her PhD in counselor education from the Ohio State University. She received her MEd in school counseling from the University of Arizona and has worked as a middle school counselor for Tucson Unified School District in Tucson, Arizona.

Cynthia Crawford, PhD, LPC, NCC, NCSC, served as a school psychologist in the North Georgia counties of Catoosa and Fannin. She then worked as an elementary school counselor in the metropolitan Atlanta area and later in Knoxville, Tennessee. She is presently assistant professor in the School of Education, Counselor Education Division, at The Citadel: The Military College of South Carolina. Dr. Crawford frequently makes presentations at local, state, and national levels.

Betty Anne Domm, MS, EdS, has been a middle school counselor for 23 years. Prior to being a counselor, she taught in an elementary school. Counseling is both her vocation and her avocation. She views mentoring new counselors as a way of continuing her love of the profession after she is no longer a full-time counselor.

John R. (Randy) Gambrell, Jr., EdS, is a former school counselor and now serves as administrator at Fannin County High School in Blue Ridge, Georgia. Randy is a *Mayberry R.F.D.* connoisseur and memorabilia collector of the TV series and has presented "Mayberry: Values for Today's Students" at various counseling conferences. Gambrell, his wife, Sherry, and kitty cat CG have their home in Knoxville, Tennessee.

Melinda M. Gibbons, PhD, NCC, is currently an assistant professor of counselor education at the University of Tennessee. Before earning her doctorate in counseling and counselor education from the University of North Carolina at Greensboro, she worked as a school counselor, primarily at the high school level. Dr. Gibbon's research interests include prospective first-generation college students, school counseling best practices, and career development.

Kristi A. Gibbs, PhD, LPC, RPT-S, previously worked as a professional counselor in both community and school settings. She has provided clinical supervision for counselors-in-training both on site and as a university supervisor. Dr. Gibbs has also supervised post-master's interns pursuing licensure or specialized training in play therapy. She is presently the Counselor Education Unit coordinator at the University of Tennessee at Chattanooga. Dr. Gibbs has presented at regional, state, and national levels. She has published one additional book chapter on supervision.

Jennifer Jordan, PhD, LPC, NCC, specializes in counseling skill development, supervision, and overseeing on-site practicum experiences. Dr. Jordan's interests include evaluating and determining appropriate intervention strategies for children and adolescents with a variety of problems utilizing play therapy and other creative techniques.

Amy Kroninger, MS, is a school counselor for grades 3–5 at a school of over 1,000 students in Knoxville, Tennessee. She is also on the advisory board for elementary school counselors in Knox County Schools. She has served as a site supervisor for practicum and internship students and is actively involved in the Smoky Mountain Counseling Association (SMCA), the local chapter of the Tennessee Counseling Association, in which she served as president.

Robin Wilbourn Lee, PhD, LPC, received her doctoral degree in counselor education and supervision from Mississippi State University. Her interests include counseling skills training, supervision, ethics, sexual assault, and domestic violence. Dr. Lee has made numerous presentations at the local, regional, state, and national levels. She has served in leadership roles in the Association for Counselor Education and Supervision, the Southern Association for Counselor Education and Supervision, the Tennessee Counseling Association, and the Tennessee Licensed Professional Counselors Association.

Virginia A. Magnus, PhD, LPC, CSC, is the school counseling coordinator at the University of Tennessee–Chattanooga. She was previously a school counselor and substance abuse counselor. Dr. Magnus presents at various professional conferences at the local, regional, state, and national levels. She is currently conducting research at a magnet middle school.

Michael Jay Manalo, MEd, NCC, is a National Certified Counselor and holds a school counseling certificate in the state of Georgia. He earned his MEd in professional school counseling from the University of Georgia and is currently a doctoral student in the counseling psychology program. His school clinical experience has included work with pre-K, elementary, and middle school students as well as supervision of school counseling students. Manalo's doctoral research is an examination of the counseling needs of Hmong students.

Aaron H. Oberman, PhD, NCC, graduated with his doctorate from the University of Tennessee, Knoxville. He is presently assistant professor and coordinator of school counseling placements at

The Citadel. Dr. Oberman's research interests include supervision, school counselor accountability, job satisfaction, and career counseling.

Shawn L. Spurgeon, PhD, teaches in the Mental Health Counseling program at The University of Tennessee at Knoxville, focusing on counseling skills techniques, formal measurement, theory and practice, and psychopathology. He has made numerous state, regional, and national presentations. Dr. Spurgeon's current research interests include African American male development over the life span and counselor identity development.

Anne E. Troutman, EdS, has been a school counselor in Knox County, Tennessee, for 15 years. She worked at Austin-East and Karns High Schools and currently serves as the chairperson for the School Counseling Department at Hardin Valley Academy. Her professional interests include career and technical education and working with at-risk students.

Mary L. (Mimi) Webster, MS, NCC, has taught special education and second grade, but for the past 22 years she has been an elementary school counselor. She has worked in suburban and inner-city settings. Webster loves having a mix of teaching, counseling, consulting, and coordinating responsibilities and especially enjoys working with primary-aged children. She also enjoys supervising graduate interns in her school.

Jolie Ziomek-Daigle, PhD, LPC, RPT-S, worked for 7 years as a school counselor in New Orleans Public Schools prior to her faculty position at the University of Georgia. She also had a part-time private practice where she counseled children, adolescents, and families. Her research interests include the clinical development of school counselor trainees; the school counselor's role in dropout prevention; and issues of retention and remediation in counselor education. She has published several book chapters and journal articles in these research areas. Some have been featured in the *Journal of Counseling and Development* and the *Professional School Counselor.*

SECTION I:

THE PRACTICUM AND INTERNSHIP JOURNEY

Getting Started

Jeannine R. Studer
Joel F. Diambra

The purpose of this chapter is to:

* Provide an understanding of the school counseling practicum and internship experiences
* Describe clinical supervision
* Allow you to self-reflect on reasons for entering the profession

This chapter is written to assist you in understanding the *what* of the clinical experiences. In other words, as you read this chapter you will hopefully have a better understanding of what the clinical experiences are, what the expectations are, and what factors need to be considered during the supervisory process. You have undoubtedly already taken several courses that have provided you with a perspective of the historical developments that have impacted the professional school counselor's role and how the American School Counselor Association (ASCA) has shaped policy to address societal concerns. If you have not taken the time to reflect on your reasons for entering this profession prior to now, take time to do so. Have you had certain experiences that have led you to this career? Or are there other factors that have influenced this decision?

As members of the school counseling profession, we meet with prospective school counseling students, and when we inquire as to the reasons they are interested in this profession, no answer is more distasteful to hear than, "I want to have time off in the summer and I know I do not want to teach, so I think this would be a good alternative." If this is one of your reasons for your career decision, perhaps you need to think in terms of whether this is the best profession for you and for those with whom you will be working. The professional school requires skill, dedication, and energy, and as you enter the clinical experiences, you are provided with an extraordinary opportunity to scrutinize your readiness for this profession.

As you begin your clinical training you will probably have conflicting feelings and thoughts. Not only will you be feeling a sense of excitement about putting the textbook concepts into practice, you will also probably be feeling anxious about beginning these new experiences. The school counseling program in which you are enrolled will provide you with specific details regarding the program requirements and policies for these experiences in a program handbook. However, this chapter will provide you with additional ideas and information about the clinical experiences, school counselor identity, and your responsibilities as a school counselor-in-training.

What Is Meant by a Counselor Identity?

The formation of a professional identity is a process that starts at the beginning of training and continues throughout one's professional career (Brott & Myers, 1999). As you have already learned from your initial classes in the school counseling curriculum, one of the major conflicts surrounding school counselors is reconciling the preparation received in the program and the realities of the work environment (Brott & Myers, 1999). Personal decisions about one's fit with the profession are often a result of performing tasks requested by the principal and other decision makers. These tasks influence the formulation of a professional identity. Unfortunately, it is not surprising that school counselors define their identity differently due to the miscellaneous tasks they choose to perform. A major goal of the ASCA is to have all professional school counselors speak with one voice regarding the definition of school counseling and to perform tasks that are consistent with the mission of the profession.

Today's professional school counselors evolved from what were formerly known as guidance counselors. These guidance counselors were trained under a traditional, reactive approach with an emphasis on services rather than student outcomes. Today, due to initiatives such as the Transforming School Counseling Initiative (TSCI) and the ASCA National Model®, the emphasis is on training school counselors as leaders of a comprehensive, developmental school counseling (CDSC) program based on measurable student outcomes.

An unfortunate truth, despite the efforts of the ASCA and many state departments of education, is that many school counseling programs have still not made the shift to a developmental program, for reasons such as too few resources, external barriers, and lack of administrative support to make the transition to one that reflects this current trend (Lambie & Williamson, 2004). In addition, there is debate as to whether the school counselor is a practitioner responsible for the mental health of students, or whether the school counselor is an educator with the responsibility of assisting teachers and other educators in the learning process. However, as future school counselors advocate for their profession through the use of collecting and analyzing meaningful data, support for a professional school counselor identity will eventually be an outcome. The application of knowledge to the real world begins through the clinical experiences.

What Is Meant by the Clinical Experiences?

The Council for Accreditation of Counseling and Related Educational Programs (CACREP) was created to standardize counselor education programs, including the clinical experiences. These experiences include the practicum and internship.

Not all school counselor programs are CACREP-accredited. At the time of this writing, there were 198 school counseling programs nationwide accredited by this organization (CACREP, 2009). Programs that do not have this accreditation follow other standards such as those mandated by their state board of education. Other non-CACREP programs may follow the recommendations of this agency, could combine these courses into one clinical opportunity, or in some cases may even use different terms such as *fieldwork*. Be certain that you are aware of the program requirements and terminology in which you are enrolled.

What Is the Difference Between Practicum and Internship?

The *practicum* provides an opportunity for counselors-in-training to work with pre-K–12 students in a school for the express purpose of improving counseling skills. For programs that are CACREP-accredited, the student will complete a minimum of 100 clock hours that include at least 40 hours of direct service in individual counseling and group experiences. The remaining 60 or more hours are considered to be indirect hours.

The *internship* is taken after the completion of the practicum. The purpose of this experience is to become familiar with a variety of professional tasks that are a normal part of the professional school counselor's regular responsibilities. Internship includes direct service to students, but it expands the learning experience to the whole of the professional school counselor job activities. CACREP-accredited programs require students to complete a minimum of 600 clock hours. Within the 600 hours, students complete at least 240 hours of direct service. As in the practicum, the remaining hours are considered indirect.

What Are Direct and Indirect Hours?

Students are often confused about the differences between direct and indirect service hours. How these hours are defined may vary from program to program, but generally *direct hours* refer to the activities in which the counselors-in-training have face-to-face contact with others such as in individual or group counseling. Or, you can think of direct service as eye-to-eye and ear-to-ear (such as phone consultations) contact with students and their families. Consulting with teachers, administrators, or community representatives in regard to a specific student would be considered direct service. *Indirect hours* are generally activities such as keeping records, meetings, making referrals, planning guidance lessons, or tasks that are not face-to-face with an individual or group. Examples of indirect hours may also include orientation to the school, reviewing procedures and policies, or general planning time—activities that cannot be directly linked to any one student or group of students.

ACTIVITY 1.1

From the following list, identify those professional school counselor practicum and internship tasks, responsibilities, or activities you consider to be indirect or direct. Mark those you think are indirect with an *I* and direct with a *D*.

	Planning the schoolwide academic calendar for the year		Making phone calls to identify an appropriate community referral for a student who is learning to speak English as a second language
	Reviewing career assessment results and postsecondary school plans with a student in your office		Chatting with a student in the hall between classes
	Conducting a parent workshop focused on study skill improvement		Eating lunch in the cafeteria surrounded by singing third graders
	Performing a puppet show to newly arrived first graders to help them transfer to your school		Facilitating a group for eight students whose parents recently divorced
	Accompanying a student and her parents to a nearby college to discuss scholarship offers		Composing thank-you letters to parents that shared their careers with the fifth-grade classes
	Assessing the academic performance of seventh graders across subjects for the previous year		Conducting a faculty meeting to share the results from a parent/student survey
	Meeting with your principal to evaluate your performance		Conducting a suicide assessment with a distraught ninth-grade boy
	Listening to a senior excitedly inform you of the colleges that have sent acceptance letters		Making copies of flyers for an upcoming new student orientation
	Monitoring detention hall		Calling a student's guardian grandparents to inform them that their granddaughter missed school again
	Entering grades into the database and analyzing results to determine player eligibility for athletic competition		Reviewing the school policy manual to determine if a moment of silence at a school function is permissible

What is it that makes some activities clear and others more ambiguous? Which of these activities do you feel are congruent with a comprehensive, developmental school counseling (CDSC) program?

You are not entering these experiences by yourself. During the practicum and internship you will be receiving supervision from both your program and school counselor supervisor at the school setting where you have been placed for the clinical experiences. These individuals will provide you with direction, assist in identifying tasks to accomplish, and give feedback and suggestions.

What Is Meant by Supervision?

According to CACREP standards, the supervisor at the school site must have at least 2 years of experience as a professional school counselor, with training in supervision. This person is often referred to as a *site supervisor*. You will also have a supervisor who is a faculty member, often referred to as a *program supervisor*, or in some cases you may be supervised by a doctoral student in a counselor education program who is being supervised by a counselor education faculty member. In this book, the students with whom you will be working will be referred to as *counselees* to avoid confusion between the student school counselors-in-training and the pre-K–12 student.

The site and program supervisors are experienced members of the counseling profession and their main priority is to create a trustful environment for you to learn the profession of counseling. In addition to supervising you, they need to be aware of the counseling needs of the counselees with whom you will be working (Lampropoulos, 2002; Lizzio, Stokes, & Wilson, 2005). At times, this is a task that requires the supervisor to be attentive of your needs as well as the counselees' needs. As an example, one of our counselors-in-training was assigned to a site supervisor who was well known for implementing many counseling groups and creating numerous activities that involved students. Our graduate student was placed with this experienced professional during the internship, but after several weeks our supervisee expressed frustration in not being able to work with counselees on her own. She explained that whenever a counselee came to see her, she was not allowed to work individually with the counselee, but instead had to notify her site supervisor, who in turn would work with the counselee while the counselor-in-training observed. When we spoke with the supervisor, she explained that she was concerned about the type of care the counselee was receiving and thought the counselee was not getting the same quality of care when she was not involved in the counseling process. The supervisor had difficulty allowing the supervisee to work independently, and even though she was an excellent counselor, our graduate student was not provided with the opportunity to work independently. Under the supervision of your site supervisor, you will be moving from a stance in which you need and desire more direction to one in which you are more autonomous. These changes are part of the supervisory developmental process that you will learn more about in Chapter 5.

During your practicum, you will meet with the program faculty supervisor or doctoral-level supervisor for an average of 1 hour each week either individually or in triadic supervision, and an additional 1.5 hours each week in which all the school counselors-in-training enrolled in the practicum will meet for group supervision. *Triadic supervision* refers to supervision in which two counselors-in-training meet with their supervisor. You will not have more than six students in your practicum class if your program follows CACREP standards.

In your internship class, there will be no more than 12 individuals, if CACREP standards are followed. Each counselor-in-training will meet an average of 1 hour each week for individual or triadic supervision with the on-site supervisor. The purpose of this supervisory experience is to listen to the counseling tapes and to discuss concerns, the counseling process, accomplishments, theoretical approach, and so forth. In addition, you will meet for an average of 1.5 hours each week of group supervision usually with the faculty supervisor. School counselors-in-training often wonder how supervision works. The questions in Activity 1.2 are designed for you to ask your site supervisor in order to get a better understanding of the expectations.

ACTIVITY 1.2

When you meet with your site supervisor, ask the following questions and write down the information for future reference.

1. When will we meet? _____
2. How often will we meet? _____
3. How long will we meet? _____
4. Where will we meet? _____
5. How will the meetings be structured and what do I need to bring? _____
6. Who else will be present when we meet? _____
7. What are some of the issues that we will discuss? _____
8. What are the procedures I need to follow when you are absent? _____
9. What is the dress code? _____
10. What is the school schedule? _____
11. What are the school policies and rules? _____
12. Who do I contact when I am ill? _____
13. Who do I contact if I am going to be late? _____
14. What contact information do I need? _____
15. What contact information do you need? _____
16. How will I be evaluated? _____

You will be asked to create a contract that outlines your personal and professional goals for each of the clinical experiences. This contract will be based on the course objectives, the site and program supervisors' requirements, and your own needs. A sample contract and guidelines for creating a contract is in Chapter 4.

Too often, students training for the school counseling profession treat the clinical courses as if they are voluntary experiences. Practicum and internship students are not volunteers because they have specific learning goals and objectives, receive supervision from both an on-site supervisor and a faculty supervisor, and are evaluated formally and regularly. Unfortunately, there are some occasions when counselors-in-training believe that since they are not being paid to work in the schools, they can attend the school site whenever they feel like it if they have other competing responsibilities. *You need to be aware that the practicum and internship experiences are not only a course requirement, but they are professional responsibilities, and are to be treated as if you were working in a professional career.* It is not only the site supervisor who relies on your attendance; students, teachers, administrators, and parents also depend upon you. Imagine what it would be like for a fifth grader who is anxiously waiting to continue counseling sessions with you, and you do not take the time to notify anyone at the school that you will not be attending. Or, think about the teacher who is planning to team-teach a guidance lesson with you and you do not put in an appearance. Your decision disappoints the fifth grader, disrupts the teacher's plans, and leaves an entire class ill-informed.

Your attitude, motivation, and willingness to learn at these sites can make a huge difference when you are seeking employment as a school counselor. It is not uncommon for employers to contact your supervisors, principal, and any other references at the schools with whom you have trained. In fact, you may be applying for full-time employment at the school where you were placed in practicum or internship.

In some cases, counselors-in-training receive payment for their services before matriculating from their school counseling program. For instance, when schools face a shortage of school counselors, it is sometimes necessary to hire an individual who has not yet finished with his or her school counseling program. In this situation, each state has certain criteria for working under these circumstances. Each state uses a different term such as *alternative, transitional,* or *interim school counselor license* for this arrangement, with various stipulations under which the school system is able to hire this individual. If you are interested in learning more about this type of license, check the Department of Education for the state in which you are interested for details.

What Happens in Supervision?

The practicum is designed to improve your counseling skills. You will be asked to audiotape, videotape, and/or transcribe counseling sessions with school-aged students. During weekly individual or triadic supervision sessions, you will be asked to review your tapes in order to discuss counseling techniques and theory, and to self-reflect while receiving feedback on your skills. Furthermore, it provides you with an opportunity to share case conceptualizations, receive feedback, have questions answered, and strategize future plans.

Some of the experiences that may be part of the supervision include

- Role-play
- Case study conceptualization
- Counseling technique demonstrations
- Listening to previously recorded counseling sessions
- Providing feedback to peers regarding taped sessions
- Discussing theory and techniques
- Sharing site concerns
- Brainstorming solutions to dilemmas encountered at the school

During group supervision you will have additional opportunities to learn about the profession with your peers who will be engaging in similar, yet unique school counseling experiences. These group experiences provide learning experiences that often center on real dilemmas and concerns in which different perspectives are discussed for working through various situations. Although direct learning occurs in group supervision, vicarious learning is more prevalent. A breadth of experiences are shared, reviewed, and thoughtfully considered, which provide greater insight from a broad perspective and help students see the bigger picture of the school counseling profession.

What Materials Are Needed?

Taping Equipment

Since audiotaping and/or videotaping is a requirement in most school counseling programs, you will need access to this equipment. If you do not have this equipment, first check with your college or university. If it does not have equipment available, ask at the school where you are conducting practicum or internship. Some schools will allow you to sign out this equipment during the academic term, but other sites may not have this equipment readily available. Be sure to check with your on-site and faculty supervisors to determine the proper format. Some supervisors require audiotaping while others mandate videotaping, and still others require both. More specifically, properly determine the desired or mandatory size and format of the audio- or videotape product. Audiotapes come in different sizes (macro and micro tapes) and can be created in digital or analog format. Videotapes come in standard and compact sizes (e.g., standard S-VHS, compact S-VHS-C cassettes). Videotaping can also be done in digital or analog format. Analog provides a more exact picture or sound; however, tape recorders and VCRs must be used to listen or to view these tapes. Digital formats are electronic media that are typically interpreted by computers to listen to or view these types of tapes (e.g., compact disk, Internet, cell phones). It is not critical that you know the differences between analog and digital format; however, the format depends on the equipment your supervisor uses to listen to or view the recordings. Be sure to check with all parties before choosing recording equipment, size, and format.

Because you will be taping counseling sessions, a private room will be needed to provide a quiet environment and ensure student confidentiality. In schools where space is a problem, school counselors-in-training are sometimes placed in a classroom that is vacant when the teacher is not teaching class or in other spaces that are less private. Using a teacher's classroom can jeopardize confidentiality, especially if the teacher needs access to the room while you are counseling students. If you have difficulty finding a secluded place for counseling, discuss this issue with your on-site supervisor.

Issues with Taping Counseling Sessions

During the clinical experiences, and the practicum class in particular, assessing your counseling skills is a primary focus. Videotaping and audiotaping have been key methods supervisors used to evaluate your skills. Yet, with increased concern for privacy and individual rights, these traditional methods are becoming more problematic. Administrators and parents may disapprove of this method due to Federal Education Rights and Privacy Act (FERPA) and Health Insurance Portability and Accountability Act (HIPAA) laws.

FERPA protects the privacy of student records and limits parental/guardian access to all student records, files, and documents maintained by school personnel. Record keeping permits school counselors to refresh memory and to increase counseling effectiveness by keeping personal notes about individual counseling sessions. However, any time notes are shared, they are no longer considered confidential. This is where confidentiality regarding taping and note taking becomes an issue; individual sessions are to be shared during supervision. HIPAA (Pub. L. 104-191) protects health information (including mental health) held by an educational institute from becoming education records unless a state law mandates differently. In other words, the HIPAA also provides protection for handwritten notes as long as the data remain private and helps the counselor recall information.

Since the counselee cannot be guaranteed confidentiality due to the need for the counselor-in-training to share information with his or her supervisor(s), parents/guardians need to be informed about the purpose of the counseling sessions and the importance of this activity for the counselor-in-training's education. Some institutions will only allow videotaping if the counselee's identity remains unknown, such as focusing the camera on the counselee's back. Erasing tapes on a regular schedule, such as at the end of the semester, can also maintain program integrity and assist with student anonymity. Check with your program supervisor regarding tape erasure protocol.

Some training institutions respond to the taping issue by providing on-site observation in which the program or site supervisor observes a live counseling session and provides feedback immediately following the session. This strategy may create other concerns such as the counselee's discomfort with the presence of another individual, the amount of time that is required, and counselors-in-training feeling not completely autonomous in conducting the counseling session. A consent form and professional disclosure statement are useful materials to communicate with parents, teachers, and administrators regarding the significance of the counseling requirement.

RELEASE FORM/PERMISSION TO TAPE

Hello. My name is _____, and I am a graduate student in the school counseling program at _____. Your son/daughter is participating in counseling interviews with me as I train to be a school counselor under the direction of the Counseling Department faculty at _____. These interviews will either be videotaped or audiotaped, and portions of the interview will be used for evaluation and/or supervision purposes only.

- Precautions will be taken to protect your child's identity.
- The taping will be used for supervision purposes only.
- After the student trainee and supervisor have met to critique the trainee's counseling skills, the tape will be erased.
- The tape/video recorder will be turned off at any time and/or any portion of the tape will be erased if requested.

If you are willing to give permission for your child to assist with this training, please sign below. If you have additional questions, you can contact my site supervisor at _____.

_____   _____
Parent/Guardian Signature   Date

_____   _____
Student Signature   Date

FIGURE 1.1   Release form/permission to tape.

Consent Form and Professional Disclosure Statement

Because you will be taping your counseling sessions with children and adolescents, you will need written permission from parents or guardians to tape their child during counseling sessions. Sometimes this creates a problem since parents/guardians may have difficulty with their child working with someone they do not know. A *consent form* explains the purpose of the counseling session with specifics about expectations. A *professional disclosure statement* describes who you are, your education, training qualifications, and how you will be supervised. When this information is provided to parents/guardians, they are usually more willing to provide consent. An example of a consent form is found in Figure 1.1, and an example of a professional disclosure statement is found in Chapter 4.

How Do I Choose a School Site for Supervision?

Location and proximity to home, the college or university, and school site are the most common motives for selecting a school site for the clinical experiences. Although these reasons are practical and understandable, they are not always the best considerations in making this choice. For instance, the potential supervisor may not have had training in supervision, may have a different philosophy regarding the school counselor's role, or may not have time to provide a quality supervisory experience. Furthermore, the school may have a homogeneous population of students that may not provide an opportunity to work with a diverse student body. You want to work with a supervisor in a school that will give you the best experience possible. To assist you with this decision, Activity 1.3 is designed to help you think about this process.

ACTIVITY 1.3

1. Which age or group of students would you be most interested in working with? Explain.

   _____

2. What age or group of students would you feel most uncomfortable working with? Write down those things that make you uncomfortable.

   _____

3. School counselors have the responsibility to work with all students, including those in special education and those who have been identified as "gifted." Identify the students with whom you feel you need additional knowledge and experiences.

   _____

How Do I Choose a Site Supervisor?

There are several methods of matching a supervisor with a counselor-in-training. Some institutions provide flexibility in allowing their students to select a supervisor based on reputation, school system, or other special characteristics. In these cases, the program placement coordinator will probably determine if this selection is appropriate before the assignment is made. It could be that the placement coordinator is aware of the strengths and weaknesses of area supervisors and may believe that a certain placement you desire may not be the best match for various reasons. For instance, one of the authors of this chapter was serving as a faculty supervisor for the practicum class, and when making a visit with a middle school site supervisor, the supervisor stated, "We teach what school counselors really need to know—not the stuff they teach at the university." This remark indicated that there was an absence of similar program goals as well as a lack of communication regarding site and academic program expectations. At the university, the benefits of a comprehensive, developmental approach to school counseling are taught, as opposed to the reactive, traditional model that many school counselors still implement. The latter was the type of program in which this particular supervisor was working. In another situation, a motivated practicum student who was excited about the opportunity to work with school-aged youth was placed with a site supervisor who showed little interest in her middle school students. The site supervisor would flippantly dismiss the practicum student's concerns about students by stating, "That's just the way they are, and we really don't have the time to help them." As a result of this experience, this practicum counselor-in-training left the experience disappointed and disillusioned with the profession. In postgraduation surveys conducted by training institutions for the purpose of evaluating program needs, many school counselor program graduates indicate that supervision was the most important aspect of their clinical experiences. Therefore, it is important that supervisors are chosen carefully.

Regardless of whether you are placed in a setting by your placement coordinator or you are choosing a supervisor, be certain that you have thought in terms of the specific supervisor characteristics that you feel may best meet your needs. Prior to beginning supervision, consider the list of questions found in Activity 1.4.

ACTIVITY 1.4

- What is the experience and training of the site supervisor? _____
- What are the grade level and ages of students with whom the supervisor works? _____
- Is equipment available for taping? _____
- What are the procedures to check out this equipment? _____
- Is there an office or room available to conduct individual or group counseling? ____
- What is the philosophy and mission of the school counseling program? _____
- Will the supervisor be available to meet for supervision at least one hour per week? ___
- What are the greatest student needs? _____
- What are the procedures to dismiss students from class for individual and/or group counseling? _____
- How receptive are parents/guardians to allowing their children to work with a practicum/intern student? _____
- Will there be opportunities to work with students representative of diverse ethnic, cultural, and gender groups? _____
- Will there be opportunities to work with students of different abilities? _____
- What is the administrator's view of counseling students in the schools? _____
- Does this individual have the time to supervise me? _____
- When does the supervisor expect me to be at the school? _____
- Will I have the opportunity to attend such events as in-service meetings or parent conferences? _____
- Will I need to make a safety plan? _____
- Will I be expected to stay after the school day is over? _____

The presence of a dual relationship is a fundamental consideration in selecting a supervisor. A *dual relationship* is one "that includes both professional and personal components" (Cotton & Tarvidas, 1998, p. 390). In fact, according to a recent study by Bodenhorn (2006), school counselors reported that dual relationships were one of the most common ethical dilemmas they have encountered. This type of conflicting relationship is more common than many practicum and internship students realize.

In the case of supervision, a dual relationship may be a supervisor whom you know in a different context, such as a friend, relative, or even a parent of your child's friend. Dual relationships could also be in relation to teachers, parents, administrators, or even if a counselor-in-training's spouse is employed in that school setting. In one situation, a difficult counselor-in-training was placed in an internship site without the placement coordinator knowing that this individual's spouse worked in the superintendent's office. The site supervisor was also unaware of this situation until the superintendent questioned the counselor-in-training's poor evaluation completed by the supervisor. The school site supervisor felt personally offended that her judgment was being questioned when the superintendent asked about the negative evaluation. There are numerous considerations in beginning the supervisory journey, and it is up to you to learn as much as you can about the expectations for this experience and to take opportunities that are available so that you can feel competent and successful when you are a fully licensed member of the profession.

Conclusion

You are starting your professional journey by working in a school as a counselor during your clinical experiences, often known as the practicum and internship. These experiences are not to be taken lightly as they are superb opportunities to get "hands-on" experience in a school counseling setting. Practicum and internship may also be the last time that you will receive formal feedback on your counseling skills because the building administrator is generally the person who supervises school counselors, and frequently this individual has no training in counseling skills and process. Therefore, it is important that your school and site supervisor are chosen wisely. This choice requires self-reflection and an understanding of both the potential supervisor's philosophy and the types of experiences that you desire for a comprehensive foundation of the school counseling profession.

Web Sites

- American Counseling Association (ACA), http://www.counseling.org/
  This Web site provides resources for counseling practitioners and students in addition to giving recent legislative information concerning the counseling profession. The salary calculator resource available from this organization provides a tool for determining salaries in various parts of the United States.

- American School Counselor Association (ASCA), http://www.schoolcounselor.org/
  This division of ACA focuses on the counseling specialty of school counseling. Numerous resources are available, as well as position papers and documents that provide timely information on numerous topics commonly impacting the profession and the stakeholders.

References

Bodenhorn, N. (2006). Exploratory study of common and challenging ethical dilemmas experienced by professional school counselors. *Professional School Counseling, 10,* 195–202.

Brott, P. E., & Myers, J. E. (1999). Development of professional school counselor identity: A grounded theory. *Professional School Counseling, 2,* 339–348.

Cottone, R. R., & Tarvydas, V.M. (1998). *Ethical and professional issues in counseling.* Upper Saddle River, NJ: Merrill.

Council for Accreditation of Counseling and Related Educational Programs (CACREP). (2009). *Directory of accredited programs.* Retrieved June 16, 2009, from http://www.cacrep.org/directory-cover-2-17-09.pdf

Lambie, G. W., & Williamson, L. L. (2004). The challenge to change from guidance counseling to professional school counseling: A historical proposition. *Professional School Counseling, 8,* 124–131.

Lampropoulos, G. K. (2002). A common factors view of counseling supervision process. *The Clinical Supervisor, 21,* 77–94.

Lizzio, A., Stokes, L., & Wilson, K. (2005). Approaches to learning in professional supervision: Supervisee perceptions of processes and outcome. *Studies in Continuing Education, 27,* 239–256.

2

Understanding the School Culture

Amy Kroninger
Betty Anne Domm
Mary L. (Mimi) Webster
Anne E. Troutman

The purpose of this chapter is to:

- Broaden your thinking about school culture
- Inform you about school cultural indicators
- Discuss how the school counselor's position is integrated into the school culture

I was at least five years into my job as a school counselor before I felt I had a grip on my job description even though my yearlong practicum/internship experience in a diverse high school concluded a very positive graduate school experience. I thought I was very prepared for the next step. What I soon realized, however, was I had barely skimmed the surface in my learning experience. Having said that, every situation is different, every school is different, every principal has different expectations, etc. Learning and understanding the school culture takes time but is critical for finding your place and gaining a vision as to where and how the counseling program functions within the school. What do I wish I had known as an intern or first year counselor? The clinical experiences include a variety of learning experiences that should be entered with an open mind, and with knowledge that flexibility and initiative are valued.

Anne Troutman, High School Counselor

Each school culture is multifaceted and unique; however, there are also commonalities across schools. Some commonalities include how people treat and feel about one another (such as feeling included and appreciated), as well as rituals and traditions that reflect collaboration and collegiality. School culture is not just about socioeconomic status, religion, race, or the size of the school; it also includes the values, rituals, and beliefs shared and demonstrated by participants within the school (Phillips & Wagner, 2003).

Three main indicators of a healthy school culture are collaboration, collegiality, and efficacy. Collaboration is characterized as the degree to which people work together, share information and instructional strategies, and have constructive discussions and debates. Collegiality is about a sense of belonging, emotional support, and inclusion as a valued member of the school, with efficacy focusing on how stakeholders view themselves and their input into the institution (Center for Improving School Culture, 2004). Although the entire school staff and faculty need to embrace these three indicators, they are particularly important for school counselors. Whereas teachers may only work directly with other teachers in their departments, counselors and school counselors-in-training will have interactions with every teacher and educational personnel in the building at some point. Thus, counselors should make it a priority to treat every stakeholder equally and with respect. A practical understanding of these indicators is essential when a counselor-in-training begins the clinical experiences and learns to manage roles and activities.

With the definition of the school culture and the three cultural indicators in mind, the focus of this chapter is to assist you in understanding the school counselor's role, as this position influences and is influenced by the school culture. Your role as a counselor-in-training in regard to discipline, safe school initiatives, No Child Left Behind (NCLB), school improvement plans, school counselor division of duties, and communication to stakeholders are highlighted.

The School Counselor's Role in Discipline

A counselor's role with regard to discipline is, for the most part, unlike any other person's in the building. Teachers will write up students for misconduct and either discipline the students themselves, or, for serious matters, send the students to a principal or assistant principal. The school counselor's role should not be one of meting out discipline because this has the potential to jeopardize the counseling relationship. Instead, the counselor can help the counselee recognize the consequences for behaviors and help the counselee remediate his or her behavior. Each school will have its own set of expectations for student conduct based on the ages of the student body as well as the school culture.

As a school counselor-in-training, be sure to implement a classroom management plan when you teach guidance lessons. Or, it may be that a teacher prefers that you use his or her own management plan when you are in a particular class. In either case, have an effective plan ready. Take advantage of your supervisor's assistance and expertise in classroom management, and take every opportunity to practice teaching classroom guidance lessons before you have a job of your own. Supervisors will want to know that a potential school counselor can teach and manage a class with confidence and skill after graduate training has ended. Refer to Chapter 9 for behavior management techniques in leading small or large groups.

Peer mediation is one effective technique that may help improve the school culture. Peer mediation can be used to resolve small issues between two students that, if left alone, might snowball into much bigger issues. The counselor often takes a leadership role in this program including selecting and training peer mediators, identifying situations where mediation could be used effectively, and scheduling mediations. If the school to which you are assigned has already implemented a peer mediation program, become involved with this plan. If not, talk with your site supervisor about instituting one as a part of your clinical experiences.

Safe School Initiatives: Harassment, Intimidation, and Bullying

School counselors want to create an environment in which all students feel safe and emotionally secure. Bullying, harassment, and intimidation typically include gestures, written, verbal, physical, and psychological acts taking place on school property, at school-sponsored functions, and on school buses. Bullying policies frequently require that schools implement specific practices to achieve safer, less violent schools, with ongoing professional education for school employees to learn about methods to prevent harassment, intimidation, and bullying. Many schools have adopted policies to prevent school violence known as *zero-tolerance* policies. These policies are usually in regard to illegal drug possession, firearms, or the commission of battery with full punishment as the consequence for any individual on the school grounds not following the policies established. Furthermore, when planning classroom guidance lessons, consider multicultural and nonstereotypical curricula. For elementary schools, *Second Step* is an effective multicultural, nonviolence curriculum that includes empathy, impulse control, and anger management within its framework.

No Child Left Behind and Implications for School Counselors

No Child Left Behind (NCLB) was signed into law on January 8, 2002 (Ed.Gov, n.d.). This standards-based education reform package is based on the belief that high expectations and measurable goals can improve student achievement. Schools must make adequate yearly progress (AYP) in reading/language arts, mathematics, and science test scores (i.e., each year, fourth graders must do better on standardized tests than the previous years), attendance, and graduation rate. No Child Left Behind requires that each state measure every child's progress in reading and math in grades 3 through 8 and at least once during grades 10 through 12. States must also administer science assessments at least once during grades 3–5, grades 6–9, and grades 10–12. Further, states must ensure that districts administer tests of English proficiency to measure oral language, reading, and writing skills in English to all limited English proficient students.

If a school fails to make adequate yearly progress toward the state benchmarks for two consecutive years, then it is put on a "high priority" list and needs to be restructured by the state to improve achievement. Because NCLB requires schools and districts to focus attention on the academic achievement of traditionally underserved groups such as students from low-income families, students with disabilities, and those from racial and ethnic subgroups, the school counselor can help by monitoring how these students are performing and offer their services when appropriate. For example, a high school counselor will work closely with students who are behind on their academic credits. Students who do not earn enough credits in four years plus one summer will be considered a nongraduate, which impacts the schools' graduation rate. Be aware of the implications of NCLB and ask your supervisor for suggestions to address the school site's report card. With educational institutions under pressure to perform and to show program effectiveness, this is an opportunity for you to engage in tasks that will assist the educational mission.

School Improvement Plans

Individual states are involved in a school improvement planning process with the purpose of helping educators use data to set student improvement goals. With the demands of NCLB, each school develops a plan that serves as the accountability document for measuring adequate yearly progress. Components of the school improvement process include school profile and collaborative process; academic and nonacademic data analysis; beliefs, mission, and vision; curricular, instructional, assessment, and organizational effectiveness; action plan development; and improvement plan and process evaluation. The school counselor is an integral person in assisting with this plan. Ask your site supervisor to show you how services and activities that are integral to the school improvement initiative are documented, and how the school counseling program objectives are aligned with those of academic course objectives. You can use information highlighted in Chapter 9 that outlines study skills strategies to assist in promoting achievement among students struggling academically.

School Counselors' Division of Responsibilities

Factors such as the school system's budget, the school's enrollment, the needs of the particular school, and the priorities of the school district all contribute to the number of school counselors that are placed in each school. As you begin your clinical experiences, you may find counselors in elementary schools assigned to more than one school and those who split time between schools. Other schools may have one full-time counselor, and still others may have two or more. If you are working in a program with more than one counselor you will need to blend philosophies, work styles, and various personalities, which requires compromise, communication, and cooperation in order to have an excellent program. Learning collaborative strategies while you are a supervisee will assist you when you begin your first school counseling position.

Middle schools and high schools with more than one counselor have different methods of assigning responsibility. Some of the more common methods of dividing responsibilities include (a) grade-level classification, in which each counselor is assigned to a particular grade level year after year, and students are assigned to a different counselor each year; (b) alphabetically, in which students have the same counselor all 4 years; or (c) by academies. There are several kinds of academy structures.

Schools with different career academies such as health and sciences may have one counselor per academy, and all students in this academy have the same counselor every year. If there are more than four counselors at a school, one may be assigned to work specifically as a college and career counselor. Make note of the division of responsibility at the school to which you are assigned, and discuss the advantages and disadvantages of this arrangement with your site supervisor.

Negotiating Responsibilities, Duties, and Tasks

Through your graduate program, you have learned about the responsibilities of a school counselor as they relate to national, state, and local standards. The challenge is to integrate these guidelines with the culture and expectations of your school. There may be principals, teachers, parents, other counselors, and various staff whose expectations of your role vary greatly from your expectations. A discussion on the importance of communication, the controversial role of testing, the role of the school counselor in regard to the special education program, and the debate surrounding teaching licensure for school counselors also contribute to the school milieu and are highlighted next.

Communication to Stakeholders

At all levels, communication is crucial. Returning phone calls and e-mails promptly will help promote a positive image for your office, and a solid reputation will be built by providing answers or solutions in a timely manner. As a school counselor-in-training, start this communication process early so that it becomes a regular part of your routine while in training, and continue this practice during your professional career. Parents of students who are failing courses or behind on their credits for

ACTIVITY 2.1

Read and respond to the following scenarios and compare your responses with those of your peers.

It is your first day as an elementary school counseling intern. Your site supervisor has informed you that you are to share your office with the speech therapist and are to counsel students in the hallway. You have been taught about confidentiality and privacy, yet you are also keenly aware that school space is very limited. Keeping in mind your values, beliefs, professional ethics and responsibilities, and the school's inadequate space, how would you respond to your site supervisor?

_____

_____

Read and respond to the following scenarios and compare your responses with those of your peers.

All teachers in your school are scheduled for bus duty throughout the year. When you began as a counselor-in-training, you were asked and agreed to help with lunch duty two days a week even though you are aware to limit your noncounseling duties. Today your site supervisor asked you to perform bus duty. How do you reconcile these multiple noncounseling related requests with your university program requirements? What factors will influence your decision and how will you proceed?

_____

_____

graduation (high school) should be communicated with on a regular basis by their teachers and counselor, or by you as a supervisee if this is one of your designated duties. In addition, school counseling Web sites should be updated regularly with information such as SAT and ACT registration deadlines, college admission deadlines, scholarships, parent meetings, and progress report distribution dates. As a supervisee, learning to update the school counseling Web site is an opportunity that you will be able to continue once you become a fully licensed member of the school counseling profession.

One of the biggest obstacles to overcome is letting your job be overtaken by clerical and testing duties. Sometimes there is a fine line between the school counselor's job and clerical work. For example, for high school counselors, as we move into the age of electronic transcripts, a lot of student record maintenance must be done to ensure accuracy. A competent secretary is able to handle this task, yet needs to be educated about confidential materials and information that may and may not be released. However, it is ultimately the responsibility of the school counselor for making sure counselees' records are accurate.

Testing

Testing is another time-consuming task that is often a large part of a school counselor's job and is influential to the school culture. Due to the enormous responsibility that accompanies year-end tests, some systems hire a test coordinator whose sole responsibility is to be accountable for the testing program. Unfortunately, many school districts simply name one of the counselors to assume this position, and rely on that counselor to make all the testing arrangements or allocate responsibilities to other individuals. Some of the tests of which you should be familiar are ACT and SAT, PLAN and PSAT, AP exams, writing assessments, as well as local and state end-of-course exams. Once test results are returned to the school, counselors need to plan a meeting to disseminate and explain the results to parents/guardians and students. This is an opportunity for you to utilize the knowledge you have acquired in your courses that addressed testing and measurement. Test orientation and interpretation are activities that you may consider including in your clinical contract.

Special Education

Although Chapter 12 contains a more comprehensive discussion concerning the role of the counselor with students with special needs, this is a population that is often overlooked by many professional school counselors. Assisting these students and their families may even be more difficult for individuals who do not have a background in education or have not taken coursework that addresses some of the legislative issues and concerns that accompany these individuals. As stated by the American School Counselor Association (2004)

> The professional school counselor takes an active role in providing a comprehensive school counseling program to students with special needs. Professional school counselors advocate for all students and provide collaborative services to students with special needs consistent with those services provided to students through the comprehensive school counseling program (¶ 50).

The elementary school counselor may include counselees with special needs in small groups, provide individual counseling, help with peer relationships, mediate problems among students, assist with improving self-confidence, or counsel for understanding behavioral consequences. Middle and high school counselors work closely with the resource teachers as students approach high school registration to assist in developing a 6-year transition plan for the students as they matriculate to high school and beyond.

Teaching Versus No Teaching Experience

When "guidance workers" first entered schools, many states required teaching credentials for individuals who entered the school counseling profession. Over the years most states eventually dropped this requirement, and today only a few states still mandate an education background for those entering the school counseling profession. Yet, there are many administrators who adhere to the belief that a background in teaching is necessary and will only consider hiring school counselors with teaching credentials.

Many elementary school counselors spend much of their time teaching classroom guidance, and middle and high school counselors visit classrooms periodically to teach guidance lessons or to provide information on topics such as testing, high school registration, and careers. Therefore, effective classroom management is an essential part of the job. Experience in behavior management is beneficial, and if you have not had much classroom experience, you will benefit from observing teachers with good behavior management techniques.

Being a former teacher may be helpful for school counselors. For example, experience in teaching lessons in front of a large group may assist in establishing credibility with teachers (Bender, 2005), particularly when consulting with teachers on classroom management strategies that worked for you as a teacher. However, for those of you who do not have a teaching background, counseling skills such as reflective listening, paraphrasing, and summarizing may come more naturally, and you will not need to "unlearn" more directive, authoritarian teaching language or behavior. Take advantage of your role as a supervisee to learn under an experienced counselor, visit highly effective teachers in your building to gain ideas, and, if possible, get experience by teaching a variety of ages in different types of settings, such as in suburban, rural, and urban schools.

If you provide guidance lessons in individual classrooms (versus students coming to your classroom), teachers may use this time to leave the room to attend to tasks they need to accomplish. However, in some schools or specific situations, you may want the teachers to stay in the room while leading the guidance class. For instance, you may be in a classroom where there are notable discipline problems or where it is important for the teacher to hear your lesson so that he or she can reinforce the teachings from it. These are instances in which communication is key in creating a collaborative partnership. The following section introduces you to some of the stakeholders with whom school counselors work on a regular basis.

Collaborative Relationship Building

The school board, school administrators, teachers, students, parents/guardians, other counseling professionals, and other school-related personnel are all integral to the school counseling program. As a school counselor-in-training, it is essential to understand how you can collaborate effectively with these individuals in the school milieu.

The School Board

School systems are governed by a group of individuals who form a school board, and as a school counselor-in-training, it would be an educational opportunity to study your school system's Web site to view the structure of the school board, the members composing this board, responsibilities of the members, and when and where meetings are held. Board members are typically elected to terms consisting of a predetermined number of years, although some school districts may have board members who are appointed to the position. School boards set policies under which school systems operate, and either appoint a superintendent or hold an election. In turn, with the approval of the school board members, superintendents hire other school personnel including building level administrators, and depending on the size of the school system, assistant and deputy assistant superintendents may be hired. The responsibilities of the school district are divided among a variety of department directors, supervisors, and specialists.

School board policies affect all school staff, faculty, and the community. Some districts hire a director of counseling who is responsible exclusively to the school counselors in the district, and often work closely with school counselor training programs in placing students in their clinical sites. Or, this person may be assigned duties that encompass supervising school counselors in addition to a broader array of responsibilities. Smaller systems may not have a supervisor specifically for counselors.

Getting to know the school board members who represent your school or district helps build a relationship, and allows the counselor to educate board members about the importance of school counseling and to advocate for counseling needs in areas such as staffing, money, materials, and the school counselor's education and training. In fact, once you are hired as a professional school counselor you may consider speaking to the school board at least one time per year so that the activities of the school counseling program are better understood. It also provides an opportunity to show appreciation to the board member who advocates for the school counseling program.

ACTIVITY 2.2

Attend a school board meeting and take notes on the topics that were discussed. Share your impressions and notes with your peers. What were your impressions of this meeting? What group dynamics did you observe?

_____

_____

_____

School Administrators

Part of a positive work environment involves administrators and counselors working closely together with mutual trust. Inform your site supervisor and principal of your activities without burdening them with minor details. You will be receiving supervision in which you will share your concerns with your site supervisor on a regular basis, and you may want to consider getting principal approval for what you are discussing in class or small groups. It is easy to venture into controversial territory with young adolescents, and it is possible that you will need the principal's support if a parent/guardian disapproves of a topic that is discussed. If there is any possibility that a discussion topic might generate controversy in the community, talk to your supervisor about sending a letter home prior to the discussion explaining what you plan to do and offer parents/guardians the option of providing alternative activities for their child if they do not want their child to participate in the activity. Any time you have a discussion with a parent that is not resolved in the way the parent/guardian hoped, inform your supervisor and principal of what transpired so that he or she has advance knowledge of the problem and is better able to assist with the issue.

ACTIVITY 2.3

Read and respond to the following scenarios and discuss your answers with your peers.

A father of one of your students makes an appointment to see you about his child's grades. He indicates that he is divorced from the child's mother (the custodial parent and he does not approve of the mother's lack of discipline). He is planning on going to court to get custody, and he wants you to testify to the child's lack of progress academically. He feels that the teachers as well as your site supervisor do not keep him as informed as they should. As he talks, he gets visibly more upset. How do you handle this?

_____

_____

You are leading a classroom guidance session on suicide that is integral to your internship contract and the goals of your school counseling training program. Your principal receives an emotional call from a parent. There has been a recent suicide in the family and the discussion in class has opened some deep wounds. As a result, the parent is angry that this topic is being discussed in school. How would you handle this situation?

_____

_____

_____

Teachers

A school counselor's relationship with faculty and staff is vital to the success of the school counseling program, and good communication will help teachers be aware of the work you do in your school. Posting your schedule outside your door in addition to posting information on the school staff bulletin, PTA newsletter, and school Web site are helpful methods in creating awareness of your role as a school counselor-in-training.

It may also be beneficial to provide a short orientation for teachers about your role as a school counselor-in-training and provide a handout with information such as your education, responsibilities, schedule, phone number, e-mail address, and so forth. Furthermore, when meeting with teachers, they can suggest certain topics such as bullying, divorce, child or sexual abuse, substance abuse, basic friendship skills, self-esteem, study skills, or peer pressure that need to be addressed. Or, these educators may suggest a particular school or community issue as an area of focus in a timely large or small group lesson. However, when scheduling time for classroom guidance, dates and times need to be arranged with teachers in advance.

You will be engaged in multiple responsibilities, and it is often difficult to accomplish everything you want to accomplish. It is even possible that you would never get out of your office or see other adults in your building. Therefore, you need to make an effort to be seen around the school. Whenever possible, try to eat lunch with different groups of teachers to build rapport with the faculty, or visit teachers during their planning time just to say hello and ask how they are doing. This attention will help tremendously in getting referrals and support for calling students from classes when you need to see them.

When you need to meet with students, stop by the teachers' classrooms to briefly speak with the teachers regarding individual students you plan to meet that day. Early morning or teacher planning times are good opportunities to do this. Exchange any relevant information, staying within the bounds of confidentiality, and ask if the teacher has any specific incidents that need to be addressed with the student when scheduling your day.

Scheduling times to see counselees can be a challenging issue, and counselors need to be very aware of protecting teachers' class time, especially in core academic subjects. Alternatives are to call students to your office before or after school, during electives, during class change time, homeroom periods, study halls, lunch, or other times that do not interfere with academics. However, if the situation is an emergency, teachers are usually understanding about interruptions.

Another mistake of many counselors-in-training is allowing a student to see them without checking whether he or she has permission to be out of class. It is not uncommon for a student to pay a visit to see you to avoid going to a class. You will create much ill will if teachers think you are allowing students to cut classes to come see you, even though this situation may happen inadvertently. If it does happen, be sure to see the teacher as soon as possible to explain or apologize.

When a teacher refers a student to you, acknowledge this referral and follow up with the teacher. If you will be seeing the student regularly, discuss this with the teacher and be sure to let him or her know that you will be checking to see if the student has made any attitudinal or behavioral changes. Even though you cannot ethically share confidential information about a student, providing general information to teachers is appreciated, and as a result many teachers are willing to make accommodations for students.

ACTIVITY 2.4

Read and respond to the following situation and discuss your response with your peers.

A critical incident happened in a classroom, in which one student was seriously harmed by another and you have been involved with counseling the victim. Staff and parents are concerned about the actions taken regarding this incident and ask you to tell them specifics about the incident and how it is being handled. How do you respond?

_____

_____

Students

Working with students is the most important thing counselors do. This can seem overwhelming at times, especially given the high student to low counselor ratio in many schools. Remember that you cannot be all things to all people, but you can be an effective presence and participant in the lives of your students. Try to get to each classroom within the first 2 weeks of school, either for a brief visit or for a regular classroom guidance lesson to introduce yourself, tell the students what you do, and how they can contact you.

Discuss with your supervisor how students can make an appointment to see you. Having students place a note on your desk or putting a mailbox outside your counseling office are typical strategies. In addition, try to familiarize yourself with a variety of individual counseling techniques. In an elementary setting these strategies might include bibliotherapy, puppetry, writing stories, playing games, art activities, and the use of props and charts.

Be a visible presence around the school whenever possible. If you have a few extra minutes, visit the lunchroom or playground, simply walk the halls, or attend students' musicals, plays, sporting events, and school festivals. However, there are certain limits that should be placed on interaction with students. As professional adults, counselors should not ever be involved with students inappropriately or in ways that would disrupt integrity. Counselors and counselors-in-training alike should not be "friends" with students on social networks such as Facebook and MySpace. There have been some incidents in which the counselor-in-training was unable to maintain appropriate boundaries with students due to unethical fraternization, which resulted in dismissal from the school counseling program.

Parents/Guardians

As a supervisee, learn how to collaborate with parents/guardians by holding informational meetings or workshops on relevant issues. Teaching parenting classes, providing information on bullying, discussing the affects of divorce, helping children with study skills, or discussing your role as a school counselor trainee are all topics that will help you in getting experience in working with parents/guardians while under supervision. Supplying handouts will help the learning process and offering snacks can add a festive mood to the meeting.

Hebert and Sergent (2006) suggest inviting parents/guardians and their children to view a movie with a school counseling theme, and then discussing the movie and its relevance in their lives. *Finding Nemo*, *The Lion King*, or *Ellen Foster* are appropriate movies that are rated G or PG with a message to share. To make movie night more enticing and fun, popcorn could be served.

When having parent/guardian conferences, be very careful with words and try to start and end every conference with something positive about the child. Keep the following suggestions in mind:

- When problem areas are being discussed, link any words of criticism to the fact that the goal is to get the student back on track so that he or she can be happy and successful.
- Be respectful and tactful about giving advice, especially if you are not a parent yourself.
- Never give the impression that you know more about the child than the parent/guardian does. Allow these caregivers to share valuable information that can help you better understand their son or daughter.
- Affirm the fact that parenting is an important and difficult job, and that you want to do your part to help with any concerns.
- Use the technique of *joining*, which means establishing rapport by making small talk with the parents/guardians, matching your communication style with theirs, and using appropriate self-disclosure to relate to their experiences. If the conference concerns grades in a particular subject, the teacher of that class should be involved.
- Stay with the facts and observations that you have gathered in your interaction with the student and look for ways to incorporate the child's strengths into the discussion with his or her parents/guardians.

Other suggestions for working with parents/guardians include normalizing children's problems through *reframing*, which means to change the negative label attributed to the child. For instance, if

---

ACTIVITY 2.5

Read and respond to the following scenario and discuss your answers with your peers.

Parents have called you to request a conference regarding their son. According to his parents, his grades are dropping, he seems unfocused, and his behavior in the classroom and with his peers is becoming a concern. They want you to tell them what is wrong with their son and how it can be fixed. How would you prepare for this conference?

_____

_____

ACTIVITY 2.6

Read and respond to the following scenario and discuss your answers with your peers.

> It is Monday morning, and you are speaking with a student's mother who is requesting that you see her child for school anxiety issues. You further explore with the student's mother what her concerns are about the student as you agree to work with the student. At the end of the conversation, the student's mother adds, "I would like you to call me each week to let me know what she is talking about with you." What do you do?
>
> _____
>
> _____

a young boy is described being "bossy," you could refer to this behavior as "likes to express himself." Another suggestion for working with parents/guardians is to start working on a library of helpful information for caregivers. This effort is something that you can begin as a school counselor trainee and continue throughout the entire span of your career. Handouts, pamphlets, books, and audio-visual materials can be included and shared with parents/guardians and teachers.

One challenging issue, particularly for school counselors-in-training, is how to balance the student's right to confidentiality without alienating the parent or guardian, who has a legitimate interest in the well-being of his or her child. Minors' ethical rights to confidentiality in the counseling relationship are often misunderstood or ignored altogether, and the demands of parents to be informed of the specific content of counseling sessions often overshadow the child's right to privacy. School counselors who develop a reputation for arbitrarily sharing students' information with others may find students reluctant to seek counseling (Glosoff & Pate, 2002). Yet, communicating the value of confidentiality as a cornerstone to the counseling relationship to parents/guardians is a major consideration in collaborating with these stakeholders.

Technology has improved methods of communicating with parents/guardians. Counselor Web sites can be updated regularly with information parents/guardians need to know, for example, ACT and SAT dates, college admission deadlines, scholarships, and opportunities for students. If you are particularly technology-savvy, you can assist your school counselor supervisor by designing a Web site for the school counseling department, which will leave a legacy for counselors-in-training to continue after you leave the school.

ACTIVITY 2.7

Read and respond to the following scenario and discuss your responses with those of your peers.

> You are part of a parent conference in which the language arts teacher mentions that the student has written something in a journal that has the teacher very concerned. The teacher mentions that a journal entry alludes to the fact that the student seems to be afraid of someone at home. The parent gets very angry and leans across the table in a threatening manner when the journal entry is mentioned. You, your site supervisor, and the teacher are the only ones in the room with this parent. How do you handle this situation?
>
> _____
>
> _____

Interaction with Other Counseling Professionals

Maintaining positive relationships with counselors at neighboring schools can have obvious benefits. For instance, students often transfer schools and counselors need to communicate with one another about transfer students' academic records, guardianship issues, grades, behavior, and so forth. In other cases, when registering eighth-grade students for high school, it is helpful for counselors from all feeder schools to meet (probably with administrators), plan, and prepare for the occasion. Talk with your site supervisor about the opportunity to observe and assist with registration so that you can learn about this responsibility firsthand. Furthermore, although time for collaboration or idea exchange among school counselors is scarce, counselors within a system may want to make an effort to meet together. It may be helpful to you as a school counselor-in-training to talk and observe counselors in neighboring systems to learn how they conduct their program.

Other School-Related Personnel

A school counselor's role also intersects with the duties of other school personnel such as secretaries, social workers, nurses, school psychologists, custodians, bookkeepers, and school resource officers. These are individuals that are not often discussed in training classes, yet they are valuable resources for learning about the role of the school counselor and collaborative relationships that impact the school culture. The following sections summarize the roles these personnel play in the school.

Secretaries

School secretaries are critical in establishing a welcoming climate as they are often the first contact with people who enter the building or call the school. The role of a secretary can be very stressful, as office personnel are extremely busy and constantly interrupted. There are some school counseling departments that are fortunate to have a clerical assistant assigned exclusively to the school counselors, whereas other schools do not have this privilege and the clerical help is restricted to one or two individuals for the entire school. As a person new to the school, you will have lots of questions, so be careful about interrupting these secretaries, and do not ask them to do small things for you that you can do yourself.

School Social Workers

Social workers are a liaison between home and school. School attendance and graduation rates are two regulations under NCLB in which schools are scrutinized as to their performance. School social workers can help with these issues by making home visits and assisting with attendance and tardiness issues. Furthermore, they are instrumental resources in connecting families with community agencies that provide such needs as clothing, food, shelter, community mental health counseling, and medical.

School Nurses

Nurses range from being at a school on a full-time basis to traveling from school site to school site throughout the school day or week. If a student requires immediate medications or procedures that are complicated, a nurse will likely be assigned to administer the necessary treatment. Furthermore, in the course of providing assistance, nurses often hear students talk about troublesome issues. For example, a child may have a stomachache and tell the nurse that his or her parents had a fight that morning. These complaints are often clues to more serious emotional concerns because children often express their emotional pain through complaints of physical symptoms rather than verbalizing their thoughts and emotions due to their developmental level. As a school counselor-in-training, make a point to talk with the school nurse about any concerns you have about counselees with whom you are working.

School Psychologists

In some school systems, there is confusion between the role of the school psychologist and that of the counselor, and in other schools the roles are more clearly understood. For example, in some schools counselors process student referrals, help with testing, and attend all or most IEP (Individualized Education Plan) meetings. In other schools, this is the role of the school psychologist. The school psychologist and school counselor can form a collaborative relationship in which each clearly understands the training and education of the other so that duties are not duplicated. As a school counselor-in-training, take time to interview the school psychologist to obtain a better understanding of his or her responsibilities.

Custodians

Custodians work long, hard hours for relatively low pay, and many are quite dedicated to the school staff and students. As a new person in the school, introduce yourself and show your appreciation for their assistance. As with the office staff, do not ask them to do minor things for you that you could do yourself. However, when you need to arrange a room or transport large materials, they can be a great help. Also, remember that custodians get to know the students on a regular basis and can be helpful resources in learning more about your students.

Bookkeeper/Treasurer

Not all school counseling programs are provided with funds to assist with purchases for counseling-related needs. Talk with your supervisor about the monies that are provided to the school counseling department and how these funds are budgeted. Hopefully, you will be given some funds to spend on your school counseling program once you are a fully credentialed member of the profession, but if not, grants are available. These funding opportunities will not only give you needed resources, they will also generate publicity for your program. As a supervisee, you may want to investigate the types of grants that are available and complete a grant application for essentials that your school site can use. In some school systems, your expenditures will be processed through the school bookkeeper. These individuals have critically important jobs that require compliance with both state and district guidelines for spending and collecting money. As a school counselor trainee, familiarize yourself with the particular bookkeeping procedures in your school and ask questions regarding funding, expenditures, and procuring funds so that you can have a better idea of how monies may be obtained for your program.

Security/School Resource Officer (SRO)

Most schools today have a security officer in the building on a full-time basis or on call when needed. These individuals are often members of local law enforcement agencies with specialty training to work in schools. The security officer's role is to protect students and school personnel from harm, to prevent dangerous situations from occurring, and to de-escalate situations that have the potential to become violent. A security officer on the premises acts as a deterrent to anyone seeking to inflict harm on school grounds, and often serves as a confidant to students. SROs establish rapport with students, serve as a resource for the staff, and are significant personnel with whom the school counselor should collaborate. For instance, you may be aware of a volatile situation that is to be reported as outlined in school policy, or the school security office may provide support with runaway students, contentious custody issues, or topics such as bullying and harassment. Be sure to learn about this individual's role in the school, particularly as the job relates to working with the school counselors.

Community Agencies

When making referrals for community services, some school counselors seek much outside assistance for students and families, while other counselors only occasionally seek help from outside agencies. Examples of referral sources used by school counselors include services for the homeless, extra clothing, investigation into suspected child abuse, mentoring relationships for children in single-parent homes, and assistance with medical or physical needs such as eyeglasses and dental care.

In addition, agencies can assist counselors by working with students who have special counseling needs. Mental health agencies facilitate groups for at-risk students, or health agencies may talk to students about issues such as pregnancy prevention or other health issues like anorexia and bulimia, weight problems, and handling diabetes. While you are a supervisee, learn about the various agencies in your community and make a list of these resources so that you are able to readily refer to them. And, if you stay in the community after graduation, you can expand this list of helpful community services.

Conclusion

This chapter provides information for you to understand the school culture and how the school counselor is a contributing person to the school milieu. In learning about the role of the school counselor, it is essential that you are knowledgeable of the various school-based initiatives and projects that contribute to the school atmosphere. In addition, you will have a deeper appreciation for the educational personnel as you familiarize yourself with the roles of these integral school and community members.

Web Sites

- For additional information on school culture particularly in smaller schools, this link contains helpful information: http://www.smallschoolsproject.org/PDFS/culture.pdf
- The article "School Context: Bridge or Barrier to Change" provides helpful information on attitudes and beliefs, attitudes toward change, and cultural norms that facilitate school improvement. This information can be accessed through: http://www.sedl.org/change/school/culture.html

References

American School Counselor Association (ASCA). (2004). *The professional school counselor and students with special needs.* Position statement. Retrieved July 13, 2009, from http://asca2. timberlakepublishing.com//files/Special%20Needs.pdf

Bender, J. M. (2005). *Ready...set...go!* Chapin, SC: Youthlight, Inc.

Center for Improving School Culture. (2004). *What is school culture?* Retrieved November 17, 2008, from http://www.schoolculture.net/whatisit.html

Ed.Gov. (n.d.). *A capsule view of the history of Federal education legislation.* Retrieved April 29, 2009, from http://www.ed.gov/policy/gen/leg/edpicks.jhtml?src=ln

Glosoff, H., & Pate, R. H. (2002). Privacy and confidentiality in school counseling. *Professional School Counseling, 6,* 20–27.

Herbert, T. P., & Sergent, D. (2006). Using movies to guide: Teachers and counselors collaborating to support gifted students. *Gifted Child Today, 4,* 14–25.

Phillips, G., & Wagner, C. (2003). *School culture assessment.* Vancouver, British Columbia: Agent 5 Design.

3

Popular Counseling Theories Used by School Counselors

Cynthia Crawford

The purpose of this chapter is to:

- Summarize the most commonly used counseling theories used in schools
- Reflect on one's personal theory of counseling as a school counselor-in-training
- Apply theory to school-related case studies

The school counselor's approach to counseling is influenced by one or more theoretical orientations. There exists a plethora of theoretical approaches within the counseling field, some representing an extension of preexisting theories of personality development and others expressing a reaction against earlier systems of thought. Overall, counseling theories explain (a) why people live productive or unproductive lives and (b) how to assist people in changing aspects within themselves that seem counterproductive (Hackney & Cormier, 2009). Regardless of one's theoretical orientation, knowledge of counseling theory is critical in accurately assessing and conceptualizing a counselee's case. Choosing a theoretical foundation is guided by the counselor's phenomenological and philosophical views from affective, cognitive, behavioral, and relational perspectives (Hackney & Cormier, 2009).

Both the counselee and counselor come to the counseling situation with a unique background of cultural experiences, which influence the counselor–counselee relationship, the counseling process, and interventions that may therapeutically meet the needs of the counselee. Because no one particular theory is best suited for all counselees, it is incumbent upon the counselor to choose a theoretical approach that best fits the needs of the counselee in terms of personality factors, background experiences, and cultural milieu (Corey, 2009a).

This chapter provides a general overview of unique contextual aspects within schools that may influence theoretical orientation and counseling theories frequently employed in school counseling settings, including person-centered counseling, reality therapy, cognitive behavioral approaches, solution-focused brief counseling, narrative therapy, and creative counseling approaches such as art, play, and music.

Contextual Aspects of Schools

Schools provide a unique environment in which to provide counseling. Although some of the aspects unique to schools are more thoroughly discussed in Chapters 2 and 13, it is important to consider the distinctive aspects of the school environment that impact school counselors' choice of theoretical orientation. Some of these aspects include children and adolescents as counselees, scope of school counselor responsibilities, and students' time availability. First, school personnel's primary aim is to educate children. Because school counselors focus their counseling energies primarily on children and adolescents, developmental issues influence choice of theoretical orientation. Second, school counselors are responsible for many tasks and activities. These responsibilities limit the amount of energy and time the school counselor has available for counseling. School counselors may not have the resources or time to adequately counsel students who present significant mental health issues, or who require unavailable resources or intensive ongoing counseling. The third aspect is the students' time availability. Students are in school to be educated. Excessive time spent in the school counseling office can take away from time spent in the classroom. In some cases, excessive counseling during school hours may impede upon a students' classroom time. These contextual considerations must be factored in when school counselors choose a counseling theory or theories.

Each of the following sections provides a brief summary of theories common to school settings, describes some unique characteristics of each approach, and indicates populations with whom each theory has been successfully applied. The following descriptions are not meant to exhaustively explain the tenets of any one particular theory, because you have undoubtedly already taken a class exclusively on counseling theories. However, this chapter serves as a reference when counseling with school-aged youth.

Person-Centered Counseling

Carl Rogers, the founder of person-centered counseling, developed it as an approach to counseling that emphasizes the counselee's inner ability to be aware of and solve his or her own problems (Monte & Sollod, 2003). Person-centered counseling represents a reaction against earlier, psychodynamic theories that viewed the counselor as an expert and interpreter of an individual's emotional distress. Through this nondirective approach, a collaborative relationship between the counselor and counselee is established that is critical to the success of therapy (Rogers, 1951). Rogers's approach challenged the assumption that "the counselor knows best" and that counselees are unable to understand and resolve their problems without direct help on the part of a counselor. In contrast, person-centered counseling compares therapy to a journey shared by two equally fallible individuals and contends that counselees are capable of self-directed growth in the presence of an unconditionally accepting counselor–counselee relationship (Corsini & Wedding, 2005a).

Rogers believed the focus of counseling should be on the person rather than the problem, that all people strive for self-actualization, and that the ultimate goal of counseling is congruence between the person's true inner self and his or her perceived self. On the part of the counselor, Rogers advocated for unconditional positive regard or nonjudgmental acceptance of the counselee; a genuine, unpretentious presentation of congruence; and accurate empathic understanding. The counselor seeks to understand the counselee's own phenomenological world and feels to the greatest extent possible, the emotions experienced by the counselee (Monte & Sollod, 2003).

Person-centered counseling skills include attentive listening and reflecting feeling, or helping the counselee to find the words to describe his or her feelings. The counselor's empathic response to the counselee's feelings may reveal fragments of the real self that have remained hidden for some time, bring these pieces of the real self to the counselee's awareness, and promote congruence between the perceived and real self (Monte & Sollod, 2003). Overall, the counselor works to provide a warm, respectful, genuine, and caring environment in which self-actualization may occur, thus allowing the counselee to problem solve independent of advice or interpretation on the part of the counselor. A central tenet of Rogers's theory was that counselees, including students, have the necessary means in themselves to resolve their own challenges, and that the counselor is responsible for establishing a therapeutic setting to enable clients to realize they have the ability for self-change and to "attain this insight themselves" (Monte & Sollod, 2003, p. 474).

Rogers once stated, "Every individual exists in a continually changing world of which he is the center" (1951, p. 483). Rogers viewed human nature from a positive perspective and contended that each individual has the power to heal the self when provided the proper psychological conditions, as described earlier. His theory emphasizes human worth and dignity, as well as the personal freedom to be, to choose, and to act (Monte & Sollod, 2003).

Person-centered counseling has been applied in a number of countries and in numerous multicultural settings. The role a counselor takes in setting aside personal values, thus completely accepting and identifying with those of the counselee, enhances the applicability of the approach with diverse populations (Sharf, 2008a). The person-centered approach has been applied with individuals, groups, and families. Basic tenets of the approach are frequently employed in educational settings from elementary to graduate school. With its emphasis on a warm, caring counselor–counselee connection, the approach is particularly applicable in crisis intervention, including traumatic disasters, extreme illness, unplanned pregnancies, and grief (Corsini & Wedding, 2005a).

ACTIVITY 3.1

Conduct a role-play using the following scenario with a partner. One person will play the role of a person-centered counselor using the philosophical approach described earlier, and the other person will role play the counselee described next.

> Ella is a fourth-grade student in a rural school that has few resources, poorly paid personnel, and nonexistent mental health agencies. The closest facility that provides counseling is in a city that is located nearly one hour away. Ella arrives in the counselor's office upset, crying, and incapable of talking about the issue that brought her to the office. It seems that her mother, her primary caregiver, was arrested the night before due to charges of drug use and abuse. Ella was sent to live with her grandparents, who live a few blocks away, until her mother is arraigned. Ella's grandparents care about Ella, but have physical difficulties that prevent them from caring for her appropriately.

Discuss what it was like to role-play the counselor and some of the challenges in using this approach. What aspects of this theory seemed to facilitate the counseling relationship?

Discuss what it was like to role-play Ella. What were some of the aspects of this counseling approach that you think assisted the counseling process? Detracted from the counseling process?

Reality Therapy or Choice Theory

William Glasser developed reality therapy in the early 1960s following his work with institutionalized delinquent adolescent girls. Presented within a friendly, collaborative counselor–counselee relationship, the essence of reality therapy, based on choice theory, is self-responsibility, or leading the counselee to take responsibility for his or her life choices (Corey, 2009b). Glasser (2001, 2005) proposed five basic essential psychological needs: survival, love and belonging, power or achievement, freedom or independence, and fun. Individuals, according to Glasser, choose their behaviors in response to the quality of relationships they experience and in an attempt to meet their perceived needs. Reality therapy suggests the underlying issue for a troubled counselee is an absence or lack of satisfaction with a significant interpersonal relationship. Therefore, as a counselor, you can facilitate a significant relationship with your student counselee.

In treating counselees for emotional disturbance, Glasser considers psychiatric symptoms to represent behaviors chosen in an attempt to meet needs stemming from an ineffective relationship. Therefore, according to Glasser, most diagnoses of mental illness are inaccurate. In working with counselees, Glasser frequently converts diagnostic descriptors such as depression, anxiety, and phobia into verb forms, expressed as *depressing*, *anxietizing*, and *phobicing*, thus implying the individual chooses the behavioral symptom and enacts it within his or her life (Sharf, 2008b).

According to Glasser (1990), an individual's total behavior consists of doing, thinking, feeling, and physiology, a concept he often illustrated in a diagram of a car. In this illustration, an individual's basic needs (survival, belonging, power, freedom, and fun) form the engine of the car. The individual's wants are responsible for steering the car. The rear wheels represent the individual's feelings and physiology, two components over which there is less control. The front wheels, controlled by the steering "wants," represent doing and thinking, and suggest a greater degree of choice and personal control. According to Glasser, behavioral change results in the individual changing what he or she thinks or does, which in turns brings about emotional as well as physiological change (Sharf, 2008b). The goals of reality therapy, therefore, are to meet one's needs by taking control of life choices.

Strategies employed by reality therapists to bring about change include questioning, optimism, humor, confrontation, and paradoxical techniques. In assessing the counselee's status in meeting his or her needs in a realistic manner, the reality therapist may employ the WDEP system (Wubbolding, 2004):

W = Wants: What do you want to be and do? Your mental picture of yourself.
D = Doing and direction: What are you doing? Where do you want to go?
E = Evaluation: Is what you are doing now working for you? Is it getting you what you want?
P = Planning: A plan to get you where you want to be, often represented by the acronym SAMIC:
    S = Simple and specific
    A = Attainable
    M = Measurable
    I = Immediate and involved
    C = Controlled and commitment (includes use of a contract)

In reality therapy, the counselor and counselee work collaboratively in creating a plan that the counselee believes will realistically meet his or her needs. Therefore, this counseling approach involves teaching individuals to make choices that will lead to desired outcomes and meet their needs through interpersonal relationships, with the counselor–counselee relationship critically important for this teaching–learning process to be successful (Sharf, 2008b; Wubbolding, 2004).

Glasser has written a number of books applying his theory to educational settings. They include *Schools Without Failure* (1969) and *The Quality School* (1998). Reality therapy is quite popular in middle and high school settings, but may be used across all grade levels by teachers, administrators, and school counselors (Sharf, 2008b).

ACTIVITY 3.2

Using the WDEP system (Wubbolding, 2004) with a partner, conduct a role-play including a counselor and a counselee using the following scenarios.

    a. A 12th-grade student who is having difficulty with career plans
    b. A 7th-grade male who is being bullied by his peers
    c. A 3rd grader who is having problems getting along with her sister

Discuss what it was like to role-play the counselor and some of the challenges in using this approach. What aspects of this theory seemed to facilitate the counseling relationship?

Discuss what it was like to role-play the student counselee. What were some of the aspects of this counseling approach that assisted the counseling process? Detracted from the counseling process?

Cognitive Behavioral Approaches

Cognitive behavioral approaches include the works of Albert Ellis (2004a, 2004b), who developed rational emotive behavior therapy (REBT) and Aaron Beck (1976, 1987), who founded cognitive therapy (CT). Each of these models combines principles from cognitive and behavioral theories into short-term therapy approaches, which are popular treatment techniques in clinical as well as school counseling settings (Corey, 2009c).

Ellis's (2004a, 2004b) REBT is based on the premise that one's interpretation of life events influences emotional and behavioral responses within the environment. Hence, by changing the interpretation or the way we think about life situations, we also change how we feel and what we do in response to our thinking. Ellis focused on altering absolutist thinking, typically represented by the words *must*, *ought*, and *should*. He contended that emotional problems are largely a result of mistaken beliefs and may be rectified by recognizing the irrational nature of one's thinking, disputing such irrational cognitions, and replacing these thoughts with more rational and effective thinking.

Rational emotive behavior therapy, directive and educational in nature, stresses thinking, judging, deciding, analyzing, and doing (Corey, 2009c; Sharf, 2008c). The counselor's role in REBT is to help the counselee realize the irrationality of mistaken beliefs, which will later be replaced by more functional thoughts and behaviors through experiential activities and behavioral homework assignments to reinforce the newly acquired behaviors.

Beck (1976, 1987) developed his theory of counseling, referred to as cognitive therapy (CT), after working with individuals suffering from depression. Although he and Ellis did not work together in developing their approaches, similarities are noted. Both require active involvement on the part of the counselee, are directive, time limited, present focused, structured, collaborative, and employ situation-specific problem identification. Differences include terminology and emphasis on empiricism to a greater degree in CT than REBT, with CT applying more structure within the counseling process and REBT using more confrontation during counseling (Corey, 2009c).

Those who are associated with CT credit emotional instability to cognitive distortions, which lead to a negative bias in thinking. Common cognitive distortions include all-or-nothing thinking, mind reading, catastrophizing, overgeneralization, labeling and mislabeling, magnification and minimization, and personalization, among others (Sharf, 2008c). Treatment involves a collaborative effort between the counselor and counselee to identify dysfunctional, distorted thinking, and challenge

---

ACTIVITY 3.3

With a partner, conduct a role-play of the following situation using a cognitive behavioral approach.

> A parent of one of your fifth graders comes to see you because she is concerned that her son, Kyle, is gay. According to Kyle's mom, he is not interested in sports or any type of physical activity that is typical for boys his age. Kyle, according his mother, is quiet and prefers to play dolls with his sister. Kyle's mom further states that it is her fault because she divorced his father when he was baby and as a result of not having a male figure in the home, Kyle is suffering the consequences.

Discuss what it was like to role-play the counselor and some of the challenges in using this approach. What aspects of this theory seemed to facilitate the counseling relationship?

Discuss what it was like to role-play Kyle's mom. What were some of the aspects of this counseling approach that assisted the counseling process? Detracted from the counseling process?

such cognitions by asking questions such as "What is the evidence for the belief?" (Sharf, 2008c, p. 349). Counselees may participate in activities such as journaling, record keeping, self-monitoring, and thought recognition as a means of examining the accuracy of their cognitions. When counselees develop an awareness of their cognitive distortions, they may again work collaboratively with the counselor to restructure their thinking and improve their problem-solving and coping skills (Corey, 2009c; Sharf, 2008c). Treatment strategies include behavioral rehearsal, role-play, and homework assignments for continued practice of positive cognitions and behaviors (Corsini & Wedding, 2005b).

Cognitive behavioral approaches have been applied successfully with children and adults demonstrating general anxiety disorders, depression, eating disorders, obsessive disorders, and substance abuse (Corey, 2009c; Corsini & Wedding, 2005b; Sharf, 2008c). The brief, didactic nature of CT and REBT make them popular approaches among school counseling interventions.

Solution-Focused Brief Counseling

Similar to the person-centered counseling approach, solution-focused brief counseling, or solution-focused therapy, is based on the assumption that everyone experiences problems and has within himself or herself the strength to implement the needed change(s) to solve such difficulties. The overall goal of the counseling process is collaborative construction of solutions between the counselee and counselor (Downing & Harrison, 1992). Earlier, traditional counseling models focused exclusively on the problem, followed by assessment to identify possible origins of the difficulty. Treatment was then designed to remediate the inadequacies of the counselee in relating to the problem (Murphy, 1997), inherently conveying to the counselee that something is wrong with him or her. Solution-focused brief counseling, in contrast, assumes the wellness and inner strength of the counselee, rather than focusing on some personality distortion or psychopathology (Downing & Harrison, 1992).

Solution-focused brief counseling was initially influenced by the work of Milton Erickson (deShazer, 1985). Erickson is regarded by many as the founder of brief therapy; the brief strategic therapy model of the Mental Research Institute in Palo Alto, California; and the solution-focused therapy model of the Brief Family Therapy Center in Milwaukee, Wisconsin. Bonnington (1993) credits the deShazer group at the Brief Family Therapy Center with development of the basic principles of solution-focused brief counseling. They include (a) the philosophy that the primary task of the counselor is to help the counselee do something different; (b) the shift of emphasis from the problem itself to a solution that may already be present within the counselee's life; (c) the idea that change, even in small increments, is productive in creating the medium for further change; and (d) goals stated in positive terms create expectations for change.

In solution-focused brief counseling, problems are viewed as being maintained by the counselee's belief that the problem is always happening and may have intensified as a result of the individual repeatedly applying the same solutions indiscriminately to each area of difficulty (LaFountain, Garner, & Eliason, 1996). At the outset of therapy, the counselor may ask the counselee not only to describe the problem, but also to think of times when the problem is either not present or present to a lesser degree (exceptions to the problem). The counselee may then be asked what was different during such times or what he or she did differently. Such dialogue implies the potential within the individual to make necessary changes (Bonnington, 1993).

Once the counselee has acknowledged the existence of a problem, the emphasis shifts to goal setting. The "miracle question" (deShazer, 1988) proposes a hypothetical situation in which the counselee is asked to imagine awakening one morning and the problem has been solved. The counselee is then instructed to process how his or her environment might be different and what he or she might be doing differently. The counselor then guides the counselee to the present reality that miracles are not likely to happen, but, since the student knows what he or she would like to be different, they have the ability to plan what they will do to bring about the desired changes. The counselor encourages the counselee to let go of previously attempted solution behaviors that have already proven ineffective in solving the problem, consider what he or she may already be doing to reach their goals, and state what behaviors he or she believes would bring about realization of goals (Bonnington, 1993). (This allows the counselee to get a vision of what is wanted rather than what is not desired.)

During subsequent sessions, the counselor assists the student in restating goals as process goals and reviews the counselee's progress. The counselor may suggest analogies that compare the process to reaching a goal in an obstacle course. Each session concludes with encouragement to reinforce behaviors that result in positive change for the counselee. Students may also be instructed to look for instances during the upcoming week that they would like to see happen more frequently. The next session then begins by discussing those events the student wishes to have repeated (LaFountain et al., 1996).

Solution-focused brief counseling techniques are applicable with students of all ages and may be applied in individual as well as group counseling settings. These techniques may be used with students demonstrating a variety of difficulties and may serve to lessen the stigma sometimes associated with certain populations that appear prevalent in group counseling programs, such as children of alcoholics or students struggling with anger or behavioral issues (LaFountain et al., 1996). Since the treatment groups focus on the strengths of the individual student, group members are able to learn from one another, thus lessening the need to identify role models.

ACTIVITY 3.4

With a partner, conduct a role-play of a school counselor and a counselee using the solution-focused counseling approach. Use one or more of the following scenarios to assist you with this process.

    a. A second grader is upset because one of her friends will not play with her or be her learning partner in class.
    b. A sophomore did not get a scholarship to attend an academic camp and believes that she will never get into a good college because of this rejection.
    c. A parent is concerned about her 17-year-old daughter who seems belligerent and will not listen to anything she has to say.

Discuss what it was like to role-play the counselor and some of the challenges in using this approach. What aspects of this theory seemed to facilitate the counseling relationship?

Discuss what it was like to role-play the counselees. What were some of the aspects of this counseling approach that assisted the counseling process? Detracted from the counseling process?

Narrative Therapy

Grounded in the principles of social theory, Michael White and David Epston (1990) are viewed as primary contributors to narrative therapy. Similar to the approaches described earlier in this chapter, narrative therapy involves a collaborative counselor–counselee relationship and empowers the counselee to take an active role in initiating life changes. In narrative therapy, an individual's reality is constructed through life stories based on past experiences and is viewed through the interpretative lens of expectations from within the dominant culture of a society (e.g., parents, peers, teachers), finally resulting in the individual's personal beliefs about him- or herself. Individual stories often conflict with stories perpetuated by the dominant societal culture, thus culminating in stress, confusion, and

ACTIVITY 3.5

With a partner, conduct a role-play of a counselor and counselee using a narrative approach. The following scenario may be used to assist with this activity:

> JoAnna is very unhappy. No matter what she tries, nothing seems to turn out the way she would like. For instance, just this morning, she took a quiz in her algebra class, and even though she spent hours studying for it, she was only able to receive a grade of a C. Furthermore, her boyfriend recently broke up with her because she tended to "drag him down," according to JoAnna. She comes to see you because she doesn't feel as if she has many friends and is lonely.

Discuss what it was like to role-play the counselor and some of the challenges in using this approach. What aspects of this theory seemed to facilitate the counseling relationship?

Discuss what it was like to role-play JoAnna. What were some of the aspects of this counseling approach that assisted the counseling process? Detracted from the counseling process?

frustration on the part of the counselee. These beliefs become the counselee's story and may serve to dictate how he or she views self and others, as well as life's challenges (Corey, 2009d).

Narrative therapy involves the counselor and counselee working collaboratively to (a) co-construct the counselee's story; (b) deconstruct "impoverishing" life stories by externalizing problems as separate and apart from the individual; (c) identify unique outcomes or times when the counselee was able to separate himself or herself from the influence of the problem; and (d) reconstruct a preferred, alternative story, thus enhancing coping and problem-solving skills, initiating goal setting, and improving self-image. Using this postmodern approach, counselees are able to reconstruct and redirect their life path to set goals for the future (Carlson, 1997; White, 1993, 1995).

Narrative therapy involves interpretation of counselee issues through the examination of a person's life stories. As in solution-focused brief counseling, the emphasis in narrative therapy is on counselee strengths and the potential for positive change, rather than on diagnosis or labeling. The counselee takes charge of interpreting his or her life story while the counselor exercises active listening and encouragement to further empower the counselee as author of his or her life story (Corey, 2009d).

The process of narrative therapy may be compared to the analysis of literary works by examining story components such as setting, plot, and themes. As counselees tell and retell their experiential narratives, the counselor listens intently for the purpose of validating the story to the counselee as well as drafting alternative extensions to the counselee's story. Through story recollection and repetition, the counselee is able to understand the experience from multiple perspectives, in some cases leading to problem solution, and in others emotional release, understanding, and acceptance as the counselee grieves aspects that have created angst within his or her own life (Neimeyer, 2000; Sharf, 2008d).

Narrative therapy may be implemented during individual or group counseling in school as well as clinical settings. Researchers have integrated the approach with creative counseling strategies, such as play and art therapy, resulting in positive therapeutic gains (Carlson, 1997; Shovlin, 1999). Narrative therapy may also be applied in career counseling settings to address developmental tasks such as understanding self-identity, building autonomy, decision making, and goal setting (Thomas & Gibbons, 2009).

Creative Counseling Approaches

Creative counseling approaches, also known as expressive therapies, are therapeutic interventions in which the counselee uses creative energies to enhance self-awareness or self-expression within a treatment setting (Robbins, 1980). Three creative counseling approaches frequently employed in school counseling settings are art therapy, play therapy, and music therapy. Such expressive approaches are often used in school counseling settings to enhance self-esteem, build self-concept, improve social interaction, and encourage multicultural awareness and acceptance among children from a variety of cultural backgrounds (D'Andrea & Daniels, 1995).

Art Therapy

Natale (1996) describes two schools of thought currently existing in the field of art therapy. First, art has for years been used as an interpretative tool to lend information regarding thoughts, memories, and feelings of individuals who may be unable or unwilling to express such verbally. Using this philosophy, the information gleaned from analysis of a counselee's art creation is analytically interpreted and used to develop a plan for reaching goals. Second, art is considered to be healing in and of itself, and may be used as a means of expressive communication with individuals who present emotional or behavioral difficulties. In this chapter, and for the purposes of school counseling, art therapy will be defined as a form of expressive communication in which the counselee expresses thoughts and feelings through creation of art products using one or more of a variety of media. Student-created art products, therefore, may provide clues to the affective status of an individual, and also serve as an expressive language, thus providing a less threatening mode of communication within the counselor–counselee relationship (Natale, 1996; Naumburg, 2001). School counselors are advised to use art therapy as a tool for self-expression and refrain from interpretation of unconscious, projected meanings unless they have received sufficient training in projective personality assessment and modern-day psychoanalysis (Naumburg, 2001).

Art therapy is easily integrated into the typical school counseling office. Art media are often readily available in school settings and include multicolored paper, pencils, crayons, markers, paints, glue, magazine cutouts for collage, modeling clay, pipe cleaners, and papier-mâché. Most materials may be stored in cabinets or file drawers until ready for use (Kahn, 1999). During the initial stage of counseling, it is important to create an atmosphere of acceptance through nonthreatening, encouraging statements, and provide a choice of art activity. During this stage, the counselor may introduce activities to enhance counselee self-awareness and encourage the examination of personal issues. Later on, goal-directed activities are recommended (Kahn, 1999). Art therapy, as a medium for self-expression and communication between counselee and counselor, may be applied by counselors in school settings to achieve similar results as other methods of brief counseling. The approach is easily integrated into theoretical models such as person-centered, cognitive behavioral, and solution-focused (Kahn, 1999; Riley, 1999).

Art therapy is suitable for counselees of all ages and areas of need, including developmental, academic, social, and emotional. The approach is considered suitable for children as well as resistant adolescent counselees, who may be less cooperative with traditional "talk therapy" approaches.

ACTIVITY 3.6

Take a blank sheet of paper and colored markers. Think about your practicum or internship experience, then draw your feelings that represent this experience. Let your mind wander while you think in terms of how you would like to represent your feelings and thoughts about this clinical experience. Do not evaluate your work and do not worry if you are unable to represent these feelings and thoughts accurately. After you are finished, put this picture away and then do this same activity at the end of your program. Compare the two pictures to see how your feelings and thoughts may have changed based on your artwork. Identify one way you might use a similar art activity with one of the students in your school.

Art provides avenues for self-expression through the defense lowering nature of concrete images depicted in drawings, paintings, and sculptures (Landreth, 2002; Riley, 1999). Allowing children to express their feelings through art also enhances coping in times of stress and separation anxiety precipitated by illness or injury (Raghurman, 1999). The approach may be an effective treatment technique for homebound students upon their return to school following medical interventions that, at times, necessitate lengthy hospital stays, surgeries, and prolonged periods of discomfort. Finally, art therapy is also recommended as an intervention for children with special needs, such as autism, to enhance expressive communication (Emery, 2004).

Play Therapy

Child-centered, nondirective play therapy is a popular treatment for children and adolescents both in school and clinical settings. Play therapy is based on the contention that play is a child's primary method of communication and cognitive processing. The child processes experiences through play and builds communicative abilities by enacting his or her perceptions of reality. Play may be used to enhance the counselor–counselee relationship, foster a sense of security on the part of the young student, and initiate individual expression through a less restricted modality independent of verbal language (Landreth, 2002).

Child-centered play therapy, based on person-centered principles, involves a complete and total acceptance of the child for the person he or she is. The therapist does not overtly direct the play session by instructing the child as to what or how to play, but instead allows the child to lead the play therapy process. The counselor uses verbal communication to reflect content and emotion following the child's actions or spoken words. A warm, permissive relationship is established between the counselor and counselee in order for the child to communicate through play what he or she may have been unable to communicate through spoken language. Play therapy allows school-aged children an avenue for expression without the constraints of formal linguistic communication (Landreth, 2002; Schaefer & O'Connor, 1983).

Play therapy incorporates a number of modalities, including representational play through the use of play objects, parallel play, interactive play between counselor and counselee (or between several children for social development), and expressive play through art making. The long-term goal of child-centered play therapy is for the child to develop congruence between his or her perceptual world based on experience and his or her self-concept (Landreth, 2002; Nordling & Guerney, 1999).

There are several counselor qualities and personality traits that may serve to enhance one's ability to successfully implement child-centered play therapy. They include (a) unconditional acceptance of the child counselee; (b) respecting the personhood of the child; (c) demonstrating sensitivity to the child's communication from both verbal and nonverbal perspectives; (d) being fully present and focused exclusively on the relationship with the child counselee at the time and moment of the therapy session; and (e) a tolerance for ambiguity (Landreth, 2002). In child-centered play therapy, the counselor is encouraged to allow the child counselee a choice to change or not to change; this is a potential challenge for many professionals since the original purpose of the counseling is often to bring about a change. Providing the child the opportunity to decide whether to change his or her behavior builds a sense of responsibility and decision making that may ultimately lead to change (Landreth, 2002).

Play therapy materials should include only toys or objects conducive to self-expression. Automated toys or toys reflecting popular celebrities or superheroes may inhibit the child's expressive communication during play. A variety of toys should be available for expression, including toys for aggressive or violent expression, including punching bags, plastic knives, plastic hammers or mallets, blocks that may be thrown, and toy guns. Most authors agree that guns do not promote violence in the real life of the child counselee (Landreth, 2002; McDonald, 1984; Trotter, Eshelman, & Landreth, 2001).

However, when using aggressive types of toys, be sure to communicate the value of these toys with administrators who enforce zero-tolerance policies.

Expressive counseling approaches such as play and art therapies are potentially effective in individual as well as group counseling interventions among school-aged children. They may serve to bridge cultural differences that exist between counselor and counselee, enhance communication with culturally diverse students, relieve stress among students as they transition to new academic settings, and improve self-esteem, thus allowing students from backgrounds different than those dominantly reflected in the school environment to achieve academic gains (Baggerly & Parker, 2005; Cochran, 1996).

ACTIVITY 3.7

Observe a child playing. Make note of this child's developmental and chronological age. Note some of the actions exhibited by this child. Compare your observations with a partner's observations and notes. Discuss how you might use play in a counseling session with one of your students.

Music in a Counseling Setting

Music has been referred to as "truly the universal language" (Vines, 2004, p. 12). Although school counselors do not conduct music therapy without obtaining proper certification or licensure, using music in large group classroom guidance and small group counseling programs may evoke thoughts and feelings among children such as awareness, self-expression, and social interaction. Music and song may be incorporated into elementary school counseling activities to enhance attentiveness, strengthen the social bond between the counselor and a group of children, and serve as a teaching aid to enhance coping during difficult life transitions such as parental divorce and relocation (Bixler, 2001; Haigh, 2005). At the middle and high school levels, music may also be employed during classroom guidance and group counseling programs to build rapport between the school counselor and student counselees. Guidance lessons and group sessions centered on popular, classroom appropriate song lyrics may stimulate self-expression among adolescent students and lead to class discussions on pertinent issues such as academic achievement, respect for diversity, and career opportunities (Veach & Gladding, 2007; Vines, 2005). Parents, teachers, and school counselors may refer students to music therapists for help in treating conditions such as attention-deficit hyperactivity disorder (ADHD), depression, low self-esteem, posttraumatic stress disorder (PTSD), and mentally or physically disabling conditions (Emery, 2004; Hendricks, 2001; Jackson, 2003; Kennedy, 2008).

ACTIVITY 3.8

Bring in music that has special meaning for you. Play the music in class and talk about the reason that the music you brought to class is meaningful to you. Describe how this music or song selection relates to your school counselor-in-training experience. How might you use a similar activity with students in your school?

Conclusion

School counselors, faced with overwhelming responsibilities and demands that are, at times, extraneous to their primary role as counselors, rarely have the luxury of 50-minute sessions considered routine by professionals in community and private settings. In addition, student counselees are often referred by parents or teachers rather than by themselves and, hence, may meet the counseling situation in a less than cooperative manner. In view of such conditions, the need arises for counseling methods that are both time effective and optimistic in nature. This chapter has provided a brief overview of several counseling theories frequently employed in school settings, which are generally time limited, collaborative, empowering, and lead to enhanced academic achievement and improved learning outcomes. School counselors are encouraged to develop an in-depth knowledge base of different counseling approaches and to select ideologies that not only appeal to themselves as practitioners within the schools, but, most important, meet the developmental and emotional needs of their counselees.

Web Sites

Person-Centered Counseling

- This YouTube depiction shows a counselor using a person-centered approach to counseling: http://video.google.com/videosearch?q=person+centered+youtube&oe=utf-8&rls=org.mozilla:en-US:official&client=firefox-a&um=1&ie=UTF-8&ei=YBf7SuWeN4HjnAfTqYD1DA&sa=X&oi=video_result_group&ct=title&resnum=1&ved=0CA4QqwQwAA#
- This link will take you to a short explanation of person-centered counseling described by Carl Rogers: http://www.youtube.com/watch?v=HarEcd4bt-s

Reality Therapy

- This link will take you to a brief discussion of reality therapy as described by William Glasser. A short scenario of this approach in practice is also shown: http://www.youtube.com/watch?v=eYJBBm7bilA&eurl=http%3A%2F%2Fvideo%2Egoogle%2Ecom%2Fvideosearch%3Fclient%3Dsafari%26rls%3Den%26q%3DReality%2BTherapy%26oe%3DUTF%2D8%26um%3D1%26ie%3DUTF%2D8%26ei%3DcFpaSoqkApGCmQf9kp2HAg%26sa%3DX&feature=player_embedded
- This link will take you to a YouTube depiction of reality therapy with an angry parent: http://video.google.com/videosearch?client=safari&rls=en&q=Reality+Therapy&oe=UTF8&um=1&ie=UTF8&ei=cFpaSoqkApGCmQf9kp2HAg&sa=X&oi=video_result_group&ct=title&resnum=12#

Cognitive Behavioral Approaches

- In the YouTube video titled *Cognitive Therapy: The Case of Tim*, you can view a fictitious counseling session using cognitive therapy: http://www.youtube.com/watch?v=LIzm4jiyvXI
- This link will take you to a counseling scenario that utilizes the strategies of cognitive therapy: http://www.youtube.com/watch?v=GqW8p9WPweQ&feature=related

Solution-Focused Brief Therapy

- This link will take you to a YouTube video titled *What is Solution Focused Brief Therapy?* Counselors describe the use of this approach in their practices: http://www.youtube.com/watch?v=R2G8UKA4yIU&feature=related
- This link will take you to a video titled *A Brief History of the Solution-Focused Approach* and the individuals who shaped this approach: http://www.youtube.com/watch?v=J0hcpLKVp7o&feature=related

Narrative Therapy

- A description of narrative therapy by Robert Rich is available on this link with examples of stories that people believe in order to continue their unhappy situations: http://anxietyanddepression-help.com/narra.html
- The following link will take you to a YouTube demonstration that was filmed for a class at the University of Texas, Austin: http://www.youtube.com/watch?v=uO5ssGiWHT8

Using Art in Counseling

- This link will take you to art therapy activities that you can adapt with the school-aged youth that you are counseling: http://www.arttherapyblog.com/c/art-therapy-activities/
- This link will take you to a page that explains art therapy and provides numerous activities that you can use in individual or group counseling: http://www.vickyb.demon.co.uk/

Play Therapy

- This link will take you to the home page of the Association for Play Therapy. An overview of play therapy, a shot media presentation describing play therapy, and links to play therapy organizations are found on this site: http://www.a4pt.org/ps.playtherapy.cfm
- This link will take you to a journal article that describes 15 effective play therapy techniques that you could adapt and implement with students in your setting: http://pegasus.cc.ucf.edu/~drbryce/Play%20Therapy%20Techniques.pdf

Music Therapy

- This link will take you to a short video that describes the use of music in counseling: http://video.google.com/videosearch?client=safari&rls=en&q=music+therapy&oe=UTF8&um=1&ie=UTF8&ei=sGJaSt3RHc6wmAfdp7TxAg&sa=X&oi=video_result_group&ct=title&resnum=4#
- This Web site from the American Music Therapy Association provides answers to frequently asked questions about music therapy: http://www.musictherapy.org/faqs.html

References

Baggerly, J., & Parker, M. (2005). Child-centered group play therapy with African American boys at the elementary school level. *Journal of Counseling and Development, 83,* 387–396.

Beck, A. T. (1976). *Cognitive therapy and emotional disorders.* New York: International Universities Press.

Beck, A. T. (1987). Cognitive therapy. In J. K. Zeig (Ed.), *The evolution of psychotherapy* (pp. 149–178). New York: Brunner/Mazel.

Bonnington, S. (1993). Solution-focused brief therapy: Helpful interventions for school counselors. *The School Counselor, 41,* 126–128.

Bixler, L. (2001). The status of the use of music as a counseling tool by elementary school counselors in Virginia (Doctoral dissertation, Virginia Polytechnic Institute and State University, 2001). *Dissertation Abstracts International, 66,* 4307.

Carlson, T. D. (1997). Using art in narrative therapy: Enhancing therapeutic possibilities. *The American Journal of Family Therapy, 25,* 271–283.

Cochran, J. L. (1996). Using play and art therapy to help culturally diverse students overcome barriers to school success. *School Counselor, 43,* 287–299.

Corey, G. (2009a). *Theory and practice of counseling and psychotherapy* (8th ed., pp. 16–35). Belmont, CA: Thomson Higher Education.

Corey, G. (2009b). *Theory and practice of counseling and psychotherapy* (8th ed., pp. 315–338). Belmont, CA: Thomson Higher Education.

Corey, G. (2009c). *Theory and practice of counseling and psychotherapy* (8th ed., pp. 272–314). Belmont, CA: Thomson Higher Education.

Corey, G. (2009d). *Theory and practice of counseling and psychotherapy* (8th ed., pp. 387–404). Belmont, CA: Thomson Higher Education.

Corsini, R. J., & Wedding, D. (2005a). *Current psychotherapies* (7th ed., pp. 131–165). Belmont, CA: Brooks/Cole.

Corsini, R. J., & Wedding, D. (2005b). *Current psychotherapies* (7th ed., pp. 238–268). Belmont, CA: Brooks/Cole.

D'Andrea, M., & Daniels, J. (1995). Helping students learn to get along: Assessing the effectiveness of a multicultural developmental guidance project. *Elementary School Guidance and Counseling, 30,* 144–153.

deShazer, S. (1985). *Keys to solutions in brief therapy*. New York: Norton.

deShazer, S. (1988). *Clues: Investigating solutions in brief therapy*. New York: Norton.

Downing, J., & Harrison, T. (1992). Solutions and school counseling. *The School Counselor, 39,* 327–332.

Ellis, A. (2004a). *Rational emotive behavior therapy: It works for me—It can work for you*. Amherst, NY: Prometheus.

Ellis, A. (2004b). *The road to tolerance: The philosophy of rational emotive behavior therapy*. Amherst, NY: Prometheus.

Emery, M. J. (2004). Art therapy as an intervention for autism. *Art Therapy: Journal of the American Art Therapy Association, 21,* 143–147.

Glasser, W. (1969). *Schools without failure*. New York: Harper & Row.

Glasser, W. (1990). *The basic concepts of reality therapy* [chart]. Canoga Park, CA: Institute for Reality Therapy.

Glasser, W. (1998). *The quality school* (Rev. ed.). New York: Harper & Row.

Glasser, W. (2001). *Counseling with choice theory: The new reality therapy*. New York: HarperCollins.

Glasser, W. (2005). *Defining mental health as a public health problem: A new leadership role for the helping professions*. Chatsworth, CA: William Glasser Institute.

Hackney, H. L., & Cormier, S. (2009). *The professional counselor*. Upper Saddle River, NJ: Pearson Education.

Haigh, G. (2005, April). Finding a voice. *The Times Educational Supplement,* 15–18.

Hendricks, C. B. (2001). A study of the use of music therapy techniques in a group for the treatment of adolescent depression (Doctoral dissertation, Texas Tech University, 2001). *Dissertation Abstracts International, 62,* 472.

Jackson, N. A. (2003). A survey of music therapy methods and their role in the treatment of early elementary school children with ADHD. *Journal of Music Therapy, 40,* 302–323.

Kahn, B. (1999). Art therapy with adolescents: Making it work for school counselors. *Professional School Counseling, 2,* 291–299.

Kennedy, A. (2008). Creating connection, crafting wellness. *Counseling Today, 5,* 34–38.

LaFountain, R., Garner, N., & Eliason, G. (1996). Solution-focused counseling groups: A key for school counselors. *The School Counselor, 43,* 256–267.

Landreth, G. (2002). *Play therapy: The art of the relationship*. New York: Brunner-Routledge.

McDonald, R. (1984, May). Violent play and nonviolent people. *Friends Journal,* 4–6.

Monte, C. F., & Sollod, R. N. (2003). *Beneath the mask: An introduction to theories of personality* (7th ed., pp. 448–488). Hoboken, NJ: John Wiley & Sons.

Murphy, J. (1997). *Solution-focused counseling in middle and high schools.* Alexandria, VA: American Counseling Association.

Natale, J. (1996). Art as healer. *The Executive Educator, 18,* 12–16.

Naumburg, M. (2001). Spontaneous art in education and psychotherapy. *American Journal of Art Therapy, 40,* 46–64.

Neimeyer, R. A. (2000). Narrative disruptions in the construction of the self. In R. A. Neimeyer & J. Raskin (Eds.), *Constructions of disorder* (pp. 207–242). Washington, DC: American Psychological Association.

Nordling, W. L., & Guerney, L. F. (1999). Typical stages in the child-centered play therapy process. *Journal for the Professional Counselor, 14,* 17–23.

Raghurman, R. S. (1999). Battling separation anxiety. *American Journal of Art Therapy, 37,* 120–129.

Riley, S. (1999). Brief therapy: An adolescent invention. *Art Therapy: Journal of the American Art Association, 16,* 83–86.

Robbins, A. (1980). *Expressive therapy.* New York: Human Science Press.

Rogers, C. (1951). *Counselee-centered therapy.* Boston: Houghton Mifflin.

Schaefer, C. E., & O'Connor, K. J. (1983). *Handbook of play therapy.* Toronto: John Wiley & Sons.

Sharf, R. (2008a). *Theories of psychotherapy and counseling: Concepts and cases* (4th ed., pp. 187–218). Belmont, CA: Thomson Higher Education.

Sharf, R. (2008b). *Theories of psychotherapy and counseling: Concepts and cases* (4th ed., pp. 374–407). Belmont, CA: Thomson Higher Education.

Sharf, R. (2008c). *Theories of psychotherapy and counseling: Concepts and cases* (4th ed., pp. 334–373). Belmont, CA: Thomson Higher Education.

Sharf, R. (2008d). *Theories of psychotherapy and counseling: Concepts and cases* (4th ed., pp. 420–428). Belmont, CA: Thomson Higher Education.

Shovlin, K. J. (1999). Discovering a narrative voice through play and art therapy: A case study. *Guidance and Counseling, 14,* 7–12.

Thomas, D. A., & Gibbons, M. M. (2009). Narrative theory: A career counseling approach for adolescents of divorce. *Professional School Counseling, 12,* 223–229.

Trotter, K., Eshelman, D., & Landreth, G. (2001). A place for Bobo in play therapy. *International Journal of Play Therapy, 12,* 117–139.

Veach, L. J., & Gladding, S. (2007). Using creative group techniques in high schools. *The Journal for Specialists in Group Work, 32,* 71–81.

Vines, G. (2004). Turn on the music. *ASCA School Counselor, 41,* 10–13.

Vines, G. (2005). Middle school counseling: Touching the souls of adolescents. *Professional School Counseling, 9,* 175–176.

White, M. (1993). Deconstruction and therapy. In S. Gilligan & R. Price (Eds.), *Therapeutic conversations* (pp. 23–51). New York: Norton.

White, M. (1995). *Re-authoring lives: Interviews and essays.* Adelaide, South Australia: Dulwich Center.

White, M., & Epston, D. (1990). *Narrative means to therapeutic ends.* New York: Norton.

Wubbolding, R. E. (2004). Professional school counselors and reality therapy. In B. Erford (Ed.), *Professional school counseling: A handbook of theories, programs, and practices* (pp. 211–218). Austin, TX: CAPS Press.

– 4 –

Overview of Supervision

Jeannine R. Studer
Joel F. Diambra

The purpose of this chapter is to:

- Assess personal readiness for supervision
- Assist in setting supervision goals
- Provide strategies for personal wellness
- Discuss technology in counseling and supervision

School counselors-in-training have identified supervision as a vital key to successful practicum and internship experiences. Furthermore, they have identified the clinical experiences as the most influential and beneficial aspect of their academic training (McClam, 2000). Therefore, practicum and internship supervision conducted by a professional school counselor who has had training in supervision and experience as a school counselor is critically important. As mentioned in Chapter 1, you may either have the opportunity to choose your own supervisor, or the program placement coordinator may select a site supervisor for you. Your placement will be based on the coordinator's knowledge of the school site counseling program, the supervisor's ability to supervise, philosophy of school counseling, and willingness to meet with you on a regular basis. In either case, you need to discuss your personal and professional goals with the placement coordinator so that your needs are known in selecting a site. Once a supervisor has been selected, meeting with this individual and learning about the school is an essential first step. The information and activities in this chapter are created to assist you in thinking about the process of supervision as you learn from an experienced professional. Making an initial contact with your supervisor, appropriate dress, understanding school policies and procedures, and methods for introducing yourself to the individuals with whom you will work are included in this chapter.

Making the Initial Contact

Remember that you are a guest in the school. The initial contact with the supervisor makes a lasting impression, and you want it to be a good one. An initial contact may be made through a phone call to the school to set up an appointment. Keep in mind that many school counselors are difficult to contact due to their varied schedule and the number of schools to which many are assigned. Therefore, sending a clear and well-crafted, error-free e-mail may be a better option (refer to Figure 4.1). When you arrive for your meeting be sure to dress professionally and arrive on time.

Dress

You are in a professional setting and the attire you are used to wearing in the classroom as a graduate student may not be acceptable in a K–12 school environment. It is better to dress up rather than face embarrassment if your inappropriate attire must be discussed with your site supervisor. Unfortunately, we know of incidents when supervisees who were inappropriately clad in revealing

---

Subject: Practicum/Internship Meeting

Dear (Ms./Mrs./Mr./Dr. Last Name of Supervisor),

I am writing to schedule an appointment with you to discuss and plan my practicum (or internship) experience with you this coming semester at (name of school). I am a master's degree school counseling student enrolled at (name of school/institution). My faculty supervisor's contact information is

Name
Title
Telephone Numbers
E-mail

I am available to meet you at your school, in your office at the following dates and times:

(Provide at least three different dates and times).

I will bring my resume, proof of liability insurance, my professional disclosure statement, and the program practicum/internship handbook for your records. Please contact me if there is anything else I should bring to our initial meeting. I look forward to meeting you and conducting my practicum (or internship) under your direct supervision.

Sincerely,

(Your full name)
(Phone number and e-mail)

FIGURE 4.1   Sample initial letter to site supervisor.

clothing were sent home by the school principal to change into more modest and professional attire. A nonprofessional look may include such things as visible tattoos and body piercings, open-toed sandals, flip-flops, shorts, jeans, revealing blouses, T-shirts, shirts with slogans, and short skirts. Studies have revealed that many employers view appearance as a reflection of an employee's work competence and social values, and decisions about the person are based on these perceptions (Kaiser, 1990, as cited in Holloman, LaPoint, Alleyne, Palmer, & Sanders-Phillips, 1996). You are an adult role model to pre-K–12 students, and your appearance and behavior influence the lives of school-aged youth more than you may realize.

The information presented here is a general guideline. Each practicum and internship school is unique, and the dress code reflects the mission of each school. As a result you are strongly encouraged to discuss the dress code with your site supervisor. Do this at the initial meeting or by telephone prior to your initial meeting.

Absences, Tardiness, and Attendance

Even though you are not being paid during your practicum and internship, you still need to act as if you were an employee of the school. When you leave the confines of the academic institution and enter the school setting, you are in direct contact with your future colleagues and potential employers. In fact, you may desire a job in the school in which you conduct your practicum or internship experience. Regardless of your employment desires, your site supervisor will likely act as a reference for you and communicate to future employers.

Make it a practice to arrive 5 to 15 minutes early. Any time you suspect that you may be tardy or absent, immediately contact your site supervisor and inform him or her of your circumstances (this is especially easy if you have entered your supervisor's telephone number on your cell phone). Tardiness and absences are preventable with adequate planning and self-discipline. However, occasionally accidents occur. When you communicate with your site supervisor, do not make excuses. Briefly inform him or her of the facts, own your responsibility in causing the tardiness or absenteeism, state that it will not happen again, and move on.

Attendance is another professional responsibility. Keep in mind that the school calendar is often different than the academic calendar where you are enrolled as a school counseling student. For liability reasons many programs are reluctant to allow their students to start or end their clinical experiences in a K–12 school building when their own training institution is not in session. Some programs allow supervisees to observe in their assigned school and accumulate indirect hours until their university/college program begins. Check with your faculty supervisor as to when you are able to begin this experience.

School Policies and Procedures

Before beginning your practicum or internship, familiarize yourself with the school policies and procedures. Ask for a faculty handbook that outlines such things as the dress code, schedule, the policy for excusing students from class, the academic calendar, and a listing of the resources and personnel in the school. In many schools any person who enters the building is required to have an identification badge that is worn throughout the day. Check with your site supervisor to see whether this is something that you will need and how you can obtain one. In addition, many school systems are requiring individuals to have a background check and drug screen test before they are able to enter the schools. Verify whether you will need to have these tests. Furthermore, teachers are often reluctant to dismiss students from their classes particularly because state and federal guidelines monitor student achievement. To create and maintain a positive working relationship with each teacher, confirm the best times to release students from classes, the procedures for excusing them from class, and the policy for returning students to class.

Introducing Yourself to the Students, Staff, and Parents

Teachers, administrators, and parents/guardians want to know who will be working with their students and are often hesitant to release a child or adolescent to someone who is unknown to them. Arrange for a time to meet and introduce yourself to these constituents. Faculty meetings provide an opportune time to meet with the faculty and staff, give them information about yourself and your credentials, and how you may be reached. Parent Teacher Association (PTA) meetings are an excellent opportunity to introduce yourself to parents/guardians. Bringing a professional disclosure statement to be distributed to faculty and parents/guardians is one strategy to help them get to know you better. This document includes such things as a description of the clinical course in which you are enrolled, education, experiences related to counseling, names of supervisors (both site and program), professional membership, nature of counseling or philosophy, and a statement regarding confidentiality.

ACTIVITY 4.1

Critical Components of a Professional Disclosure Statement

Complete the following information:

1. Name and contact information _____
2. Education and training _____
3. Experiences related to counseling _____
4. Names of supervisors _____
5. Nature of counseling/philosophy _____
6. Professional memberships _____
7. Professional code of ethics _____
8. Hours and days available _____
9. Confidentiality statement _____

ACTIVITY 4.2

Develop your Professional Disclosure Statement by following the sample below and filling in your information given in Activity 4.1.

Professional Disclosure Statement

Date

Jane Doe
1234 Alphabet Street
City, State Zip
Telephone Numbers
E-mail Address

I earned my B.A. degree in psychology from the Quality University in 2010. Currently I am a working toward earning my school counseling master's degree in school counseling from Exemplary University. My anticipated date of graduation is May 2011. I have been a camp counselor at Camp Have a Good Time for three consecutive summers and completed my practicum experience last semester at South Middle School.

For my internship, my site supervisor is Ms. Good Heart (phone 987-654-3210) and my faculty supervisor is Dr. Long Ago (phone 012-345-6789).

Briefly, my philosophy of school counseling is embedded in reality theory. I believe students make choices and are responsible for the choices they make (whether or not they are aware of the choices they have made). Therefore, I strive to help students gain awareness of their own responsibility in their lives and to make purposeful and productive choices that lead to or accomplish their self-determined goals.

(continued on next page)

ACTIVITY 4.2 (continued)

I am an active member in the local counseling association chapter. The local chapter is affiliated with the state counseling association, Best State Counseling Association, and American School Counseling Association, both of which I am a member. I adhere to the American School Counseling Association (ASCA) Code of Ethics and am accountable to my supervisors, local, state, and national associations.

As per agreement with my site and faculty supervisors, I plan to be on the Cool Middle School campus to conduct my internship Mondays, Wednesdays, and Fridays from 8:00 a.m. to 3:30 p.m. throughout the school year.

The information students share with me will be held in confidence except for the following reasons: my supervisor needs to be aware of the nature of the issue to provide the best care to the student; the student requests, in writing, that I share the information with a specified person; the student shares information that implies s/he could harm her/himself, or someone else putting someone in immanent danger. In these situations a caregiver has a legal right to this information.

Signature _____ Date _____

You will also need a plan for meeting with students to introduce yourself, your role in the school, and how you can be contacted. When students know who you are they are more willing to work with you, and your site supervisors can help make arrangements for you to meet students. At times school counselors-in-training will arrange a time in advance with the teachers to enter the classroom to introduce themselves to the students. The introduction needs to be based on the age of the students and their level of understanding. For younger students, simple terminology and creativity helps to keep their attention and assists in helping them remember who you are. Several activities to consider for introductions are

1. Stand in the hallways when students are changing classes and introduce yourself as they pass by in the halls. Shake their hands and tell them who you are and how they can contact you.
2. Post brightly colored paper with your photograph explaining who you are, days and times you are available, where you are located, and how they can contact you.
3. Make up business cards so that older students or adults can put them in their wallets or purses. Include your name, contact information, and where you can be reached. GigglePrint.com offers a site where you can select free business cards that can be customized.
4. Attend extracurricular activities. Students appreciate your attendance and you will have an opportunity to understand different aspects of the school environment.
5. Design a crossword puzzle that includes keywords such as your name, what you do, where you can be reached, and so forth. There are several online resources available for quickly and easily creating crossword puzzles. You simply need to identify key words and then a clue for each word. Computer programs can automatically create a crossword puzzle from these key words and clues. A few Web sites that help create crossword puzzles are provided in the following list for your convenience. If you have trouble accessing these sites, simply use a search engine (e.g., Google) and seek "Create Crossword Puzzles."

http://www.crosswordpuzzlegames.com/create.html
http://www.armoredpenguin.com/crossword/
http://www.eclipsecrossword.com/

ACTIVITY 4.3

Brainstorm other ways that you could introduce yourself to parents, students, and teachers.

_____

_____

_____

_____

Self-Reflection of Readiness for Supervision

The practicum and internship are designed to build your school counseling knowledge, skills, and values through application of theory to practice in a real work setting. Too often counselors-in-training look at these experiences as "something that has to be done to fulfill the degree requirements." If this last statement reflects your thinking, you are not ready for either of these experiences, and may need to reconsider your decision to enter the school counseling profession, because you are preparing to directly influence the lives of numerous children. These clinical experiences are designed to help you become an excellent school counselor, and it is up to you to use these opportunities to help yourself grow personally and professionally.

Research indicates that early counseling-related experiences are influential to counseling effectiveness (Reupert, 2006). However, other factors such as the counselor's age, gender, education, and personality also influence the process. In fact, the counselor's personal qualities are often considered as the most important factors (Reupert, 2006) impacting the counseling relationship. This leads to the question, "What are the qualities that are essential to be an effective counselor?" Behaviorists express the importance of empathy and rapport (Lazarus, 1985, as cited in Reupert, 2006). Person-centered counselors mention empathy in addition to qualities of genuineness, congruence, and respectfulness (Meador & Rogers, 1984, as cited in Reupert, 2006). Systems theorists identify self-disclosure and understanding as vital to building an alliance with counselees (Oke, 1994, as cited in Reupert, 2006) in addition to personal self-awareness (Kondrat, 1999, as cited in Reupert, 2006). The American Counseling Association (ACA) and its Code of Ethics also identify characteristics essential to effective counseling relationships (Engels et al., 2004).

ACTIVITY 4.4

What personal qualities do you think an effective counselor should have? Write your responses below.

_____   _____   _____

_____   _____   _____

_____   _____   _____

Now, compare your list with those of your peers. What are some of the similarities? Differences?

_____

_____

_____

ACTIVITY 4.5

The following is a list of characteristics associated with effective counseling. Circle those traits you believe are your personal qualities. When you are finished, give this list to someone who knows you well and ask that person to circle those qualities that they believe apply to you.

My Personal Qualities

(Circle the qualities that you believe best describe you.)

Empathetic	Culturally Aware
Genuine	Validates Other's Concerns
Good Communication Skills	Integrity
Congruent	Uses Humor Appropriately
Respectful	Cooperative
Self-Aware	Acknowledges Mistakes
High Tolerance for Stress	Able to Make Appropriate Decisions
Maintains Good Mental Health	Professional Demeanor
Encouraging	Dependable
Composed in Stressful Situations	Responsible
Patient with Other's Progress	Intelligent
Creative	Intentional
Sensitive	Honest
Leader	Insightful
Consistent	Motivated

Now, compare your list with the list provided by your significant person and discuss the similarities and differences between the two lists. If there are discrepancies between your view of self and their perceptions, prompt them to give you specific examples. Recognizing your strengths and areas in which you need to improve gives you an opportunity to set personal goals for your practicum and internship experiences. Include these goals on your practicum and/or internship contract and strategies to reach these objectives.

Goal Setting

When you have a good understanding of the practicum and internship experiences, you are less likely to be disappointed. Likewise, the supervisor also needs a thorough understanding of the clinical experience and his or her role in supervision. Not everyone enters the clinical experiences with the same training or education. For instance, those with a background in education usually have a better knowledge of such things as the school structure, policies, and classroom management. Those who have a human services background may have a better understanding of the counseling process.

After you have reflected on your strengths and areas in which you need more experience, gather ideas from the counselors at your school site to determine specific projects they would like to accomplish. Some examples include updating and formalizing the school critical incident management plan, creating a college scholarship resource handbook for college-bound students, collecting community agency information for referral purposes, or implementing a group for students from divorced parental homes. A contract that outlines the expectations for the supervisory relationship and the activities you are to perform is essential. The contract, then, serves as a type of "job description" that outlines what you are going to do.

The American School Counselor Association (ASCA) promotes a comprehensive, developmental school counseling (CDSC) program. The ASCA National Standards outlines the knowledge and skills that pre-K–12 students need to be able to know and do in the academic, career, and personal/social domains. The standards serve as a foundation for the ASCA National Model® that was developed as a prototype for school counselors to use when developing their own program (ASCA, 2003). However, many school counseling programs have not yet made the transformation to a comprehensive and developmental program. Even if you are assigned to a school with a traditional school counseling program, many activities that the counselor/supervisor performs are reflective of those in the ASCA National Model. It is up to you to identify the activities that support a CDSC program during your clinical experiences in order to be prepared to take a leadership role in developing such a program when credentialed as a school counselor.

The following story illustrates one example of how a school counseling intern contributed to the school through a public relations activity that is a component of the management element of the ASCA National Model.

During her internship, one student polled the school counselors and identified a need to raise money to supplement school supplies for students from lower-income families. After thought and discussion, the intern determined she would create a recipe book to sell to faculty and parents. First, she created a flyer explaining the purpose of the project. She distributed the notice to students who were instructed to take the form to their parents/guardians, and put copies in faculty mailboxes with a request to send in a favorite recipe. Soon recipes flooded in that were representative of students from all grades and ethnic groups. The intern typed, formatted, and sorted the recipes into logical food categories, and requested students to generate a creative cover design and category names unique to the school. While she organized the recipe book, she contacted publishing companies, and one company agreed to publish her book. Although she realized that she would not be able to complete the entire project by the end of her internship, she asked her program supervisor if a future intern could complete the project. Through a collaborative discussion between the intern, site supervisor, and program supervisor, an upcoming intern agreed to complete the project. The recipe books were printed and sold to faculty and parents/guardians who were anxious to see their recipe in print. Within one month 1,500 copies were sold for $12.95 each. The money not only helped needy students, but another unexpected result was the positive and widespread public relations outcome for the school counseling program. This public relations activity is an element within the system support component of the ASCA National Model Delivery System.

ACTIVITY 4.6

Review the ASCA National Model in Chapter 6, Figure 6.1. In consultation with the program supervisor and your on-site school counseling supervisor, identify professional and personal goals that you wish to accomplish during your practicum and internship experiences. When you think about the activities to include on your contract, be sure they are supported in a CDSC program. Figure 4.2 represents an internship contract based on the ASCA standards and model.

The school counseling faculty promotes a developmental, comprehensive school counseling program, and request that the activities provided to the school counselor intern correspond with this model. The ASCA National Standards were developed for pre-K–12 students. However, school counselors perform activities that meet these standards, and interns are expected to perform activities that correspond with the ASCA National Model such as those indicated in the following contract.

Professional Goal	Performance Activities	Evaluation	ASCA Program Component
To develop a needs assessment	1. Develop a needs assessment for students 2. Administer the needs assessment 3. Interpret results	1. Feedback from school supervisor	Management

Personal Goal	Performance Activities	Evaluation	ASCA Program Component
To learn classroom management	1. Observe classroom teachers 2. Practice effective management skills in a guidance class	1. Feedback from classroom teacher	Accountability

Supervisory Activities Using the ASCA National Model®

Professional Goal	Performance Activities	Evaluation	ASCA Program Component

Personal Goals	Performance Activities	Evaluation	ASCA Program Component

The ASCA National Model components include:

Accountability
    Intervention and Performance Assessment
Delivery Service
    School Guidance Curriculum
    Individual Student Planning
    Responsive Services
    System Support

Foundation
    Beliefs and Philosophy
    ASCA National Standards
    Mission Statement
Management System
    Agreements
    Use of Data
    Action Plans
    Calendar

If the above meets the approval of the counselor and supervisors, please sign below.

School Counselor-in-Training _____ Date _____
Faculty Supervisor _____ Date _____
School Supervisor _____ Date _____

FIGURE 4.2   Sample internship contract.

Another preparation plan you may need to consider is a personal safety plan. You may be placed in a school setting that is located in what is regarded as a high-crime area. In situations such as these, you will need to consult with your supervisor on making a safety plan.

Personal Safety Plan

No one enters the school counseling profession thinking in terms of school violence, but the reality of the situation is that violence is very real in schools today (Fishbaugh, Berkeley, & Schroth, 2003). Some school-aged youth could pose a threat to your safety as well as others. At one time we had a graduate student in our school counseling program who grew up in a small, upper-middle class suburban area of Ohio that was characterized as fairly homogeneous and "safe." He attended a small liberal arts college with a student body similar to that of his high school. When he found out he was placed in an urban high school for his practicum, he was concerned about his safety and immediately sought out the program placement coordinator to request a different setting. He was instructed to talk with his site supervisor about the school safety plan and to ask for assistance in making up his own personal safety plan. Reluctantly, he agreed to do this. After only one week, he began to speak enthusiastically about his practicum school and relayed how much he was learning from this unique experience. Eventually, he actually thanked his placement coordinator for not transferring him to a different site. After graduation, and as a result of this experience, he was able to secure a position as a school counselor in an urban middle school. No school is exempt from school violence, and although well-being is a definite concern in preparing for your clinical setting, preparation is a key for personal safety.

Most schools have adopted a policy that specifies procedures for alerting teachers and faculty when an emergency occurs. This plan outlines the action each person is to take, including the school counselor's crisis management responsibilities. Every person who works in the school should know how to implement the plan, and you are no exception. In fact, it is possible that you will be a key player in crisis intervention if a crisis plan needs to be activated. Consider the following:

- When you are working with a student who is angry, keep the office door open and ask your supervisor to sit in on the session.
- If your supervisor is not available, it may be best to speak with an angry student in the hall or waiting area if there is one available.
- Look for signs of mounting tension, irritability, and so forth. When potential violence is evident, ask the student to discuss his or her feelings. Verbalizing feelings is better than having the counselee act out these feelings (Star, 1984).
- Speak in a calm, quiet voice to calm the student.
- Park in a well-lighted area in the parking lot.
- Leave the school building with another person.
- Leave expensive jewelry and clothing at home.

ACTIVITY 4.7
Read the school safety plan at your clinical site and compare this plan with those of your peers. Develop your own safety plan.

Taking Care of Yourself as a Professional

A talented writer and late university colleague of ours, Dr. Ted Hipple, could be depended upon to sign off on all of his written correspondence with the words, "Be Well." Hipple understood the bottom line: health makes all the difference. I have heard it said, "If you haven't got your health,

ACTIVITY 4.8

List five stressful situations you have encountered in the past year. Now list specific ways you attempted to manage each stressful situation.

Situation	Stress Management Strategy(ies)
_____	_____
_____	_____
_____	_____
_____	_____
_____	_____

Now put a plus (+) in front of the strategies that are positive, or ones that are healthy and bring about constructive results. Put a minus (−) next to those strategies that are negative, or ones that bring about unhelpful consequences. How successful are the strategies you use? If you note unhelpful strategies, it is time to try some new ways of managing your stress. Be sure to listen carefully as your peers share strategies they use to help them handle difficult situations.

you haven't got anything." Those of us who are showing our age or who have experienced poor health seem to understand the importance of promoting and maintaining good health easier than our younger friends. (I didn't say we older folks follow our own advice, mind you.)

Burnout is defined as emotional exhaustion, disconnection, and a lack of concern (Haddad, 1998, as cited in Butler & Constantine, 2005). The increased levels of stress impact physical, emotional, and intellectual difficulties that can result in poor performance and negative feelings among school counselors as well as with those with whom they work (Wilkerson & Bellini, 2006). Some of the stressors reported by school counselors include not enough time to see students, too much paperwork, professional job overload, too much clerical work, an unmanageable case load, role ambiguity, counseling a child in which there is a suspicion of abuse (Sears & Navin, 1983), lack of decision making among administrators, low salary, and poor relationships with teachers and administrators (Wilkerson & Bellini, 2006).

You will be performing many school counselor activities and, as in starting a new job, this requires learning and experiencing various responsibilities in short periods of time. On top of these stresses, many supervisees continue to take additional classes while in their clinical courses and even choose to be employed while completing practicum and internship. This makes for a full and stressful schedule. Furthermore, there is the added responsibility of making new relationships at the school, with parents, and others. Taking care of yourself is vital, and time must be scheduled to ensure physical, emotional, and psychological health, or your progress may be delayed and could negatively affect your performance.

One technique for managing stress is to consider how you perceive stress. For instance, when people define stress as a problem, it is viewed as something that is beyond their control. When taught to redefine stress as a challenge rather than as a problem, people can feel as if they have control over these demanding situations (Stensrud & Stensrud, 1983) rather than being controlled by the stress. Several other stress management techniques include

- Assertiveness
- Goal setting
- Problem-solving strategies
- Exercise
- Social support
- Meditation
- Massage
- Biofeedback
- Yoga

The Use of Technology in Counseling and Supervision

Practicing school counselors depend on computers to be more effective on the job, and awareness of the different types of technology used by school counselors will be beneficial to you as you enter your clinical experiences. However, it is wise to balance any temptation to become technology dependent. For example, Carlson, Portman, and Bartlett (2006) warn counselors who rely on e-mail communication that they may miss opportunities for instrumental face-to-face communication necessary for developing trust and rapport in counseling relationships.

On the positive side, computer-literate counselors are able to contribute to education reform, and knowledge of available technology can assist in time management (Casey, 1995, as cited in Sabella & Booker, 2003). Counselors use technology to create and store student information, track courses, develop schedules, disseminate career information, find professional development opportunities, provide greater visibility of the school counseling program, and administer tests. Internet convenience is also helpful when counselors want to assist teachers and parents develop an awareness of such things as cyberbullying (also known as harassment, intimidation, or threats) by providing links to credible Internet resources.

Computers can also assist in finding accessible professional development opportunities. By joining an electronic mailing list (or listserv) such as that provided by the ASCA, discussion board questions can be posted to which numerous school counseling professionals can respond. This format is also useful for identifying professional concerns from archived questions and responses. However, even an electronic mailing list poses challenges. Almost anyone can join an electronic mailing list, so empirically based and accurate responses are not always provided. You are professionally responsible to take reasonable steps to ensure the information you receive and disseminate is sound, valid, and research based.

Counselors also use computers as accommodations for students with disabilities. For instance, software can translate written text to spoken text. This can be used with a student who has impaired vision. For a student with a hearing loss, verbal instructions can be converted to text. And for a student with a fine motor physical disability, a touch screen may be a helpful accommodation (Wall, 2004).

As a school counselor-in-training you may have better technology skills than your supervisor. This may be an opportune time for you to teach your supervisor technology skills that could make tasks as a school counselor more manageable. Carlson et al. (2006) found that 92.7% of school counselors at all grade levels reported that they felt at least somewhat comfortable using computers; however, 76.9% reported being anxious or very anxious in using a variety of software. Technology may provide an opportunity for you to contribute to your school site. You may be able to introduce

---

ACTIVITY 4.9

List six different forms of technology you use everyday. Now, identify one possible method this technology could be used in a school counseling program. Compare your list with your peers' lists.

Form of Technology	Skills	Use in School

current software, teach your supervisor basic technology skills to make cumbersome tasks more manageable, or develop efficient spreadsheets for combining and compiling counselee data.

Although there are many advantages to technology, these are accompanied by safety and ethical concerns, such as awareness of antivirus software to prevent malicious computer viruses from infecting and damaging data files. Additionally, installing and updating security software is a must to keep others from accessing computer-stored confidential records.

Conclusion

This chapter provides essential information to consider as you are preparing for your clinical experiences. Advance preparation assists in making these new opportunities less stressful. Identifying and starting activities such as contacting your site supervisor, and learning about the school policies and procedures, attendance policy, and crisis plans will orient you and help you feel comfortable. Developing a contract aligned with the ASCA National Model will identify site supervisor expectations and will assist you in gaining an understanding of how a school counselor assumes a leadership role in a CDSC program. Developing a personal safety plan is essential as you enter and leave the building, is a consideration in whatever setting you are placed, and is related to your own physical and mental health. The wellness practices you begin now will likely translate into the patterns of personal health you continue as a professional school counselor. Finally, be aware of computer uses in the school and how your skills may contribute to a more efficient school counseling program.

Web Site

This link provides links, publications, sample documents, and journal articles: http://www.schoolcounselor.org/resources.asp. You must be an ASCA member to access this site.

References

American School Counselor Association (ASCA). (2003). *ASCA National Standards for Students*. Alexandria, VA: Author.

Butler, S. K., & Constantine, M. G. (2005). Collective self-esteem and burnout in professional school counselors. *Professional School Counseling, 9*, 55–62.

Carlson, L. A., Portman, T. A. A., & Bartlett, J. R. (2006). Professional school counselors' approaches to technology. *Professional School Counseling, 9*, 252–256.

Engels, D. W., & Associates. (2004). *The professional counselor: Portfolio, competencies, performance guidelines, and assessment* (3rd ed.). Alexandria, VA: American Counseling Association.

Fishbaugh, M. S. E., Berkeley, T. R., & Schroth, G. (Eds.). (2003). *Ensuring safe school environments: Exploring issues, seeking solutions*. Mahwah, NJ: Lawrence Erlbaum Associates.

Holloman, L. O., LaPoint, V., Alleyne, S. I., Palmer, R. J., & Sanders-Phillips, K. (1996). Dress-related behavioral problems and violence in the public school setting: Prevention, intervention, and policy—A holistic approach. *Journal of Negro Education, 65*, 267–281.

McClam, T. (2000). *Follow-up studies of graduates*. Unpublished manuscript, University of Tennessee, Knoxville.

Reupert, A. (2006). The counsellor's self in therapy: An inevitable presence. *International Journal for the Advancement of Counselling, 28*, 95–105.

Sabella, R., & Booker, B. L. (2003). Using technology to promote your guidance and counseling program among stakeholders. *Professional School Counseling, 6*, 206–213.

Sears, S. J., & Navin, S. L. (1983). Stressors in school counseling. *Education, 103*, 333–337.

Star, B. (1984). Patient violence/therapist safety. *Social Work, 29*, 225–230.

Stensrud, R., & Stensrud, K. (1983). Coping skills training: A systematic approach to stress management counseling. *Personnel and Guidance Journal, 62*, 214–218.

Wall, J. E. (2004). *Enhancing assessment through technology.* Alexandria, VA: ASCA School Counselor.

Wilkerson, K., & Bellini, J. (2006). Intrapersonal and organizational factors associated with burnout among school counselors. *Journal of Counseling & Development, 84*, 440–450.

A Developmental Passage
Models of Supervision

Kristi A. Gibbs
Virginia A. Magnus

The purpose of this chapter is to:

• Provide an overview of supervision models
• Highlight challenges in supervision

School counselor education programs do not typically include formal training in supervision for master's-level practitioners (Dollarhide & Miller, 2006). Rather, courses in clinical supervision are typically found in doctoral programs (Council for Accreditation of Counseling and Related Educational Programs [CACREP], 2009). However, the clinical supervision of counselors is most often provided by master's-level practitioners, many of whom have not received adequate training in supervision (Britton, Goodman, & Rak, 2002; Dollarhide & Miller, 2006; McMahon & Simons, 2004). This is troublesome, especially given the legal and ethical ramifications of counseling and supervision (Herlihy, Gray, & McCollum, 2002).

Magnuson, Norem, and Bradley (2001) stated that when "counselors without adequate preparation assume responsibility for supervising trainees, they may inadvertently portray supervision as a superficial requirement and miss the opportunity to adequately prepare individual members of the next generation of counselors" (p. 214). Furthermore, the Ethical Guidelines for Counseling Supervisors (Association for Counselor Education and Supervision, 1995) indicate, "supervisors should have had training in supervision prior to initiating their role as supervisors" (Section 2.01, p. 272). Researchers (Dollarhide & Miller, 2006; Herlihy et al., 2002) have cited lack of training in supervision as one reason that school counselors-in-training may receive inadequate supervision. Accordingly, the intent of this chapter is to provide you with a basic overview of several models of supervision along with challenges you might encounter in supervision, thereby providing a basic framework for engaging in clinical supervision.

Right about now you may be saying, "I'm a student. Do I really need to read about supervision models and challenges? Who cares if I have a basic framework for supervision?" The answer is yes, you are a student, and no, you are probably not going to be supervising anyone this semester. However, you need to know what to expect from supervision so that you will be better prepared for this experience. Furthermore, you may find yourself in a position to supervise another school counselor-in-training in as little as 2 to 3 years, at which point you will reflect back on this chapter and say, "Wow, I actually know what a supervisor is supposed to do because I read about it in my school counseling book." Also, having this knowledge may provide you with tools to be a better consumer of supervision yourself, as you are undoubtedly receiving supervision right now. So, let's get started talking a little more about supervision.

Supervision Roles

The professional literature (Bernard & Goodyear, 2009; Studer, 2006) broadly identifies three categories of supervision models: (1) developmental models, (2) integrated or social role models, and

(3) models grounded in a specific counseling theory. The first two categories include models developed specifically for supervision, whereas the last category contains models that may more accurately be identified as extensions of a specific counseling theoretical orientation. Due to practicality and limitations of space, we will only discuss the first two categories in this chapter.

Developmental Models

Developmental models of supervision focus primarily on how you will grow and change over time through training and supervision (Bernard & Goodyear, 2009). Basic assumptions of developmental models of supervision include the belief that supervisees move through stages that are qualitatively different from one another. These stages require interventions and interactions from the supervisor, which differ across developmental levels (Bernard & Goodyear, 2009). Stated simply, developmental models suggest that in the first weeks of your practicum you will be at a specific developmental stage that is qualitatively different from your stage of counseling development in the last month of internship. Accordingly, you may benefit from a different supervisory environment, inquiries, and interventions in the beginning of the supervised experience when compared to later stages in the internship. Furthermore, you will grow in both confidence and skill over time, calling for awareness and flexibility from your supervisor.

In this section, we will provide an overview of what Bernard and Goodyear (2009) have described as the most widely used developmental model of supervision, the integrated developmental model (IDM). This model was originally developed by Stoltenberg (1981) and expanded upon with Delworth in 1987. These authors (Stoltenberg & Delworth, 1987) describe counselor development as occurring through four stages: (1) the beginning of the journey, (2) trial and tribulation, (3) challenge and growth, and (4) integrated. Additionally, the supervisee (that's you!) is described as "progressing in terms of three basic structures—self- and other-awareness, motivation, and autonomy" (Stoltenberg & Delworth, 1987, p. 35). Interactions between these three structures and the four levels of development are described in the following.

Level One: The Beginning of the Journey

In the first stage of counselor development, you enter the supervisory relationship with limited training and experience (Bernard & Goodyear, 2009). At this stage you are dependent on the supervisor, seeking to imitate skills and techniques rather than embracing your own style (Stoltenberg, 1981). It is our hope that as counselors and as future supervisors you will always remember the feelings associated with the beginning of this journey. Recalling memories of the early stages in your own development can help you gain confidence in your growth as a counselor. It may also help you to more effectively supervise school counselors-in-training in the future. For additional information, let us turn our focus to the aforementioned structures as they relate to level one supervisees described by Stoltenberg and Delworth (1987).

Self- and Other-Awareness
Awareness of both others and self is typically low at this stage of development. You may be extra-sensitive about any sort of evaluation. You may benefit from activities of reflection that help you understand yourself and others in the school context.

Motivation
High levels of motivation and anxiety are evident at level one. At this stage you may find yourself very attentive and focused, and you probably want to know the "right" answer as it pertains to interventions with counselees. Because you are new to the school, you may also be concerned with learning and retaining a plethora of new information coupled with a desire to perform adequately. Naturally, these competing pressures cause some anxiety.

Autonomy

The supervisee at this level is highly dependent on the supervisor, typically expecting the supervisor to provide structure in supervision. If you are at this stage you may need more positive feedback. You may not yet be ready to work by yourself and as a result may benefit from regular input and encouragement.

ACTIVITY 5.1

Spend 10 minutes with one or two other peers. Reflect back to when you first began your practicum or internship experience and share with each other your thoughts and feelings regarding your self- and other-awareness, motivation, and autonomy level at that time. Consider your supervision expectations, too.

Motivation

_____

_____

Autonomy

_____

_____

Self- and Other-Awareness

_____

_____

Expectations of Supervisor

_____

_____

Level Two: Trial and Tribulation

Level two supervisees are in conflict, seeking some autonomy while continuing to be somewhat dependent on the supervisor (Stoltenberg & Delworth, 1987). According to Stoltenberg (1981), counselors at this stage are increasing self-awareness while also striving for independence. Supervisors might expect supervisees in the second or third semester of training to be at this stage of development. If you are at this stage, you may begin to find yourself more independent, but this can result in a tumultuous time for the supervision process. To help with understanding what may contribute to supervisory tension, turn your attention to the structures proposed by Stoltenberg and Delworth (1987).

Self- and Other-Awareness

The supervisee becomes more able to focus increasingly on the counselee. You may begin to distinguish your own values and issues from those of the counselee; however, improved consciousness also includes self-recognition of less productive thoughts, habits, and values. This increased awareness may cause frustration for you as countertransference develops.

Motivation

Motivation and confidence are fluctuating at this stage. This may be partially due to the more advanced school counselor-in-training taking on counselees who are more difficult. You may feel confident in one moment and confused or unsure in the next. This confusion can impact motivation, so that you appear motivated at times for specific tasks and lack motivation at other times for different tasks, akin to an approach–avoidance response.

Autonomy

Supervisees are more assertive, choosing to implement new interventions of their own choosing. At this stage, you may no longer be imitative of your supervisor. However, dependency on the supervisor may still occasionally be present. Supervisor input may be more desired when you encounter a new counseling situation, an ambiguous ethical dilemma, or responsibility for a unique school activity.

Level Three: Challenge and Growth

At the next stage of development, supervisees should be coming into their own style; supervisees are able to understand their role in counseling. Stoltenberg and Delworth (1987) call this stage the "calm after the storm" (p. 93).

Self- and Other-Awareness

The supervisee is aware of self, including both strengths and weaknesses. You may develop a sense of professional confidence to grow in areas of weakness. Empathy allows you to be fully in the moment with the counselee but also to pull back when appropriate.

Motivation

The level three supervisee is relatively stable in terms of motivation and commitment to the profession. At this stage, the school counselor-in-training may still have doubts about the profession, but these doubts should not be immobilizing. You might begin to recognize that doubts and concerns may occasionally be a natural part of the developmental process.

Autonomy

Primarily autonomous, the supervisee seeks assistance from the supervisor for specific things. However, most decisions are made independently. Supervision tends to be more collegial in nature.

Level Four: Integrated

We all start out as beginning counselors in the initial stages of development. With perseverance and supervision, many of us are privileged to practice as counselors and eventually attain this ultimate stage in counseling development. Stoltenberg and Delworth (1987) called this stage *integrated* to signify the integration of the supervisee across all three domains: motivation, autonomy, and self–other awareness. These authors also assert a belief that most counselors require at least 5 or 6 years of professional experience to reach this level. So be patient and do not expect to be perfect immediately.

Self- and Other-Awareness

The supervisee is aware of self, including specific strengths and weaknesses. He or she has developed professional confidence and readily seeks input from others for self-improvement. Empathy allows the counselor to fluidly adjust from being fully in the here and now with the counselee to pulling back when therapeutic.

Motivation

The level three supervisee is motivated and committed to the counseling profession. When you reach this stage, you should have few doubts about the profession and realize that occasional doubts and concerns are a natural part of the developmental process.

Autonomy

At this stage you should be very autonomous. Most decisions should be made independently with occasional assistance from your supervisor for specific things. Supervision is collegial in nature.

ACTIVITY 5.2

Identify a counselor you think personifies level three, integrated characteristics. Write down ways this counselor demonstrates integration.

Motivation

_____

_____

Autonomy

_____

_____

Self- and Other-Awareness

_____

_____

In the preceding pages, we provided an overview of Stoltenberg and Delworth's (1987) developmental model of supervision. Our focus with the developmental model was on stages of supervisee development across time. In the pages that follow, we shift our focus to the supervisor and specific roles that might be utilized in the supervision relationship. However, before we move on, we would like to encourage you to take a few minutes to reflect and think about where you are, developmentally, in your journey toward becoming a professional school counselor. Keep in mind the four levels offered by Stoltenberg and Delworth (1987): (1) the beginning of the journey, (2) trial and tribulation, (3) challenge and growth, (4) integrated, and be mindful of your own levels of awareness, motivation, and autonomy.

Social Role Models

Social role models as described by Bernard and Goodyear (2009) delineate different roles that the supervisor might employ during the course of supervision. Three roles specifically identified in the literature are teacher, counselor, and consultant (Bernard, 1979; Bernard & Goodyear, 2009). However, it is important to note that although supervision has similarities to the aforementioned roles, it is a qualitatively different skill. Douce (as cited in Bernard & Goodyear, 2009, p. 101) stated that "supervision is a separate skill similar to teaching—but different; similar to counseling—but different; and similar to consulting—but different." As we discuss one social role model of supervision, Bernard's (1979) discrimination model, give special attention to the nuances of each of the roles: supervisor, teacher, counselor, and consultant.

TABLE 5.1   Examples of the Discrimination Model

Focus of Supervision	Teacher	Counselor	Consultant
Process skills or intervention	Counselor would like to learn a specific skill Supervisor teaches the skill	Counselor rarely addresses feelings during sessions Supervisor attempts to help counselor determine how discussing feelings impacts him or her and how this might be limiting his or her ability to focus on feelings in session	Counselor wants to use a sand tray technique in session Supervisor works with counselor to identify resources that provide information about the technique
Conceptualization skills	Counselor is unable to identify themes between counseling sessions Supervisor points out connections between sessions, helping counselor identify overarching themes	Counselor is unable to identify appropriate goals for counselee Supervisor helps counselor identify personal triggers that may be blocking ability to identify goals in session	Counselor would like to conceptualize counselee from a different theoretical orientation Supervisor discusses beliefs of that particular theory and how conceptualization might look
Personalization skills	Counselor is unaware that his or her tendency to maintain direct eye contact makes counselee uncomfortable Supervisor talks about multicultural diversity and the fact that making eye contact is considered disrespectful in some cultures	Counselor becomes defensive when counselee indicates preference for a different counselor Supervisor discusses why being liked is so important to the counselor	Counselor would like to feel more comfortable and competent working with gay or lesbian counselees Supervisor helps counselor to identify several things that might help to increase both his or her comfort and competence with counselees who are gay or lesbian

The discrimination model (Bernard, 1979) identifies three supervisor roles and three areas of focus for supervision. The focus areas are *intervention skills* (overt behaviors of the supervisee), *conceptualization skills* (covert behaviors including how the supervisee understands what the counselee is saying and recognizes themes), and *personalization skills* (ability of the supervisee to hear feedback from both counselee and supervisor, and ability to recognize and be comfortable with the counselor's own feelings, values, and attitudes).

According to the discrimination model (Bernard, 1979) the supervisor must first determine the area of focus and then choose a role from which to respond. As previously indicated, the roles include teacher, counselor, and consultant. Bernard cautions the supervisor to remember that there are nine choices for the supervisor to consider and that each circumstance should be approached as a unique situation. As shown in Table 5.1, each of the supervisor roles is identified with a particular focus for supervision.

Thus far we have discussed two models of supervision: The integrated developmental model (Stoltenberg & Delworth, 1987) and the discrimination model (Bernard, 1979). Although both were developed for the explicit purpose of supervising counselors, some (Luke & Bernard, 2006; Wood & Rayle, 2006) have wondered whether traditional models of counselor supervision are meeting the supervision needs of school counselors-in-training given the tasks they are expected to perform as part of their comprehensive, developmental school counseling (CDSC) programs. To address that gap, we will provide an overview of an expanded version of the discrimination model that was developed specifically for school counselors (Luke & Bernard, 2006).

ACTIVITY 5.3

Consider and answer the questions to the following scenario and compare your responses with those of your peers.

> Amy is a practicum student in an elementary school. Juanita, a third-grade student, comes to see Amy because she is concerned about her brother, Miquel, who is being deployed with the Army. Amy has difficulty working with Juanita because it brings up her own feelings for her father, who is also being deployed to a foreign country.

What role should the supervisor assume in the focus areas of process, conceptualization, and personalization skills?

School Counseling Supervision Models

School counseling supervision must attend to functions of the school counselor-in-training, which are not necessarily limited to individual and group counseling (Luke & Bernard, 2006). Accordingly, Luke and Bernard (2006) identified four domains of CDSC programs that should be addressed in supervision with school counselors-in-training: (1) large-group guidance; (2) responsive counseling and consultation; (3) individual advisement; and (4) programmatic planning, coordination, and evaluation.

The school counselor supervision model (SCSM) (Luke & Bernard, 2006) is an extension of the discrimination model, which includes the four aforementioned domains. Accordingly, the SCSM is conceptualized as a 3 × 3 × 4 model addressing three supervisor roles, three foci of supervision, and four points of entry.

Supervisor role: teacher, counselor, consultant
Focus of supervision: intervention, conceptualization, personalization
Point of entry: large-group intervention; counseling and consultation; individual and group advisement; planning, coordination, and evaluation

Group Advisement: Planning, Coordination, and Evaluation

School counselors engage in many tasks on any given day, but most duties will fall into one of the four categories designated as a point of entry. Therefore, the first step for a supervisor utilizing the SCSM is to identify which domain (point of entry) is being addressed in supervision (Luke & Bernard, 2006).

Once the domain is determined, the supervisor should be more readily able to identify the focus of supervision and finally the supervisory role. However, when conceptualizing the SCSM model as an extension of the discrimination model, it is important to remember that "the supervisor uses the same template ... but broadens the focus of supervision to include the interventions, conceptualization, and personalization that are involved in successfully implementing all aspects of a CSCP [comprehensive school counseling program]" (Luke & Bernard, 2006, p. 286).

ACTIVITY 5.4

Spend 10 minutes with one or two other peers. Reflect back to your last supervision session. Can you identify a supervision intervention your supervisor used that addressed one of the points of entry issues identified in the SCSM model? Once you have identified a point of entry, try to determine which role your supervisor responded in and, finally, which focus area was addressed.

Point of Entry

Large group intervention; counseling and consultation; individual and group advisement; planning, coordination, and evaluation

_____

_____

_____

Supervisor Role

Teacher, counselor, consultant

_____

_____

_____

Focus Area

Intervention, conceptualization, personalization

_____

_____

_____

It is vital that supervisors be grounded in some theory from which to conceptualize supervision. However, it is also important to attend to the supervisory relationship and the inherent challenges presented within that dyad. Therefore, we will transition our focus to an overview of the supervisory relationship and your role in this process.

Supervisory Relationship and Supervision Challenges

Although it is essential to understand supervision models and their function in the supervision process, it is equally important for you to understand the supervisor–supervisee relationship now as well as in the future when you may become a supervisor. Bernard and Goodyear (2009) describe the supervisory relationship as the feelings and perceptions individuals have in relation to one another. Some believe that the supervisor–supervisee relationship may be at the heart of a successful practicum and internship. Although there is still much to be learned about this unique and multifaceted relationship, it is a vital element of supervision (Borders & Brown, 2005; Ladany, Walker, & Melincoff, 2001). It is important to note that the relationship that emerges is integral to your growth, education, and progress, and is an essential component of the supervisory process (Holloway, 1999; Watkins, 1997). The working alliance, individual differences, and evaluation are also integral components of the supervisory relationship and are discussed next.

Working Alliance

The development of a working alliance is perceived to be as important as the supervisory relationship (Bordin, 1983; White & Queen, 2003). Bordin's concept of the supervisory working alliance has been utilized in the supervision process and is defined as "a collaboration for change … involving three aspects: 1) mutual agreements and understandings regarding the goals sought in the change process; 2) the tasks of each of the partners; and 3) the bonds between the partners" (1983, p. 35). White and Queen (2003) maintain that the working alliance is central to understanding the supervisory relationship, given that it can influence the counseling relationship between the school counselor-in-training and his or her counselees. Furthermore, establishing safety, a trusting atmosphere, and reciprocal regard between supervisor and school counselor-in-training enhances supervisee willingness to receive suggestions and training, and to modify behavior (Borders & Brown, 2005).

Individual Differences

Individual differences add to the complexity of the relationship. According to Borders and Brown (2005), "each supervisee and supervisor brings unique personalities, life experiences, interpersonal histories, professional motivations and goals to the supervisory context" (p. 68). For example, not all supervisors and supervisees interact with others in a similar manner or react to the same situation in the same way. Each is influenced by his or her respective distinctiveness.

Evaluation

Another distinguishing feature and significant part of supervision is evaluation. Indeed, evaluation is a necessary component of supervision and is inherent to the supervisory process. Baird (2002) defined evaluation as "the process of giving and receiving feedback about the quality of one's performance" (p. 78). According to Campbell (2000), the purpose of evaluation is to identify goals for subsequent knowledge instead of a reexamination of previous work. Haynes, Corey, and Moulton (2003) assert that evaluation is necessary for the accomplishment of the four goals of supervision: fostering development, ensuring counselee welfare, acting as gatekeepers for the profession, and developing autonomous professionals.

Given that the evaluation process has the potential to cause you, as a counselor-in-training, discomfort, stress, and anxiety, it is important for the supervisor to discuss evaluation openly at the outset of supervision (Baird, 2002; Borders & Brown, 2005; Haynes et al., 2003). Evaluation is a delicate balancing act: You need honest and helpful feedback in order to learn and grow, yet the supervisor must strive to maintain the bonds established in the relationship.

The evaluative component of supervision further complicates the supervisory relationship for several reasons, including, but not limited to, the following: it may be the first time you have experienced supervision, you may fear supervisor disapproval, and you may be anxious about having your performance and skills examined (Kiser, 2008). Evaluation can cause difficulties, because there is an inherent power differential ever-present in the process. This unequal distribution of power can produce stress and conflicts in the relationship because "supervisees are asked to be vulnerable and self-disclose their professional inadequacies and their personal biases to the same person who will grade them, write letters of recommendation, or complete reference forms for licensure" (Borders & Brown, 2005, p. 67). Borders and Brown (2005) further state that power differences should be acknowledged in view of the fact that evaluation is an integral part of the supervisory process.

In sum, the supervisor–supervisee relationship is an essential component of supervision. The interactions between participating individuals can enhance or impede your training and, therefore, must be carefully considered.

ACTIVITY 5.5

Think of a time when you received evaluative feedback from your supervisor. Was the feedback helpful? If so, why? If not, why not?

1. How might your supervisor give you feedback that would be more helpful?

_____

_____

2. Did you implement the feedback you received? If so, how?

_____

_____

Other Challenges

Several other challenges underlie the basic principles of the supervisory relationship. For example, multicultural influences, supervisee anxiety and resistance, the parallel process, and dual roles/relationships warrant discussion and are included in the next sections.

Multicultural Influences

The environment and community in which we develop and mature influence each of us. Additionally, we are oriented to family norms, attitudes, and family culture. These same norms and values can be expected to influence the counselee–counselor relationship as well as your relationship with your supervisors. To work successfully with individuals from diverse backgrounds, it is vital to be aware of your personal history, other individuals' personal histories, and the impact of both on the counseling and supervision relationship (Baird, 2002; Borders & Brown, 2005). As maintained by Borders and Brown (2005), some supervisees may not be able to identify problems or issues stemming from multicultural concerns; thus, "it is the supervisor's responsibility to introduce multicultural issues early in the supervision relationship, check in about them often, and invite the supervisee to discuss them at any time" (p. 70). You are likely to encounter multicultural issues you may not know how to manage. In such situations, it will be important for you to discuss the situation with your supervisor during group supervision. At the same time, it is an opportunity for self-discovery, self-evaluation, and for expanding your knowledge and awareness of multicultural issues.

Multicultural issues, different worldviews, and unique values will likewise be present within the supervisor–supervisee relationship. In addition to dealing with these issues related to your counselees, it is important for you and your supervisor to discuss your own diverse life experiences, thoughts, and perspectives. This open discussion, mutual respect, and willingness to learn from one another models a healthy counselor–counselee relationship. Diversity as it relates to differences in schools is discussed in greater detail in Chapter 12.

Anxiety

Anxiety is an expected facet of practicum and internship. In fact, Borders and Brown (2005) suggest that it is a known aspect of supervision. Furthermore, Bernard and Goodyear (2009) contend that supervisees feel apprehension not only when working with counselees, but also during supervision. Certainly, observation and evaluation are customary components of both practicum and internship, and can be very intimidating, particularly if you have never experienced supervision. Supervisees often feel incompetent, vulnerable, and unskilled as they begin to put knowledge and skills into practice. Nonetheless, anxiety in and of itself can be beneficial because it encourages you to be prepared for supervision. Conversely, too much anxiety may interfere with your effectiveness and the ability to recall needed skills during sessions.

As previously mentioned, the evaluative nature and power differential in supervision can influence supervisee anxiety. Even if you have successfully completed the academic part of the program, you must also successfully complete the practical experience under the watchful eyes of supervisors and peers. Feelings of anxiety may also stem from fears associated with performance. During the practicum and internship, you will present cases, videotapes, and audiotapes, and experience site observation that can cause feelings of anxiety (Bernard & Goodyear, 2009; Borders & Brown, 2005; Haynes et al., 2003).

Performance anxiety can threaten your sense of competence and ability; it is not unusual for you to have an unrealistic view of the counseling process and set high expectations for yourself even though you lack experience. Your anxiety will decrease over time, however, as you understand that feelings of anxiety, concerns about counseling skills, receiving feedback, and having to self-disclose are normal and expected elements of supervision. Also, keep in mind that feelings of anxiety decrease with experience and change in any given situation. Once you recognize that dealing with the anxiety in supervision is normal and helpful, you will be able to learn from it and in turn grow from it (Haynes et al., 2003).

Resistance

A consequence of anxiety is resistance, and it is a common aspect of the supervisory process that you may experience as a counselor-in-training. Borders and Brown (2005) state that "supervisees necessarily must find ways to handle their anxiety, and sometimes their attempts are not productive … resistance may reflect the supervisees' attempt to reduce anxiety to a manageable and productive level" (p. 72). Some of the underlying factors related to supervisee resistance include rigidly holding to a specific theory, giving advice or problem solving before the counselee has identified the problem, confrontation surrounding taping, and vulnerability associated with the evaluation process (Borders & Brown, 2005; Haynes et al., 2003; Watkins, 1997).

Resistant activities, as with anxiety, can impede the learning process; therefore, recognizing the basis for the resistance and finding ways to diminish the supposed threat will increase your ability to deal with resistance in a positive manner. Open and honest discussion of resistance in supervision can increase awareness of resistant behaviors and in the process enhance your development.

Parallel Process

Parallel process is similar to transference and countertransference, traditional concepts in psycho-analytic theory. Searles (1955) was the first to make use of the concept of parallel process, which he referred to as "the reflective process." He defined parallel process as "the process at work currently in the *relationship between* patient and therapist are often reflected in the *relationship between* therapist and supervisor" (p. 135). Furthermore, Friedlander, Siegel, and Brenock (1989) explain parallel process by stating, "supervisees unconsciously present themselves to their supervisors as their counselees have presented to them. The process reverses when the supervisee adopts attitudes and behaviors of the supervisor in relating to the counselee" (p. 149). In summary, exploration and reflection of the parallel process in supervision can be constructive when it enhances your ability to gain insight into the way you interact with counselees (Bernard & Goodyear, 2009; Borders & Brown, 2005; Haynes et al., 2003).

Dual Roles

Kiser (2008) defines dual roles or relationships as follows: "Dual relationships occur when a helping professional assumes a second role with a counselee or colleague in addition to the professional role" (p. 253). The American School Counselor Association (ASCA) Code of Ethics (2004), states in Section A.4.a. Dual Relationships, that the professional school counselor should, "Avoid dual relationships that might impair his/her objectivity and increase the risk of harm to the student." This same ethical code applies to you as well. According to Studer (2006), school counselors-in-training may need help in clarifying actions or behaviors that interfere with the ability to be objective in a counseling or supervisory relationship and consequently cause harm. Supervisors are responsible for helping you avoid, identify and correct, and to learn from dual relationships.

Haynes et al. (2003) indicate that dual role or relationship issues oftentimes come up during fieldwork and clinical experiences, and supervisees must learn to work through and come to terms with boundary issues. Borders and Brown (2005) suggest two possible types of dual roles: social and sexual.

ACTIVITY 5.6

Read and respond to the following case study. Compare your answers with those of your peers.

Caroline is in her fourth year working as an elementary school counselor when one of her former professors asks if she would be willing to take a school counselor intern. Not sure initially, Caroline hesitates. With encouragement from her former professor, she cautiously agrees. The following semester James, a timid intern, shows up at Caroline's school ready to begin his internship. As expected, James is thrown right in. With Caroline's assistance, he begins leading classroom guidance lessons, starts two groups with first- and third-grade girls, and even sees two students for individual counseling. When the university instructor goes to the school for a site visit, both James and Caroline report that everything is great.

Seven weeks into the semester, James is watching the evening news, shocked at the tragedy unfolding on the television. An automobile accident involving multiple cars has traffic backed up on the interstate as helicopters are airlifting victims to nearby hospitals. James thinks back about 10 years to a time when he first heard that his 16-year-old sister had died after a truck ran a stoplight, hitting the car she was driving. As James goes to sleep that evening, he is saddened by the possibility of fatalities connected with the car accident he had witnessed earlier in the evening.

It is not until early the following morning that James begins to realize the full extent to which this event is going to affect his life. Two of the victims from the accident were an 8-year-old boy and his father. The child attended the school where James is interning and the boy's 6-year-old sister was in one of James's groups. He had no idea where to begin as he attempted to focus on helping the students while grappling with his own reactions to the tragedy. Fortunately, James has a supervision session scheduled for the following day. Conceptualizing supervision from the school counseling supervision model how would you proceed with James?

1. Where do you think the supervising counselor should begin in working with James?
2. What focus area would you want your supervisor to take if you had a situation similar to James? Process skills? Conceptualization? Personalization?
3. What role would you want your supervisor to assume? Teacher? Counselor? Consultant? Why?

Social role boundaries may be less difficult for the school counselor to maintain with students, given that their counselees are usually younger than they are. However, the possibility of social relationships increases when working with parents similar in age and interests, and with whom you may develop a personal relationship. Maintaining constructive and professional boundaries may be more challenging with students' adult parents or caregivers. Be mindful that your professional obligations and responsibilities to your students supersede social relationships, and remember that you should avoid any social interaction that might cause loss of objectivity (Borders & Brown, 2005; Haynes et al., 2003).

Sexual involvement with a counselee is prohibited by virtually all ethical codes. Even given the legal and professional liability and consequences, sexual relationships between students and school professionals continue to be in the news media; it is clear that these sexual relationships do occur from time to time. What happens to well-intentioned school professionals that leads to misconduct and poor professional judgment? Counseling, by its very nature, can be isolated and intimate. As part of the therapeutic process, counselees share private information, in confidence, with the school counselor or with you, as the school-counselor-in-training. These interactions are often conducted in a private or semiprivate setting. Counseling session interactions may occur on a sporadic or regular basis over a long period of time. All of these factors are similar to more personal and intimate relationships outside of counseling and can be confusing to the counselee and to you. Role confusion occurs and builds when the school counselor or you, as a school counselor-in-training, fail to regularly review and maintain the primary reason or goal of the relationship, which is helping the counselee to change or adapt to environmental conditions or relationships outside the counseling setting or relationship. It is paramount that you establish, review, and maintain this therapeutic focus with your counselees. It is equally important that your supervisor do this with you.

Role confusion and dual roles are issues for you to discuss and clarify during supervision. Undoubtedly, sexual relationships confound and impede the counseling and supervision relationship and cause injury to the counselee or supervisee. Therefore, it is imperative that sexual relationships are avoided at all costs and any potential issues be brought up in supervision.

Finally, Borders and Brown (2005) suggest that the closeness of the supervisory relationship and the power differential make it difficult to avoid dual role problems. As a means of prevention, Haynes et al. (2003) suggest that supervisors clarify their role at the beginning of supervision; supervisors who set up appropriate professional boundaries are good role models and teach you how to develop appropriate boundaries.

Conclusion

School counseling students graduating from a Council for Accreditation of Counseling and Related Educational Programs (CACREP)-accredited school counseling program typically receive an average of approximately 100-plus hours of supervision (combined site and university) over the course of a 700-hour field experience. The considerable amount of time devoted to supervision provides perspective about the importance of the supervisory relationship. Given this significance, it is our sincere hope that reading this chapter has provided you with the necessary information to approach supervision in an intentional manner, informed with theory about models of supervision and challenges of the supervisory relationship.

References

American School Counselor Association (ASCA). (2004). *Ethical standards for school counselors.* Alexandria, VA: Author.

Association for Counselor Education and Supervision. (1995). Ethical guidelines for counseling supervisors. *Counselor Education and Supervision, 34,* 270–276.

Baird, B. N. (2002). *The internship, practicum, and field placement handbook: A guide for the help-ing professions* (3rd ed.). Upper Saddle River, NJ: Prentice Hall.

Bernard, J. M. (1979). Supervisor training: A discrimination model. *Counselor Education and Supervision, 19*, 60–68.

Bernard, J. M., & Goodyear, R. K. (2009). *Fundamentals of clinical supervision* (4th ed.). Boston: Allyn & Bacon.

Borders, L. D., & Brown, L. L. (2005). *The new handbook of counseling supervision.* Mahwah, NJ: Lahaska Press.

Bordin, E. S. (1983). A working alliance based model of supervision. *The Counseling Psychologist, 11*(1), 35–42.

Britton, P. J., Goodman, J. M., & Rak, C. F. (2002). Presenting workshops on supervision: A didac-tic-experiential format. *Counselor Education and Supervision, 42*, 31–39.

Campbell, J. M. (2000). *Becoming an effective supervisor: A workbook for counselors and psycho-therapists.* Philadelphia: Accelerated Development.

Council for Accreditation of Counseling and Related Educational Programs (CACREP). (2009). *2009 standards.* Retrieved January 15, 2009, from www.cacrep.org/2009standards.pdf

Dollarhide, C. T., & Miller, G. M. (2006). Supervision for preparation and practice of school coun-selors: Pathways to excellence. *Counselor Education and Supervision, 45*, 242–252.

Friedlander, M. L., Siegel, S. M., & Brenock, K. (1989). Parallel process in counseling and supervi-sion: A case study. *Journal of Counseling Psychology, 36*(2), 149–157.

Haynes, R., Corey, G., & Moulton, P. (2003). *Clinical supervision in the helping professions: A practical guide.* Pacific Grove, CA: Brooks/Cole.

Herlihy, B., Gray, N., & McCollum, V. (2002). Legal and ethical issues in school counselor supervi-sion. *Professional School Counseling, 6*, 55–60.

Holloway, E. (1999). A framework for supervision training. In E. Holloway & M. Carroll (Eds.), *Training counseling supervisors: Strategies, methods, and techniques* (pp. 8–36). London: Sage Publications.

Kiser, P. M. (2008). *The human services internship: Getting the most from your experience* (2nd ed.). Belmont, CA: Thompson Brooks/Cole.

Ladany, N., Walker, J. A., & Melincoff, D. S. (2001). Supervisory style: Its relationship to the super-visory working-alliance and supervisor self-disclosure. *Counselor Education and Supervision, 40*(4), 263–275.

Luke, M., & Bernard, J. M. (2006). The school counseling supervision model: An extension of the discrimination model. *Counselor Education and Supervision, 45*, 282–295.

Magnuson, S., Norem, K., & Bradley, L. J. (2001). Supervising school counselors. In L. J. Bradley & N. Ladany (Eds.), *Counselor supervision: Principles, process, & practice* (3rd ed., pp. 207–221). Philadelphia: Brunner-Routledge.

McMahon, M., & Simons, R. (2004). Supervision training for professional counselors: An explor-atory study. *Counselor Education and Supervision, 43*, 301–309.

Searles, H. F. (1955). The informational value of the supervisor's emotional experiences. *Psychiatry, 18*, 135–146.

Stoltenberg, C. D. (1981). Approaching supervision from a developmental perspective: The coun-selor complexity model. *Journal of Counseling Psychology, 28*, 59–65.

Stoltenberg, C. D., & Delworth, U. (1987). *Supervising counselors and therapists.* San Francisco: Jossey-Bass.

Studer, J. R. (2006). *Supervising the school counselor trainee: Guidelines for practice.* Alexandria, VA: American Counseling Association.

Watkins, C. E., Jr. (1997). *Handbook of psychotherapy supervision.* New York: Wiley.

White, V. E., & Queen, J. (2003). Supervisor and supervisee attachments and social provisions related to the supervisory working alliance. *Counselor Education and Supervision, 43*(3), 203–218.

Wood, C., & Rayle, A. D. (2006). A model of school counseling supervision: The goals, functions, roles, and systems model. *Counselor Education and Supervision, 45*, 253–266.

SECTION II:

THE AMERICAN SCHOOL COUNSELOR ASSOCIATION (ASCA) NATIONAL MODEL AS A STRUCTURE FOR UNDERSTANDING THE ROLE OF THE PROFESSIONAL SCHOOL COUNSELOR

The American School Counselor Association (ASCA) National Model and Components as a Supervisory Guide

Jeannine R. Studer
Joel F. Diambra

The purpose of this chapter is to:

- Review the American School Counselor Association (ASCA) National Model®
- Introduce the ASCA National Model as a template for supervision
- Review time percentage recommendations as a tool to guide supervisory activities within the ASCA National Model

In recent years, the school reform movement has provided a catalyst for all school personnel to demonstrate how their programs contribute to the growth of all their students; school counselors and are no exception. Although some people believe that educational accountability is a recent focus, it is not a new consideration. Since guidance workers, now known as professional school counselors, first entered schools in the early part of the 20th century, people have been curious as to how these professionals make a difference in the lives of students (Gysbers, 2004), as school counselors have been remiss in demonstrating their contributions to student success. By now you have probably been introduced to a traditional approach to school counseling, and how this method is being replaced with a comprehensive, developmental school counseling (CDSC) program focus. We do not intend to repeat this information in this chapter, but instead our intent is to assist you in better understanding school counselor activities that mirror programming advocated by the ASCA while you are in a clinical setting.

A Brief Historical Overview of the Counseling Profession

Throughout school counseling's relatively brief history, counselors have performed numerous but different tasks, which occur for several reasons. Initially, the push to explore space and compete with the Russian's *Sputnik*—the space race—drove the first guidance counselors to direct or guide students into the fields of math and science. Making a difference was measured by increased student enrollment in math and science majors in colleges and universities. In the 1970s, the burgeoned free spirit movement linked with the 1960s brought about greater recognition of concerns such as civil rights, women's issues, and students with special needs. Schools had a responsibility to change with legislative mandates and requirements, and concerns were increasingly causing school counselors to respond to issues rather than proactively engaging in prevention activities. Slowly, there was a shift in evaluating essential tasks performed by school counselors, and with this awareness there was a change in the vocational title from guidance counselor to professional school counselor. (Although, we are aware that, even among school counselors, this title is evolving at a leisurely pace.)

The ASCA took an active role and responded to the demand for educational reform by standardizing the school counselor role and demonstrated how school counselors make a difference in the lives of students by developing the ASCA National Standards. Initially implemented in 1997, these standards identify student competencies in the academic, career, and personal/social domains. Six years later, these standards were incorporated into the ASCA National Model that was developed as a prototype CDSC program (ASCA, 2003) to assist in legitimatizing the school counseling profession (Schwallie-Giddis, ter Maat, & Pak, 2003). The introduction of this model helped school counselors reorganize and reconstruct their traditional approach to working with students and other constituents. From these efforts, stakeholders recognized benefits that the ASCA (2003) outlined. See Table 6.1 for a summarization of the benefits.

It seems clear that there is much to gain from implementing a complete and effective school counseling program following the ASCA National Model. However, implementation, time, data collection, and analysis, coupled with sound research practices, are needed to substantiate the benefits claimed.

TABLE 6.1   Benefits for School Counseling Programs Based on the ASCA National Model

Benefits for students
- Ensures every student receives the benefit of the school counseling program by designing content curriculum for every student
- Monitors data to facilitate student improvement
- Provides strategies for closing the achievement gap because some students need more
- Promotes a rigorous academic curriculum for every student
- Ensures equitable access to educational opportunities
- Fosters advocacy for students
- Supports development of skills to increase student success

Benefits for parents
- Provides support in advocating for their children's academic, career, and personal/social development
- Supports partnerships in their children's learning and career planning
- Ensures academic planning for every student
- Ensures access to school and community resources
- Provides training and informational workshops
- Connects to community- and school-based services
- Provides data for continuous information on student progress
- Ensures every student receives the content of the school counseling curriculum
- Promotes a philosophy that some students need more and seeks to ensure they receive it

Benefits for teachers
- Promotes an interdisciplinary team approach to address student needs and educational goals
- Increases collaboration with school counselors and teachers
- Supports development of classroom-management skills
- Provides a system for cofacilitation of classroom guidance lessons
- Supports the learning environment
- Promotes teaming to increase student achievement
- Analyzes data to improve school climate and student achievement

Benefits for school counselors
- Defines responsibilities within the context of a school counseling program
- Seeks to eliminate non-school-counseling program activities
- Supports access to every student
- Provides a tool for program management, implementation, and accountability
- Recognizes school counselors as leaders, advocates, and change agents
- Ensures the school counseling program's contribution to the school's mission

Benefits to counselor educators
- Builds collaboration between counselor education programs and schools
- Provides a framework for school counseling programs
- Provides a model for site-based school counseling fieldwork or internships
- Increases data collection for collaborative research on school counseling programs
- Establishes a framework for professional development to benefit practicing school counselors
- Promotes alliances with other educator training programs

Benefits for postsecondary education
- Enhances articulation and transition of students to postsecondary institutions
- Prepares every student for advanced educational opportunities
- Motivates every student to seek a wide range of substantial, postsecondary options, including college
- Encourages and supports rigorous academic preparation
- Promotes equity and access to postsecondary education for every student

(continued on next page)

TABLE 6.1 (continued)   Benefits for School Counseling Programs Based on the ASCA National Model

Benefits for administrators	Benefits for student services personnel
• Aligns the school counseling program with the school's academic mission	• Defines the school counseling program
• Provides a school counseling program promoting student success	• Maximizes collaborative teaming to ensure individual student success
• Monitors data for school improvement	• Uses school counseling program data to maximize benefit to individual student growth
• Provides a system for managing a school counseling program	• Increases collaboration for utilizing school and community resources
• Articulates a process for evaluating a school counseling program	
• Uses data to jointly develop school counseling goals and school counselor responsibilities	
• Provides useful data for grant applications and funding sources	
• Provides a proactive school guidance curriculum addressing the students' needs and enhancing school climate	

Benefits for the boards and departments of education	Benefits for community: business, labor, and industry
• Provides a rationale based on data for implementing a school counseling program	• Increases opportunities for business, industry, and labor to actively participate in the school counseling program
• Ensures equity and access to a quality school counseling program for every student	• Builds collaboration, which enhances a student's postsecondary success
• Demonstrates the need for appropriate levels of funding	• Connects business, industry, and labor to students and families
• Articulates appropriate credentials and staffing ratios	• Supports the academic preparation necessary for students' success in the workforce
• Informs the community about school counseling program success	
• Supports standards-based programs	
• Provides data about improved student achievement	

Source: From *The ASCA National Model: A Framework for School Counseling Programs,* by ASCA, 2003, Alexandria, VA: ASCA, which was adapted from *Sharing the Vision: National Standards for School Programs*, by C. A. Campbell and C. A. Dahir, 1997, Alexandria, VA: ASCA.

Summary of a CDSC Program

The fundamental philosophy underlying ASCA-supported programs is to assist student growth across the academic, career, and personal/social domains through counseling goals that mirror the student outcomes deemed essential by school districts (Adelman & Taylor, 2002, as cited in Sink & Stroh, 2003). Part of the hope of the ASCA National Model is summed up by Dahir: "The National Model reinforces the importance of linking the National Standards with the process of implementing a comprehensive, developmental results-based program that is consistent with the current educational reform agenda and responsive to state, district and building-level needs" (ASCA, 2003, p. 31).

The foundation, the delivery, accountability, and management components provide the organization of the ASCA National Model, and provide structure for school counselors in leading a CDSC program (ASCA, 2003). In addition, core themes of leadership, advocacy, collaboration and teaming, and systemic change are integrated throughout the model (Education Trust, 2007). The ASCA National Model is shown in Figure 6.1

Historically, the school counselor's role and identity has changed as economic, political, and social variables influence educational themes. The ASCA addressed how school counselors are integral to the educational mission of the institute, yet there continues to be debate as to the primary role of professional school counselors. Today, with the growing numbers of students at risk for academic

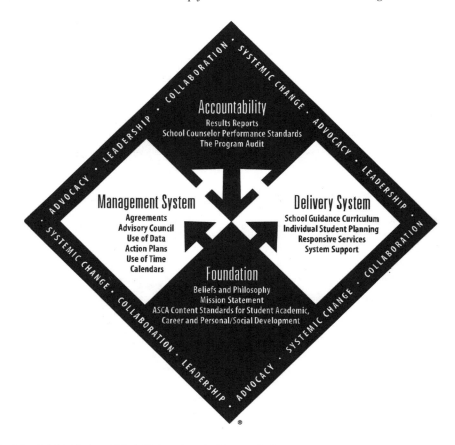

FIGURE 6.1   The ASCA National Model®. Reprinted with permission.

failure, some researchers (Keys, Bemak, & Lockhart, 1998) believe the school counselor's primary role is to "address the critical needs of at-risk youth" (p. 381). Others (Brown & Trusty, 2005) believe that school counselors can show their contributions to student growth by "establishing the efficacy of interventions that increase academic achievement" (p. 14). In a study by Amatea and Clark (2005), administrators believed that the school counselor is a collaborator with other teachers, parents, administrators, and so forth, to improve student growth. To add even more confusion, the ASCA position statement on the role of the professional school counselor states "the professional school counselor is a certified/licensed *educator* trained in school counseling with unique qualifications and skills to address all students' academic, personal/social and career development needs" (ASCA, 2004, ¶ 1). Therefore, a fundamental professional identity question remains: Is the school counselor a mental health expert who works in an educational setting, an educator who works with social/personal and career concerns to increase academic growth, or a collaborator with others? Discuss these issues with your site supervisor and learn about his or her perceptions of school counseling.

Regardless of how you or your school defines the school counselor's role, the ASCA National Model can be used as a template for school counselors to follow when developing their own program. The *Foundation* component includes the program philosophy and beliefs, as well as student standards and outcomes that are deemed essential for student growth. The *Delivery System* describes program presentation through such means as the classroom curriculum, individual planning, responsive services, and system support. The *Accountability System* identifies measurable student and program outcome activities, and the *Management System* identifies individuals responsible for activities, the time frame for implementing the activities, and how time is spent within the various areas.

Four thematic elements of school counselor responsibilities are integrated within the model: leadership, advocacy, collaboration and teaming, and systemic change. Leadership includes assisting student success by recognizing and overcoming barriers that impede growth (ASCA, 2003). Some researchers (Amatea & Clark, 2005) believe this leadership task is a role change in that rather than providing assistance and support as in traditional school counseling programs, school counselors are now asked to assume a position of authority and decision making. As an advocate, counselors assist all students and serve as a support for students who have not had the same opportunities afforded to more advantaged students. As a collaborator, the school counselor works cooperatively with others rather than assuming responsibility that others can assume (Amatea & Clark, 2005). Finally, as a systems change agent, the school counselor addresses and tries to transform school and community policies and procedures to best meet student needs. Each of the ASCA National Model components and your role in each of these areas will be discussed in the following chapters.

As you discover the advantages of working within a CDSC program, you will probably be eager to put these concepts to work during your training. Yet, it is important to remember that the CDSC philosophy and the ASCA National Model are relatively new. Many existing school counselors were not trained in them and may not be familiar with this approach to school counseling.

The Professional School Counselor Standards: School Counselor Competencies

You are entering the profession at a time of significant transition. School counselor supervisors may lack familiarity with the new model, and this may create an understandable tension, one that is often coupled with anxiety. When you are in a school site with school counselor supervisors who have not transitioned into a school counseling model aligned with the CDSC program philosophy, you may express disappointment that you are unable to fully put CDSC concepts into practice. Even if tension occurs, it is important to remember that traditional school counselors still perform many of the tasks supported by a CDSC program, even if their program is not organized in the same manner.

If you are placed in a school that has not yet transformed the school counseling program, you are encouraged to track the activities that you and your school counselor site supervisor perform that complement those supported by a CDSC program. Tracking these activities has several benefits. First, this procedure will help you gain a better understanding of how school counselors operate in a traditional type of a program. Second, you can share the list of corresponding activities with your school counselor supervisors to inform them of the specific ways they already embrace the contemporary philosophy and model. Third, you can provide the ASCA National Model guidelines and allow the school counselors to compare the corresponding activities with those that are not yet conducted on a routine basis. Sharing this tracked data may provide new insight and encourage system change.

Direct service to counselees has traditionally been one of the most challenging counseling components for school counselors. Administrators and teachers experience enormous amounts of pressure to perform and complete ever-growing responsibilities. Teachers were trained for their unique and specific classroom responsibilities, and administrators are often experienced teachers who returned to school for administrative training. Therefore, most administrators understand the role of the teacher and their role as administrator. However, few teachers and administrators were informed as to the roles and responsibilities of the school counselor; therefore, requests for school counselor assistance by teachers and administrators are based on their perceptions. However, school counselor responses to requests of this type must be measured carefully. Helping others often creates a natural tension for the school counselor as he or she asks the question, "Can I help others and still fulfill my responsibilities within a reasonable amount of time?" The ASCA National Model provides a foundation from which school counselors can make these everyday decisions.

School counselor performance standards are identified within the ASCA National Model document (2003) to define school counselor activities as they assume leadership within their school counseling program. However, these standards were strengthened in a recent publication by an ASCA publication titled *School Counseling Standards: School Counselor Competencies* (ASCA, n.d.) to standardize school counselor activities. These competencies are integrated within the four components and themes of the National Model and assist in identifying the competencies that school counselors need to be effective. Activity 6.1 is designed as a checklist for you to use in observing your supervisor and as a guide for conducting your own supervisory activities. It can also be used as a guideline for developing your own contract objectives and goals during the clinical experiences.

ACTIVITY 6.1

Read through the following list of competencies and discuss with your site supervisor the types of activities that he or she ordinarily performs. This list of competencies can also be used to assist you in determining the competencies that you have already accomplished, those that can be incorporated into your clinical contract, and those that can be conducted once you enter the profession of school counseling. Indicate those activities that you would like to accomplish during the clinical experience.

	Supervisor Activities	Counselor-in-Training Activities
A. Plans, organizes, delivers, and evaluates the comprehensive school counseling program that aligns with the ASCA National Model		
1. Creates a vision statement examining the professional and personal competencies and qualities that are required by a school counselor		
2. Describes the rationale for a comprehensive school counseling program		
3. Articulates the school counseling themes of advocacy, leadership collaboration, and system change		
4. Describes in detail the tenets of a comprehensive school counseling program and critiques their use as a basis for designing a program		
5. Describe the benefits of a comprehensive school counseling program for all stakeholders		
6. Describes, defines, and identifies the qualities of an effective school		
7. Describes the history of comprehensive school counseling programs		
8. Uses technology effectively and efficiently to plan, organize, deliver, and evaluate the CSDC program		
9. Demonstrates multicultural competencies in planning, organizing, delivering, and evaluating the CDSC program as reflected in the ASCA Ethical Standards		
B. Advocates, leads, collaborates, and acts as a system change agent for student success		
Leadership		
1. Defines leadership and its role in comprehensive school counseling programs		
2. Identifies and applies a model of leadership to a comprehensive school counseling program		
3. Identifies and demonstrates professional and personal qualities/skills of effective leaders		
4. Identifies and applies components of the ASCA National Model that require leadership		

ACTIVITY 6.1 (continued)

	Supervisor Activities	Counselor-in-Training Activities
5. Creates a plan to challenge the non-school-counseling-related tasks that are assigned to school counselors		
Advocacy		
1. Defines advocacy and its role in comprehensive school counseling programs		
2. Identifies and demonstrates benefits of advocacy with school and community stakeholders		
3. Describes school counselor advocacy competencies, which include dispositions, knowledge, and skills		
4. Reviews advocacy models and develops a personal advocacy plan		
5. Understands district policy procedures and development and the legislative process		
Collaboration		
1. Defines collaboration and its role in comprehensive school counseling programs		
2. Identifies and applies models of collaboration for effective use in a school counseling program and understands the similarities and differences between consultation, collaboration, and counseling and coordination strategies		
3. Creates role delineation statements for student service providers (i.e., school social worker, school psychologist, school nurse) and identifies best practices for collaborating to impact student success		
System Change Agent		
1. Defines system change and its role in comprehensive school counseling programs		
2. Develops plan to deal with personal and institutional resistance impeding the change process		
3. Understands the impact of school, district, and state educational policies, procedures, and practices that support and/or impede student success		
Foundation		
C. Develops the beliefs and philosophy of the school counseling program that align with current school improvement and student success initiatives at the school, district, and state level		
1. Examines personal, district, and state beliefs, assumptions, and philosophies about student success … and then writes an overview of personal beliefs in a clear manner		
2. Demonstrates knowledge of a school's particular educational philosophy and mission		
3. Conceptualizes and writes a personal professional philosophy		
4. Understands and knows how to apply a consensus-building process to foster agreement in a group		

(continued on next page)

ACTIVITY 6.1 (continued)

	Supervisor Activities	Counselor-in-Training Activities
D. Develops a school counseling mission statement that aligns with the school, district, and state mission		
1. Critiques a school district mission statement and identifies or writes a mission statement that aligns with beliefs		
2. Writes a sample mission statement that is specific, concise, clear, and comprehensive, describing a school counseling program's purpose and a vision for how the program benefits every student		
3. Communicates the philosophy and mission of the school counseling program to all appropriate stakeholders		
E. Utilizes student standards to drive the implementation of a comprehensive school counseling program		
1. Crosswalks the ASCA Student Standards with other appropriate standards		
2. Prioritizes student standards that align with the school's goals		
F. Applies the ethical standards and principles of the school counseling		
1. Practices ethical principles of the school counseling profession and adheres to the legal aspects of the role of the school counselor		
2. Understands the legal and ethical nature of working in a pluralistic, multicultural, and technological society		
3. Understands and practices in accordance with school district policy and local, state, and federal statutory requirements		
4. Understands the unique legal and ethical nature of working with minor students in a school setting		
5. Advocates responsibly for school board policy, local, state, and federal statutory requirements that are in the best interest of students		
6. Resolves ethical dilemmas by employing an ethical decision-making model appropriate to work in schools		
7. Models ethical behavior		
8. Continuously engages in professional development and uses resources to inform and guide ethical and legal work		
9. Practices within the ethical and statutory limits of confidentiality		
10. Continually seeks consultation and supervision to guide legal and ethical decision making and to recognize and resolve ethical dilemmas		
11. Understands and applies an ethical and legal obligation not only to students but to parents, administration, and teachers as well		
Delivery System		
G. Implements the school guidance curriculum		
1. Crosswalks ASCA Student Standards with appropriate guidance curriculum		
2. Develops and presents a developmental guidance lesson plan that addresses curriculum for all students including closing-the-gap activities		

ACTIVITY 6.1 (continued)

	Supervisor Activities	Counselor-in-Training Activities
3. Demonstrates classroom management and instructional skills		
4. Develops materials and instructional strategies to meet student needs and school goals		
5. Encourages staff involvement to ensure the effective implementation of the school guidance curriculum		
6. Knows, understands, and uses a variety of technology in the delivery of guidance curriculum activities		
7. Understands multicultural and pluralistic trends when developing and choosing guidance curriculum		
8. Understands the resources available for students with special needs		
H. Facilitates individual student planning		
1. Understands individual student planning as a component of a comprehensive program		
2. Develops strategies to implement individual student planning		
3. Helps students establish goals and develops and uses planning skills in collaboration with parents or guardians and school personnel		
4. Understands career opportunities, labor market trends, and global economics and uses various career assessment techniques to assist students in understanding their abilities and career interests		
5. Uses various tools, including technology, to assist students in academic, career, and personal/social goal setting and planning		
6. Understands the relationship of academic performance to the world of work, family life, and community service		
7. Understands methods for helping students monitor and direct their own learning and personal/social and career development		
I. Provides responsive services		
1. Understands how to make referrals to appropriate professionals when necessary		
2. Lists and describes issues addressed in responsive services, such as consultation, individual and small-group counseling, crisis counseling, referrals, and peer facilitation		
3. Compiles resources to utilize with students, staff, and families to effectively address issues in responsive services		
4. Understands appropriate individual and small-group counseling theories and techniques		
5. Demonstrates an ability to provide counseling for students during times of transition, separation, heightened stress, and critical change		

(continued on next page)

ACTIVITY 6.1 (continued)

	Supervisor Activities	Counselor-in-Training Activities
6. Understands what defines a crisis, the appropriate response, and a variety of intervention strategies to meet the needs of the individual, group, or school community before, during, and after a crisis		
7. Provides team leadership to the school and community in a crisis		
8. Involves appropriate school and community professionals as well as the family in a crisis situation		
9. Applies appropriate counseling approaches to promoting change among consultees within a consultation approach		
10. Understands and is able to build effective and high-quality peer helper programs		
11. Understands the nature of academic, career, and personal/social counseling in schools, and the similarities and differences among school counseling and other types of counseling within a continuum of care		
12. Understands the role of the school counselor and the school counseling program in the school crisis plan		
J. Implements system support activities for the comprehensive school counseling program		
1. Creates a system support planning document addressing the school counselor's responsibilities for professional development, consultation and collaboration, and program management		
2. Provides activities that establish, maintain, and enhance the comprehensive school counseling program as well as other educational programs		
3. Conducts in-service training for other stakeholders to share school counseling expertise		
4. Understands and knows how to provide supervision for school counseling interns consistent with the principles of the ASCA National Model		
5. Understands how to facilitate group meetings to effectively and efficiently meet group goals		
6. Knows how to use and analyze data to evaluate the counseling program and research activity outcomes, and to identify gaps between and among different groups of students		
Management		
K. Negotiates with the administrator to define the management system for the comprehensive school counseling program		
1. Discusses and develops the components of the school counselor management system with the other members of the counseling staff and have agreement		
2. Presents the school counseling management system to principal and finalizes an annual school counseling management agreement		
3. Discusses the anticipated program results when implementing the action plans for the school year		
4. Participates in professional organizations		

ACTIVITY 6.1 (continued)

	Supervisor Activities	Counselor-in-Training Activities
5. Develops a yearly professional development plan demonstrating how the counselor advances relevant knowledge, skills and dispositions; also communicates effective goals and benchmarks for meeting and exceeding expectations that are consistent with the administrator counselor agreement and district performance appraisals		
6. Uses personal reflection, consultation, and supervision to promote professional growth and development		
L. Establishes and convenes an advisory council for the comprehensive school counseling program		
1. Uses leadership skills to facilitate vision and positive change for the comprehensive school counseling program		
2. Determines appropriate education stakeholders for advisory council		
3. Develops meeting agenda		
4. Reviews school data, school counseling program audit, and school counseling program goals with the council		
5. Records meeting notes and distributes as appropriate		
6. Analyzes and incorporates feedback from advisory council related to school counseling program goals as appropriate		
M. Collects, analyzes, and interprets relevant data to monitor and advantage student behavior and achievement		
1. Analyzes, synthesizes, and disaggregates data to examine student outcomes and to identify and intervene as needed		
2. Uses data to identify policies, practices, and procedures that lead to systemic barriers, successes, and areas of weakness		
3. Uses student data to demonstrate a need for systemic change in such areas as course enrollment patterns; equity and access; and the achievement, opportunity, and information gaps		
4. Understands and uses data to establish goals and activities to close the achievement, opportunity, and information gaps		
5. Knows and understands theoretical and historical bases for assessment techniques		
N. Organizes and manages time to implement an effective program		
1. Identifies appropriate distribution of school counselor's time based on delivery system and school's data		
2. Creates a rationale for school counselor's time to focus on the goals of the comprehensive school counseling program		
3. Identifies and evaluates "fair share" responsibilities, which articulate appropriate and inappropriate counseling and non-school-counseling-related activities		
4. Creates a rationale for the school counselor's total time spent in each component of the delivery system		

(continued on next page)

ACTIVITY 6.1 (continued)

	Supervisor Activities	Counselor-in-Training Activities
O. Develops calendars to ensure the effective implementation of the school counseling program		
1. Creates annual, monthly, and weekly calendars to plan activities to reflect school goals		
2. Demonstrates time-management skills that include scheduling, publicizing, and prioritizing time and task		
P. Implements data-driven action plans that align with school and school counseling program goals		
1. Uses appropriate academic and behavioral data to develop guidance curriculum and closing-the-gap action plans and to determine appropriate students for the target group or intervention		
2. Identifies ASCA domains, standards, and competencies being addressed by the plan		
3. Determines the intended impact on academics and behavior		
4. Identifies appropriate activities to accomplish objectives		
5. Identifies appropriate resources needed		
6. Identifies data-appropriate strategies to gather process perception and results data		
7. Shares results of action plans with staff, parents, and community		
Accountability		
Q. Uses data from results reports to evaluate program effectiveness and to determine program needs		
1. Uses formal and informal methods of program evaluation to design and modify comprehensive school counseling programs		
2. Uses student data to support decision making in designing effective school counseling programs and interventions		
3. Measures results attained from school guidance curriculum and closing-the-gap activities		
4. Works with members of the school counseling team and with the administration to decide how school counseling programs are evaluated and how results are shared		
5. Collects process, perception, and results data		
6. Uses technology in conducting research and program evaluation		
7. Reports program results to professional school counseling community		
8. Uses data to demonstrate the value the school counseling program adds to student achievement		
R. Understands and advocates for appropriate school counselor performance appraisal process		
1. Conducts self-appraisal related to school counseling skills and performance		
2. Identifies how school counseling activities fit within categories of performance appraisal instrument		

ACTIVITY 6.1 (continued)

	Supervisor Activities	Counselor-in-Training Activities
3. Encourages administrators to use performance appraisal instrument that reflects appropriate responsibilities for school counselors		
S. Conducts a program audit		
1. Completes a program audit to compare current school counseling program implementation to the ASCA National Model		
2. Shares the results of the program audit with administrators, the advisory council, and other appropriate stakeholders		
3. Identifies areas for improvement for the school counseling program		

Recommended Percentage of Time Performing School Counseling Activities

From the school counselor competencies listed in Activity 6.1, it is obvious that the school counselor performs myriad activities and has a responsibility for gaining the knowledge, skills, and behaviors that are needed to perform the job effectively. Yet, too often the school counselor's time is disproportionately spent in some areas and not others. Gysbers and Henderson (2000) recommend specific amounts of time school counselors are to spend in the delivery system, with 80% of the school counselor's time to be spent in delivering direct service.

Even when these criteria are met, Gysbers and Henderson (2000) provide more specific recommendations of time usage within the Delivery System across the three school levels (refer to Table 6.2). As a counselor-in-training, you will probably receive requests to assist with activities that do not meet the philosophy and intent of a CDSC program. In a few cases, we had some students who directly refused to participate in an activity that they felt was beyond the scope of their supervisory contract. This is not an appropriate time to decline, and may even create ill will. Instead, go ahead and participate in the experience so that you can take what you learned to advocate for yourself when you are hired as a professional school counselor.

TABLE 6.2   Recommended Percentage of Time Spent in the Delivery Components

Delivery System	Elementary School Counselor	Middle School Counselor	High School Counselor
Guidance curriculum	35%–45%	25%–35%	15%–25%
Individual student planning	5%–10%	15%–25%	25%–35%
Responsive services	30%–40%	30%–40%	25%–35%
System support	10%–15%	10%–15%	15%–20%

Source: From *Developing and Managing Your School Guidance Program* (3rd ed.), by N. C. Gysbers and P. Henderson, 2000, Alexandria, VA: American Counseling Association.

ACTIVITY 6.2

Chapter 8 contains a data tracking sheet that can be used to monitor where time is spent. Use this form or one that you have designed and observe your school counselor supervisor for one week. Note how much time he/she spends in each of these delivery areas. Each week, compute the time spent by delivery area and compare your results with the recommended percentages in Table 6.2.

As you perform your school counselor tasks, track how your time is spent in these areas. After accumulating one week of data for your supervisor and one week of data for yourself, compare the time you spent on tasks with those of your supervisor. Keep in mind that time differences may be due to your program responsibilities and tasks that need to be performed by an experienced professional with more advanced skills. You may also want to identify strategies for learning some of the tasks that are reserved for more experienced counselors.

- How are your Delivery System component activities similar or different?
- How do your Delivery System activities and time spent on these activities compare with those recommended by school level, according to Gysbers and Henderson (2000).

SUPERVISOR TIME

	Guidance Curriculum	Individual Planning	Responsive Services	System Support
Time engaged in Delivery System component activity (measure in .25 hour increments)				

SCHOOL COUNSELOR-IN-TRAINING TIME

	Guidance Curriculum	Individual Planning	Responsive Services	System Support
Time engaged in Delivery System component activity (measure in .25 hour increments)				

What strengths and limitations did you identify in the school counseling delivery system?

_____

_____

How might you attempt to begin a systemic change?

_____

_____

Conclusion

The ASCA National Model was designed as a template for school counselors to use when developing a CDSC program. Within this chapter the various components were summarized along with practical strategies for you to consider as you delve into the school counselor's role in a school counseling program. A number of key concepts were reviewed: a brief history of the development of the ASCA National Model; benefits gained; a summary of the school counselor's role; the various components and themes within the National Model; recommendations for tracking and introducing the National Model to school counselors-in-training; school counselor competencies; time percentage recommendations to help maintain the school counselor's role within the delivery system component; and activities to begin using these practices.

As you engage in activities during your clinical experiences, note how your supervisor spends time within the ASCA National Model components and the activities you perform that complement the spirit of this prototype. Even though your clinical experiences may not be in a school setting that has transformed its school counseling program to one that reflects the philosophy and goals of a CDSC program, note the myriad activities performed by the school counselor that easily fit within this model so that you can begin to understand your role as a school counselor in a CDSC program.

References

Amatea, E. S., & Clark, M. A. (2005). Changing schools, changing counselors: A qualitative study of school administrators' conceptions of the school counselor role. *Professional School Counseling, 9,* 16–27.

American School Counselor Association (ASCA). (2003). *The ASCA national model: A framework for school counseling programs.* Alexandria, VA: Author.

American School Counselor Association (ASCA). (2004). *The role of the professional school counselor.* Retrieved October 19, 2007, from http://www.schoolcounselor.org/content.asp?pl=325&sl=133&contentid=240

Brown, D., & Trusty, J. (2005). The ASCA national model, accountability, and establishing causal links between school counselors' activities and student outcomes: A reply to Sink. *Professional School Counseling, 9,* 13–15.

Campbell, C. A., & Dahir, C. A. (1997). *Sharing the vision: The national standards for school counseling programs.* Alexandria, VA: American School Counselor Association.

Education Trust. (2007). *Professional development.* Retrieved October 19, 2007, from, http://www2.edtrust.org/EdTrust/Transforming+School+Counseling/Metlife.htm

Gysbers, N. C. (2004). Comprehensive guidance and counseling programs: The evolution of accountability. *Professional School Counseling, 8,* 1–14.

Gysbers, N. C., & Henderson, P. (2000). *Developing and managing your school guidance program* (3rd ed.). Alexandria, VA: American Counseling Association.

Keys, S. G., Bemak, F., & Lockhart, E. J. (1998). Transforming school counseling to serve the mental health needs of at-risk youth. *Journal of Counseling & Development, 76,* 381–388.

Schwallie-Giddis, P., ter Maat, M., & Pak, M. (2003). Initiating leadership by introducing and implementing the ASCA national model. *Professional School Counseling, 6,* 170–173.

Sink, C. A., & Stroh, H. R. (2003). Raising achievement test scores of early elementary school students through comprehensive school counseling programs. *Professional School Counseling, 6,* 350–364.

The Foundation Component

Caroline A. Baker
Sibyl Camille Cato

The purpose of this chapter is to:

- Explore foundational aspects of a school counseling program within various school environments
- Examine your personal and professional values in relation to the school community
- Develop a personal and program philosophy of school counseling, while exploring school counseling program vision and mission statements
- Relate school, district, and state standards to the American School Counselor Association (ASCA) National Model® and Standards

It is likely that you have already learned about the components and elements within a comprehensive, developmental school counseling (CDSC) program from courses you have taken in your school counseling curriculum. Of the four elements outlined in the ASCA National Model, the Foundation component serves as the structure from which the Management and Delivery System components build, and it is integral to the Accountability component. And now, as you embark on your school counseling practicum and internship experiences, you should begin to see aspects of the ASCA National Model at work within your placement school. As you are performing myriad school counselor tasks at your school site, it is essential that you take the time to reflect on your beliefs surrounding school counseling, and on the professional you are becoming, to build on your understanding of the school counselor as a vital force within the school.

This chapter will help you begin the process of appreciating the ideals and values inherent to a CDSC program, and how the mission and philosophy of the school counseling program support the school counselor's role. In addition, recognizing how your own values and beliefs fit into those of the larger school system is an essential process for determining your fit into the profession. Once you acknowledge the direction you and your program are heading, and how these goals integrate within the school, the groundwork has been set; it is now up to you to fervently carry out the goals you identified. Yet, this cannot occur without a thorough knowledge base of who you are, and of the core values and beliefs from which the ASCA has built its convictions surrounding the role of the school counselor.

Through this chapter, you will identify foundational components of a school counseling program by examining your personal and professional belief system in relation to students, parents, school personnel, and other key educational figures. Furthermore, developing a personal philosophy of school counseling, outlining what you would like a school counselor program to become in the future, and choosing ASCA Standards to meet these ideals, are all discussed in this chapter. Finally, you will be able to tie your reflections about and knowledge of school environments to the ASCA National Standards as well as to your state and district standards. The ultimate goal of a "comprehensive, developmental, and systematic school counseling program" requires a solid foundation to ensure every student receives the necessary services to help them succeed (ASCA, 2003).

Although you may have developed philosophy and mission statements as an assignment in one of your graduate classes, keep in mind that as you gain more experience in understanding the school counselor's role your beliefs and philosophy will change. You will develop new insights and knowledge with each person you work, and in turn these opportunities will impact your thoughts about yourself and the profession. Therefore, your philosophy is ever-evolving, and what you think is essential to the profession at this time may not be a priority in the future. As you read this chapter, the activities are designed to help you rethink these initial efforts or to help you begin the process of developing these fundamental declarations if you have not had an opportunity before this time.

ACTIVITY 7.1

Ask your site supervisor to share the school counseling mission, philosophy, and vision statement. What are some of the key themes that stand out for you? Compare these statements with those of your peers. What similarities and differences are evident?

_____

_____

Personal and Professional Values

What is a value? Although there are numerous definitions, a definition provided by the American Psychological Association (2007) states that a value is "a moral, social, or aesthetic principle accepted by an individual or society as a guide to what is good, desirable, or important" (p. 975). How do you, as a person training for the school counseling profession, determine what is just, necessary, and valuable? To answer this question, it would be helpful for you to gather information about the school and community in which you are performing your clinical experiences, including your personal beliefs about students, parents, educators, and your own capabilities? How are your beliefs similar or different from these stakeholders? Finally how would you answer the question, "What are the behaviors, skills, and knowledge that I believe all youth should have upon graduating from high school?" Give these questions serious thought as you progress through your graduate program; your future duties and actions as a school counselor hinge upon the foundation of your program, which are built from your personal and professional values.

School counselors do not work independently in the school environment to serve the students. Who are the other professionals in the school building who interact with the students? You may immediately think about teachers, principals, and perhaps other specialists in the building, but many more people than this affect the success of each student. Administrative assistants, custodians, bus drivers, school superintendents, lunch staff, the Parent Teacher Association, and others contribute to the academic experience of every student. There may be times when you need to consult one or more of these professionals to gather all relevant information to help a student, and they may, in turn, expect to know what is happening with that student. How do your values intersect with the ethics of our professional counseling association? Are there any of your beliefs that may conflict with our ethical principles? For instance, what do your values and beliefs say about maintaining confidentiality while also maintaining positive, collaborative working relationships? How do you tactfully navigate such tricky situations without cutting off relationships with the important people in the students' lives? This ambiguous aspect of being a school counselor is not easily defined, although on the surface it appears to be black and white. When you get into your practicum and internship sites, pay close attention to how your site supervisor handles these situations and ask questions to gain an understanding of the reasons events were handled in a certain manner. Do you feel comfortable with the way in which he or she talks to other school professionals about certain students and certain confidential situations? If not, how would you handle it? Similarly, school personnel may seek a

ACTIVITY 7.2

Complete the following chart, entering notes about your values and beliefs regarding the intersection of each aspect of a school counseling program. For example, what personal beliefs do you hold regarding the school counselor's role as a leader in regard to students in the school? What professional values surround school counselor leadership and students? To assist you with this process, a few examples are provided.

	Leadership	Advocacy	Teaming/ Collaboration	Counseling/ Coordination	Assessment/ Use of Data
Students	Personal: Students are able to make decisions, and at times need assistance. Professional:			All students can benefit from a partnership with teachers.	
Parents	Personal: Professional:	Parents need to advocate for their student.			
Teachers/ School staff	Personal: Professional:		There are some teachers with whom it is difficult to form a partnership.		
Advisory board	Personal: Professional:				Advisory board members can only understand program effectiveness when they see reports that highlight results.
Achievement	Personal: Professional:	Sometimes school counselors need to show how they assist in student achievement.			
Other	Personal: Professional:				

(continued on next page)

ACTIVITY 7.2 (continued)

After you have identified your beliefs and values in regard to each of the areas above, identify and list the themes that serve as a basis for your values and beliefs regarding the school counseling program. Discuss your belief system with those of your peers.

Themes

_____   _____   _____

_____   _____   _____

_____   _____

Now, take these themes and rewrite them as belief statements by filling in the following blanks.

I believe _____

I believe _____

I believe _____

Now that you have noted your beliefs, refer to these statements in writing your philosophy and mission statements. Or, if you have already written a philosophy or mission statement, use these beliefs as a basis for revision.

counseling relationship with you; you will need to identify how to maintain appropriate professional and role boundaries.

Other ethical situations may come up, such as cases that challenge your personal values or that might require referrals to outside agencies. You almost certainly will meet with a student from a background different from yours and your relationship with this child will require you to seek information and understanding of that student's culture. How do your personal and professional values support this relationship? Your school counseling program foundation proclaims the ability to serve every student, so what does that actually look like? Counseling is very rarely confined to neat, clean categories; you will make ethical decisions often and must know your own values that strengthen your philosophy before embarking as a school counselor.

In 1996, the Education Trust, along with the Wallace Reader's Digest Fund, outlined a *Transforming School Counseling Initiative* (TSCI) that works in conjunction with the ASCA National Model. The base of this initiative is formed from the focus areas of leadership, advocacy, teaming and collaboration, counseling and coordination, and assessment and use of data (Education Trust, 2003). TSCI supports ASCA and offers these themes as integral to the basic components outlined in the National Model. Take some time to work on Activity 7.2 to identify how your values and beliefs align with these foundational components.

Developing a Philosophy of School Counseling

According to the *Merriam-Webster Dictionary* (2009), a philosophy is defined as "a search for a general understanding of values and reality by chiefly speculative rather than observational means." Determining how your values fit within a philosophy of school counseling is the next step in formulating your thoughts about the school counseling profession. Reflect on the courses and assignments that have shaped your understanding of what a school counselor does within a school and community. What ideas stand out to you? Why? You might recall your own school counselor and school culture when you were a student in grades pre-K–12. What was that program like? What did they do to help you succeed, and what messages did they send out about their program? As you review your experiences, you are creating and molding your personal philosophy of what an ideal school counselor is and the role you believe he or she plays in schools. Identifying the values and beliefs that hold priority for you will lend to the formation of a strong program philosophy and mission statement with the ultimate goal of receiving an endorsement by the decision makers for the school programs. Knowing what you believe is essential to weaving into the fabric of the school community, as it strengthens your position, particularly when you are able to show how your program facilitates student growth.

Professional school counselors who believe in and follow the principles behind the ASCA National Model, and who effectively meet the needs of their school, serve as excellent resources for describing and modeling a school counseling identity. These professionals have integrated their training, values, and beliefs with the existing school and district philosophy and mission statements to form a collaborative alliance that functions as a framework to facilitate student success. If you are provided with the opportunity to create or revise a philosophy for your school building or school counseling program, be aware that the task will not be simple. There may be people involved in the process who are attached to traditions and resistant to change. These individuals can hinder the process and create an unfavorable group dynamic. Keep in mind, however, that the reason you are creating a vision is to pave the way toward greater student and school success.

While you are performing your clinical experiences, observe and speak with school counselors who prescribe to a CDSC program, as you will receive invaluable knowledge about forming a counseling philosophy that supports school counseling and is integrated to the school. These professional school counselors are living their school counseling philosophy.

ACTIVITY 7.3

Using your belief statements from Activity 7.2 as a base, begin to develop your personal and professional philosophy of school counseling. Use the following questions to guide this activity. Compare your philosophical statement with those of your peers.

- Who are the stakeholders with whom the school counselor works?
- What is the school counselor's role in advocacy?
- How does the school counselor contribute to data collection and assessment?
- How can the school counselor serve as a leader of the school counseling program with respect to administrators and teachers?
- What is the school counselor's role in collaboration?
- How are students different as a result of school counseling?

_____

_____

_____

Discuss your philosophy with your supervisor and continually modify it as you grow throughout your practicum and internship experience; it will be a significant addition to your counseling portfolio. School systems are constantly changing and adapting to research and reforms geared to meet the needs of the student population. School counseling programs must respond to this fluid change while keeping in mind the direction they wish to go. To do this, school counselors need to establish a shared vision with the school community. Examining both the school counselor's strengths and limitations and those of the school counseling program, facilitate the creation of these statements. School counselors should explore what needs to be accomplished in 1 year, 5 years, 10 years, and into the future. Your philosophy of the school counseling program should parallel that of the school district and be approved by the school board. Therefore, these statements are to be considered in your program documents. After you have reflected on your philosophy of school counseling, the next step is forming a mission statement, or a vision of how you would like yourself and your program to look like in the future, to provide a guiding focus.

What Is a Mission Statement?

Mission statements are brief depictions of the vision of a company, organization, or in this case a school, and are written at the district, school, and school counseling program level. The school counseling program's mission must align with the philosophy of the school and the district. According to the ASCA National Model (2003), the mission statement should

1. Keep the school counseling program's focus on the beliefs, assumptions and philosophy of those involved
2. Establish a structure for innovations
3. Create one vision
4. Provide an anchor in the face of change

Creating a mission statement from scratch is not an easy task, especially if the school counselor is new to the role or to the school building. It is necessary to get each counselor involved in this process to ensure that each person contributes their beliefs and values to the shared vision of the school counseling program. In addition, the focus of the mission statement should have each student in the forefront, with an indication of the long-range objectives for all students.

ACTIVITY 7.4

Ask your site supervisor to share the mission statement created for the school counseling program. What are some of the themes that stand out in this statement? If your site school has not yet developed a mission statement, one of your contributions to the school and school counseling program should help create one. Share your school site's school counselor mission statement with your peers, or the mission statement that you created if your school has not yet adopted one.

Standards and Competencies in a CDSC Program

Standards and competencies are essential to educational reform in that they identify target areas for student growth; CDSC programs are no exception. This section summarizes standards and competencies for you to consider as you perform your clinical experiences.

In 1997, the ASCA governing council recognized the need for school counseling programs to identify standards that would identify targeted knowledge, skill, or behavior changes in school-aged youth as a result of participating in a school counseling program. These standards are related to the mission of the school to promote equal access to school counseling services for all students (ASCA, 1998), and are included in the three broad domains of academic, career, and personal/social development. Three standards within each of these domains are identified with specific competencies and indicators integral to each of the standards. Although you have probably been introduced to these ASCA Standards, they are outlined in Table 7.1 for you to use as a reference. Choosing competencies on which to focus depends on communication with faculty/staff and an examination of the school's philosophy and mission.

TABLE 7.1   ASCA National Standards, Competencies, and Indicators Academic Development

ASCA National Standards for academic development guide school counseling programs to implement strategies and activities to support and maximize each student's ability to learn.

Standard A: Students will acquire the attitudes, knowledge, and skills that contribute to effective learning in school and across the lifespan.

A:A1 Improve Academic Self-Concept

A:A1.1 Articulate feelings of competence and confidence as learners

A:A1.2 Display a positive interest in learning

A:A1.3 Take pride in work and achievement

A:A1.4 Accept mistakes as essential to the learning process

A:A1.5 Identify attitudes and behaviors that lead to successful learning

A:A2 Acquire Skills for Improving Learning

A:A2.1 Apply time- and task-management skills

A:A2.2 Demonstrate how effort and persistence positively affect learning

A:A2.3 Use communications skills to know when and how to ask for help when needed

A:A2.4 Apply knowledge and learning styles to positively influence school performance

A:A3 Achieve School Success

A:A3.1 Take responsibility for their actions

A:A3.2 Demonstrate the ability to work independently, as well as the ability to work cooperatively with other students

A:A3.3 Develop a broad range of interests and abilities

A:A3.4 Demonstrate dependability, productivity, and initiative

A:A3.5 Share knowledge

Standard B: Students will complete school with the academic preparation essential to choose from a wide range of substantial postsecondary options, including college.

A:B1 Improve Learning

A:B1.1 Demonstrate the motivation to achieve individual potential

A:B1.2 Learn and apply critical-thinking skills

A:B1.3 Apply the study skills necessary for academic success at each level

A:B1.4 Seek information and support from faculty, staff, family, and peers

A:B1.5 Organize and apply academic information from a variety of sources

A:B1.6 Use knowledge of learning styles to positively influence school performance

A:B1.7 Become a self-directed and independent learner

A:B2 Plan to Achieve Goals

A:B2.1 Establish challenging academic goals in elementary, middle/junior high, and high school

A:B2.2 Use assessment results in educational planning

A:B2.3 Develop and implement annual plan of study to maximize academic ability and achievement

A:B2.4 Apply knowledge of aptitudes and interests to goal setting

A:B2.5 Use problem-solving and decision-making skills to assess progress toward educational goals

A:B2.6 Understand the relationship between classroom performance and success in school

A:B2.7 Identify postsecondary options consistent with interests, achievement, aptitude, and abilities

Standard C: Students will understand the relationship of academics to the world of work and to life at home and in the community.

A:C1 Relate School to Life Experiences

A:C1.1 Demonstrate the ability to balance school, studies, extracurricular activities, leisure time, and family life

A:C1.2 Seek co-curricular and community experiences to enhance the school experience

A:C1.3 Understand the relationship between learning and work

A:C1.4 Demonstrate an understanding of the value of lifelong learning as essential to seeking, obtaining, and maintaining life goals

A:C1.5 Understand that school success is the preparation to make the transition from student to community member

A:C1.6 Understand how school success and academic achievement enhance future career and vocational opportunities

(continued on next page)

TABLE 7.1 (continued)   ASCA National Standards, Competencies, and Indicators
Academic Development

Career Development

ASCA National Standards for career development guide school counseling programs to provide the foundation for the acquisition of skills, attitudes, and knowledge that enable students to make a successful transition from school to the world of work, and from job to job across the lifespan.

Standard A: Students will acquire the skills to investigate the world of work in relation to knowledge of self and to make informed career decisions.

C:A1 Develop Career Awareness

C:A1.1 Develop skills to locate, evaluate, and interpret career information

C:A1.2 Learn about the variety of traditional and nontraditional occupations

C:A1.3 Develop an awareness of personal abilities, skills, interests, and motivations

C:A1.4 Learn how to interact and work cooperatively in teams

C:A1.5 Learn to make decisions

C:A1.6 Learn how to set goals

C:A1.7 Understand the importance of planning

C:A1.8 Pursue and develop competency in areas of interest

C:A1.9 Develop hobbies and vocational interests

C:A1.10 Balance between work and leisure time

C:A2 Develop Employment Readiness

C:A2.1 Acquire employability skills such as working on a team, problem solving, and organizational skills

C:A2.2 Apply job-readiness skills to seek employment opportunities

C:A2.3 Demonstrate knowledge about the changing workplace

C:A2.4 Learn about the rights and responsibilities of employers and employees

C:A2.5 Learn to respect individual uniqueness in the workplace

C:A2.6 Learn how to write a résumé

C:A2.7 Develop a positive attitude toward work and learning

C:A2.8 Understand the importance of responsibility, dependability, punctuality, integrity, and effort in the workplace

C:A2.9 Utilize time- and task-management skills

Standard B: Students will employ strategies to achieve future career goals with success and satisfaction.

C:B1 Acquire Career Information

C:B1.1 Apply decision-making skills to career planning, course selection, and career transition

C:B1.2 Identify personal skills, interests, and abilities and relate them to current career choice

C:B1.3 Demonstrate knowledge of the career-planning process

C:B1.4 Know the various ways in which occupations can be classified

C:B1.5 Use research and information resources to obtain career information

C:B1.6 Learn to use the Internet to access career-planning information

C:B1.7 Describe traditional and nontraditional career choices and how they relate to career choice

C:B1.8 Understand how changing economic and societal needs influence employment trends and future training

C:B2 Identify Career Goals

C:B2.1 Demonstrate awareness of the education and training needed to achieve career goals

C:B2.2 Assess and modify their educational plan to support career

C:B2.3 Use employability and job readiness skills in internship, mentoring, shadowing, and/or other work experience

C:B2.4 Select course work that is related to career interests

C:B2.5 Maintain a career-planning portfolio

Standard C: Students will understand the relationship between personal qualities, education, training, and the world of work.

C:C1 Acquire Knowledge to Achieve Career Goals

C:C1.1 Understand the relationship between educational achievement and career success

C:C1.2 Explain how work can help to achieve personal success and satisfaction

C:C1.3 Identify personal preferences and interests influencing career choice and success

TABLE 7.1 (continued)   ASCA National Standards, Competencies, and Indicators
Academic Development

C:C1.4 Understand that the changing workplace requires lifelong learning and acquiring new skills

C:C1.5 Describe the effect of work on lifestyle

C:C1.6 Understand the importance of equity and access in career choice

C:C1.7 Understand that work is an important and satisfying means of personal expression

C:C2 Apply Skills to Achieve Career Goals

C:C2.1 Demonstrate how interests, abilities, and achievement relate to achieving personal, social, educational, and career goals

C:C2.2 Learn how to use conflict-management skills with peers and adults

C:C2.3 Learn to work cooperatively with others as a team member

C:C2.4 Apply academic and employment readiness skills in work-based learning situations such as internships, shadowing, and/or mentoring experiences

Personal/Social Development

ASCA National Standards for personal/social development guide school counseling programs to provide the foundation for personal and social growth as students progress through school and into adulthood.

Standard A: Students will acquire the knowledge, attitudes, and interpersonal skills to help them understand and respect self and others.

PS:A1 Acquire Self-Knowledge

PS:A1.1 Develop positive attitudes toward self as a unique and worthy person

PS:A1.2 Identify values, attitudes, and beliefs

PS:A1.3 Learn the goal-setting process

PS:A1.4 Understand change is a part of growth

PS:A1.5 Identify and express feelings

PS:A1.6 Distinguish between appropriate and inappropriate behavior

PS:A1.7 Recognize personal boundaries, rights, and privacy needs

PS:A1.8 Understand the need for self-control and how to practice it

PS:A1.9 Demonstrate cooperative behavior in groups

PS:A1.10 Identify personal strengths and assets

PS:A1.11 Identify and discuss changing personal and social roles

PS:A1.12 Identify and recognize changing family roles

PS:A2 Acquire Interpersonal Skills

PS:A2.1 Recognize that everyone has rights and responsibilities

PS:A2.2 Respect alternative points of view

PS:A2.3 Recognize, accept, respect, and appreciate individual differences

PS:A2.4 Recognize, accept, and appreciate ethnic and cultural diversity

PS:A2.5 Recognize and respect differences in various family configurations

PS:A2.6 Use effective communications skills

PS:A2.7 Know that communication involves speaking, listening, and nonverbal behavior

PS:A2.8 Learn how to make and keep friends

Standard B: Students will make decisions, set goals, and take necessary action to achieve goals.

PS:B1 Self-Knowledge Application

PS:B1.1 Use a decision-making and problem-solving model

PS:B1.2 Understand consequences of decisions and choices

PS:B1.3 Identify alternative solutions to a problem

PS:B1.4 Develop effective coping skills for dealing with problems

PS:B1.5 Demonstrate when, where, and how to seek help for solving problems and making decisions

PS:B1.6 Know how to apply conflict-resolution skills

PS:B1.7 Demonstrate a respect and appreciation for individual and cultural differences

(continued on next page)

TABLE 7.1 (continued)   ASCA National Standards, Competencies, and Indicators
Academic Development

PS:B1.8 Know when peer pressure is influencing a decision

PS:B1.9 Identify long- and short-term goals

PS:B1.10 Identify alternative ways of achieving goals

PS:B1.11 Use persistence and perseverance in acquiring knowledge and skills

PS:B1.12 Develop an action plan to set and achieve realistic goals

Standard C: Students will understand safety and survival skills.

PS:C1 Acquire Personal Safety Skills

PS:C1.1 Demonstrate knowledge of personal information (i.e., telephone number, home address, emergency contact)

PS:C1.2 Learn about the relationship between rules, laws, safety, and the protection of rights of the individual

PS:C1.3 Learn about the differences between appropriate and inappropriate physical contact

PS:C1.4 Demonstrate the ability to set boundaries, rights, and personal privacy

PS:C1.5 Differentiate between situations requiring peer support and situations requiring adult professional help

PS:C1.6 Identify resource people in the school and community, and know how to seek their help

PS:C1.7 Apply effective problem-solving and decision-making skills to make safe and healthy choices

PS:C1.8 Learn about the emotional and physical dangers of substance use and abuse

PS:C1.9 Learn how to cope with peer pressure

PS:C1.10 Learn techniques for managing stress and conflict

PS:C1.11 Learn coping skills for managing life events

At this point in your academic career, it should come as no surprise to you that a road map is needed to point the direction to where you are heading; all of the Foundation elements that we have discussed so far assist in navigating this map. The goals of the school counseling program should be reflected in the domains in the ASCA Standards, as well as in the state and district standards, and should provide structure for the program.

Crosswalking has been described as one way school competencies and standards can be related to the ASCA National Model (2003). Crosswalking involves comparing the school counseling competencies with the school's standards to show links to the current curriculum. The crosswalk can serve as a checklist to show what the school counselor is doing and what activities need to be done to eliminate gaps in the philosophy, mission, and standards of the school community.

ACTIVITY 7.5

Compare your school and state standards and competencies with those outlined by the ASCA. Now, look at your clinical contract. Which of the activities in your contract are performance criteria that can be used to meet some of these standards and competencies? Complete the table as you reference this information.

ASCA Standard/ Competency/Indicator	State Standard/ Competency/Indicator	District Standard/ Competency/Indicator	Contract Activity

Compare your chart with those of your peers.

Finally, the ASCA recognizes data-driven, comprehensive school counseling programs through the Recognized ASCA Model Program (RAMP). To become a RAMP school, information and an application are available on the ASCA Web site at http://ascamodel.timberlakepublishing.com/content.asp?pl=11&contentid=11. When you view this Web site, note that a philosophy statement, mission statement, and competencies are needed documentation for the application.

Conclusion

School counselors play vital roles in the success of all students and are essential in integrating the school counseling program with the mission and philosophy of the school district. Because school counselors do not exist in isolation, collaborative relationships must be built with other school professionals and with the community; these relationships benefit the school and model effective working relationships for students. To form a successful comprehensive, developmental school counseling program, you need to examine your personal and professional values and beliefs through self-reflection, by observing existing school counseling programs and counselors, and by spending time taking into account various aspects of the school in relation to the goals and philosophy inherent in the ASCA National Model. Once you have taken the opportunity for this in-depth reflection, you can sketch a personal philosophy and mission of school counseling from which to build the foundation of your school counseling program. Your vision for school counseling may complement the school site in which you are performing your clinical experiences, or it could be quite different. When you transition into a fully credentialed member of the profession, searching for school sites with a similar philosophy as yours is a huge consideration. After all, you would not be able to successfully perform your duties in an environment that does not support how you envision the profession.

After completing these crucial steps to ensure a successful school counseling program, you will apply and adapt your personal philosophy to your specific school environment in which you will identify the standards and competencies that identify knowledge, skill, and behavior outcomes to assess student achievement. Once you have completed these steps, you are well on your way to understanding the foundational components of a school counseling program. Outlining a foundation paves the way for designing a delivery and management system, which will ultimately lead to a school counseling program run on a solid basis and influenced by accountability.

References

American School Counselor Association (ASCA). (2003). *The ASCA national model: A framework for school counseling programs*. Alexandria, VA: Author.
American Psychological Association. (2007). *Dictionary of psychology*. Washington, DC: Author.
Education Trust. (2003). *Scope of work*. Retrieved January 29, 2009, from http://www2.edtrust.org/EdTrust/Transforming+School+Counseling/scope+work.htm
Merriam-Webster. (2009). *Philosophy*. Retrieved July 27, 2009, from http://www.merriam-webster.com/dictionary/philosophy

– 8 –

The Management System Component

Jeannine R. Studer
Joel F. Diambra
John R. Gambrell, Jr.

The purpose of this chapter is to:

- Present an overview of the management system in a comprehensive, developmental school counseling program
- Discuss office location, layout, and atmosphere considerations
- Represent agreements and ideas to build and maintain the school counseling program
- Share the importance of data in program management
- Suggest public relations and action plan strategies

A program cannot exist without people who are responsible for certain duties, a plan for when activities will occur, and approval from the administration for program organization. Additionally, a hierarchy exists in each school that provides structure for supervision and communication patterns. When you first enter the school, policies and procedures will already be in place, yet it is up to you to determine how your academic training requirements can be fulfilled within the parameters of the school mission and goals. Therefore, you need to be aware of how you will fulfill your responsibilities within the scope of the existing school, management structure, and hierarchy, as well as where time is spent and how data is used.

The Management System, like all the components in the American School Counselor Association (ASCA) National Model®, does not stand by itself. This component can be compared to a general contractor building a house, who is responsible for balancing multiple roles that are scheduled on a master calendar. The general contractor must have oversight control and agreements among the subcontractors, all of whom need to be aware of the scheduled completion dates and how each person will work with other individuals involved with the project. Finally, consideration needs to be given to how stakeholders will view the final results (e.g., the home buyer's satisfaction with the completed home). Much like the layout of a home, the school structure will partially dictate when and where you will conduct activities. School structure is influenced by the physical floor plan of the school (e.g., the location of offices, classrooms, cafeteria, gymnasium, theater, etc.).

The School Counselor's Office

The location of the school counselor's office and office space arrangement may determine how often people come to see you, and may contribute to making people feel comfortable when they come to your office. At times, school counselors-in-training have complained that other educational resource personnel (e.g., school psychologist, speech therapist, etc.) share the space they were given for counseling purposes. Obviously, these shared space arrangements make scheduling individual counseling sessions challenging. In one case, a student counselor-in-training was frustrated when no office space was available, and only after her site supervisor helped her reframe her predicament was this situation viewed as an opportunity to be creative. She adapted by conducting counseling sessions while walking around the school track with some of her counselees.

ACTIVITY 8.1

Tour the school building to which you are assigned and pay attention to space arrangements such as the administrator's office location in relation to the school counselors' offices. Consider the following questions: Where are the school counseling offices located? Are they labeled School Counseling or something else (e.g., guidance counselor)? Is there enough room to conduct individual and group counseling? Is the office decor and furniture arrangement inviting? Is the office in a private place for counseling to occur? Do the walls and space allow for voices to be overheard? Is there an appropriate place for students and others to wait outside the office? Will students be greeted by someone at a front desk or a sign directing them to the location of a school counselor? Is there clerical assistance available and accessible to the school counselors? Are there adequate spaces for books and other materials? Is there ample storage for materials and electronic equipment? Is there computer space available that can be accessed privately? Is there a printer/fax located in an area where the printed material can remain confidential? Does the equipment need to be shared with other personnel? Is there a common area with bulletin board space available for advertising counseling events or college or career information? What suggestions for improvements would you make?

_____

_____

_____

_____

_____

Sometimes the school counselor's office is located in close proximity to the administrator's office, causing students to associate visiting the school counselor with "being in trouble." This can be problematic until you establish your role apart from dispensing discipline. School counseling offices located in a thoroughfare area open to visitors, administration, staff, and students may be easily accessible, but may not provide the privacy that counseling students requires. In other schools, the school counselors' offices are located in remote settings that are difficult to find. This may significantly diminish the number and frequency of students who seek school counselor assistance.

Although the list of questions in Activity 8.1 is quite long, you may soon realize that the list only begins to address some of the issues related to an efficient and effective work space for conducting some of the school counseling tasks.

The school's physical floor plan is just one factor that influences where and when school counseling activities will occur. Management hierarchy, flow of communication, and agreements made in collaboration with the administration impact school counseling activities, too.

School Organizational Charts

Most school districts have an organizational chart that indicates relationships between the school board, superintendent, school principals, and other school stakeholders. A school's organizational chart provides a visual image of school personnel, their relationship to one another, and the hierarchy of supervision. Typically the principal is responsible for the organization of the school, and the school board is responsible for the school system hierarchy. Because each school is unique and each principal perceives management, hierarchy, and lines of communication differently, few schools are organized or managed in the same way. A generic school organizational chart is provided in Figure 8.1.

ACTIVITY 8.2

Sketch a picture of the school counselor's office, including the available office facilities and furniture location. When you are finished, compare your sketch with those of your peers and discuss an ideal or alternate office arrangement. For example, is the counselor's desk situated in a position that serves as a barrier between the counselor and counselee? Is there open space between the counselor and those seeing the counselor that creates an inviting impression for those who visit?

What is your first impression of the school counselor's office? Some offices have stacks of papers and books on the desk and floor, giving the perception that the counselor is disorganized. Other counselors have their desk and office completely empty of all materials, giving the impression that the counselor has little to do. Other considerations for an inviting office may include decor placed on walls; the furniture style, color, and texture; desk decorations; paint color; carpet/rug versus linoleum floors; and so forth. For instance, if the counselor has religious/spiritual artifacts in the office, these could make students uncomfortable or comfortable depending on if they think their beliefs would or would not be accepted. Your first impressions may be similar to others' first impressions. Take the time to consider how you could make your school counseling space inviting.

ACTIVITY 8.3

In the space next to each of the items listed next, place an *I* next to the items that would make the counseling office inviting, and place a *U* next to the items that would make the counseling office uninviting for students and other visitors. Add items of your own to the list and compare with your peers.

_____ Family pictures		_____ Posters of athletics	
_____ Confederate flag		_____ College/university diploma	
_____ Rainbow symbol		_____ Candy jar	
_____ Symbolic jewelry		_____ National Rifle Association certificate	
_____ Bible		_____ Candles or scents	
_____ College diplomas/professional licenses		_____ School mascot memorabilia	
_____ Counselor wearing casual clothing		_____ Kleenex	
_____ "Right to Life" poster		_____ Pictures of pets	
_____ College posters		_____ Motivational quotes	
_____ Wooden-seat chairs		_____ Orange-colored walls	
_____ Aquarium		_____ Music playing	

ACTIVITY 8.4

Examine the organizational chart of the school to which you are assigned. Are there any positions for which you are unsure of the role expectations? Talk with these individuals and learn how these positions integrate within the school structure. Compare the organizational chart of the school to which you are assigned with those of your peers.

_____

_____

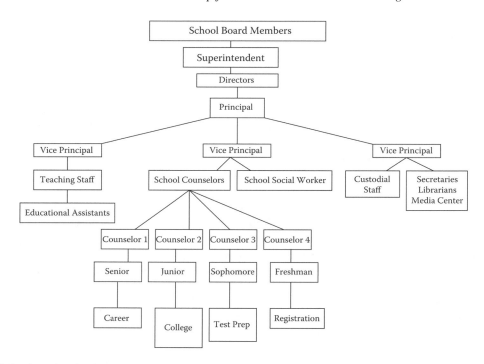

FIGURE 8.1 Sample school organizational chart.

The school counselor may be able to positively influence the organizational schema by communicating the school counselors' roles and responsibilities to the principal. Explaining tasks for which the school counselor is trained may take on several forms such as through management agreements, the use of a personal or program calendar, or through the provision of a needs assessment with data collection to reveal program results. Each of these strategies is discussed next.

Management Agreements, Calendars and Time Management, Data, Needs Assessments, and Schedules

Management Agreements

All individuals who are essential to the school counseling program should be included in the management plan so that everyone involved is aware of who is responsible for each activity, when and where it will occur, and the supplies or equipment that are needed. The school counseling program is an integral component of the school mission in which school counselors work in collaboration with other educational programs. For example, multiple standards in the ASCA National Model (e.g., Personal/Social Domain, Standard PS:C *Students will understand safety and survival skills*, Competency PS:C1 *Acquire Personal Safety Skills,* Indicator PS:C1.1 *Demonstrate knowledge of personal information (i.e., telephone number, home address, emergency contact)*) can be addressed in a classroom in partnership with the school counselor and teacher. Or, the school social worker or community social service workers may be invited into the school to discuss substance abuse. In some cases, a written contract that identifies monetary arrangements will be needed for outside individuals who assist with programming. Before making these types of arrangements, the building administrator or your supervisor is to be informed of all contractual agreements or individuals outside of the school system who are facilitating program activities.

TABLE 8.1   Master Schedule Example

Activity	Person(s) Responsible	Date and Time	Location	Audience	Comments
PS: C1.1 Demonstrate knowledge of personal information	School counselor, fifth-grade health teacher	September 15 @ 2:00	Teacher's classroom/ 45 minutes	Fifth graders (49)	No contract needed
Drug/alcohol awareness	Counselor, local police task force	November 16 @ 9:30	Auditorium; One hour	All middle school students (226)	Written contract with task force needed

Calendars and Time Management

Having a clear plan that is scheduled on a yearly calendar can provide an opportunity for all interested personnel to be aware of when events will occur and their responsibilities in meeting program standards. Table 8.1 is an example of how activities can be identified on a master calendar to indicate the activity, person(s) responsible, date, location, audience or recipients, and additional comments.

Keeping track of all the activities that a counselor performs each day is difficult, and, as a result, school counselors have learned to organize themselves according to a system that works best for them. This can be in the form of a personal daily calendar of activities or a weekly file divided into compartments for each day of the week with the appropriate information filed in each section.

Several managerial strategies that you can utilize while conducting your activities in the clinical setting include

- Set up a daily paperwork system to prevent paper from piling up, becoming disorganized and potentially lost. Categories can be created based on the types of documents that come across your desk or computer. Some categories to consider include applications, financial aid, letters of recommendation, and so forth.
- Divide projects by those that take precedence and categorizing these tasks into priorities such as A = important and urgent; B = important but not urgent; C = urgent but not important; D = delegate to more appropriate personnel. From our experiences, it seems that most counselors are good at managing A-level priorities but are not as adept at handling B-, C-, and D-level activities.
- Other helpful time-saving organizational tools are electronic or notebook calendars, master lists, file folders, large accordion folders, and computerized systems.
- Before leaving the office at the end of the day, review all your unfinished tasks and calendar to identify upcoming activities. Prioritize tasks that need to be addressed the next day.

ACTIVITY 8.5

Ask your supervisor to show you his or her personal calendar of events. Ask him or her how it is organized and what managerial strategies have been most helpful. For instance, some elementary counselors use a different color marker for each grade level. When that color appears on the calendar it serves as a reminder that an activity is to occur for a particular grade. Other counselors have a different personal calendar for each grade level. In a few sentences, describe the management system used by your supervisor.

_____

_____

Use of Data and Needs Assessment

The Accountability component discussed in Chapter 10 is closely aligned with the Management System. Yet, data collection alone is not sufficient. Data must be reviewed, studied, analyzed, categorized, and used when considering future plans. Data are used to reassess plans and to educate decision makers. These data are categorized as process, perception, and results.

Process Data

Process data, referred to as enumerative data, indicates where, when, and with whom the counselor spends time. Some school counselors track daily activities and tally their activities to share with their administrator, and, using this system, a picture is created of where time is spent at different times of the academic year so that it becomes evident how the school counselor is spending his or her time (see Table 8.2).

ACTIVITY 8.6

Use Table 8.2 (or one you have created) to track the time you spend each day in the various components of the ASCA National Model. In which areas do you spend the majority of your time? How does your time compare with those of your peers? Use the information to compare how your time is spent in relationship to the recommended time distributions discussed in Chapter 6.

In our experience, some school counselors-in-training have the mistaken belief that their work day is over when the final school bell rings. School counselors-in-training are often surprised when they learn that the school counselor may need to schedule events or meetings in the evenings to meet with individuals who are not able to attend during the regular school day. In some cases, our school counselors-in-training decided to take on supplemental school activities such as coaching without realizing the amount of time involved and the time schedules required to adequately fulfill their school counselor responsibilities. It is essential to first take care of your own needs and personal health, and then, second, to fulfill your school counselor responsibilities. Be careful not commit to activities that require too much time and dedication. You will become a better judge of the time and energy commitment required after you work a couple of years as a school counselor.

Perception Data

Perception data includes learning other individuals' perceptions of what they know or believe about the school counseling program. In one case, a mother of a star football player was outraged at the school counselor who she perceived was responsible for making her son ineligible to play in the state football championship. The parent was quite vocal about the "incompetent school counselor." The mother told other parents and students that the school counselor would be responsible if the team lost the state title due to her son not being able to play in the game. This mother was understandably upset; however, she failed to recognize that her son was ineligible to play due to his inadequate academic performance, tardiness to class, and poor attendance. In this situation, it was the athletic director who was responsible for monitoring eligibility, but it was the school counselor who was responsible for informing the player and parent. Information such as this is valuable for school counselors so that they have a better understanding of how others see their role. Perceptions and misperceptions, when made known, can encourage school counselors to publicize and inform others of their professional responsibilities.

TABLE 8.2   Daily Activity Chart

Time	Management: Agreements, Advisory, Council, Use of Data, Use of Time, Action Plan, Schedules and Calendars	Delivery System: Guidance Curriculum, Student Planning, Responsive Services, System Support	Foundation: Beliefs, Philosophy, Mission Statement, Domains, ASCA Standards	Accountability: Results Report, Counselor Standards, Program Audit
7:00–7:30				
7:30–8:00				
8:00–8:30				
8:30–9:00				
9:00–9:30				
9:30–10:00				
10:00–10:30				
10:30–11:00				
11:00–11:30				
11:30–12:00				
12:00–12:30				
12:30–1:00				
1:00–1:30				
1:30–2:00				
2:00–2:30				
2:30–3:00				
3:00–3:30				
3:30–4:00				
4:00–4:30				
4:30–5:00				
5:00–5:30				
5:30–6:00				
6:00–6:30				
6:30–7:00				
7:00–7:30				
7:30–8:00				
8:00–8:30				
8:30–9:00				

ACTIVITY 8.7

Walk around campus, your neighborhood, or even the school to which you are assigned, and randomly ask various people the following question: "What do you think school counselors do?" Note the responses you receive and share them with your peers. What did you learn? How do these answers influence what you hope to do when you enter the school counseling profession?

_____

_____

_____

Results Data

Results data reveal how interventions and activities have been effective in reaching goals. Data can be collected immediately, over a certain period of time, at an indicated point in the future, or ongoing. Immediate data measures the direct impact of a one time activity or intervention. For instance, when giving a group guidance lesson, students can be given a brief pretest at the beginning of the lesson to determine how much they know about the subject to be taught. Immediately after the lesson is presented, students can be given a posttest. Score comparison can determine how much learning occurred as a result of the specific lesson to this group of students.

Summative and formative evaluations are useful data collection strategies for revising goals and activities. *Formative evaluation* utilizes data collected while an activity is occurring so that revisions or alterations can be made before the intervention ends. For instance, you may be leading a small counseling group on relationship building, and to determine whether the group goals are being met, you may evaluate the group participants midway through the strategy and learn that the members need more practice in demonstrating assertiveness. From this information you may decide to engage the students in additional role-plays to more appropriately learn these skills. Because summative data depends on formative evaluation, an assessment conducted at the end of the intervention, referred to as *summative evaluation,* is conducted to determine intervention value (Studer, 2005).

Needs Assessments

A comprehensive needs assessment that takes into account the opinions from students, parents, teachers, administrators, school board members, and other interested individuals forms the foundation for program design and implementation. These opinions may be compared with other school data, such as those on the school report card, and can assist in determining program goals, competencies, and indicators for student success in the academic, career, and personal/social domains. The ASCA Web site (www.schoolcounselor.org) has examples of needs assessments that can be adapted for your particular school.

The graph in Figure 8.2 is an example of the results of a needs assessment that was given to teachers. Teachers indicated the areas they believed were most needed by the students in their school, and their top needs and responses were categorized by topics. The responses were tallied and data presented in a chart. If you are unfamiliar with creating computer-generated graphs, a helpful Web site that can assist you in converting data into graph form is available from the National Center for Education Statistics at the "Kids' Zone" graph link at http://nces.ed.gov/nceskids/createagraph/default.aspx

ACTIVITY 8.8

Go to the ASCA Web site (www.schoolcounselor.org). You must be an ASCA member to access this site. Locate the "School Counselors & Members" link, then the "Resource Center" link. Locate the "Sample School Counselor Forms/Needs Assessments" topic and view the links, publications, and sample documents that are associated with this topic. Share your findings with your peers.

_____

_____

_____

These data can be beneficial to your site supervisor in determining areas to address with the school counseling curriculum, and your efforts may create a legacy in the school for others to continue.

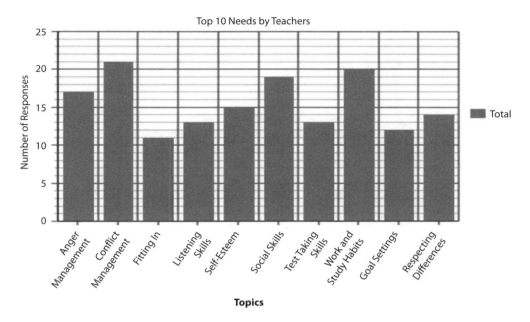

FIGURE 8.2   Top ten needs by teachers. (Reprinted with permission by the National Center for Education Statistics.)

Public Relations

Sharing information with others outside the immediate school community is essential in building and sustaining good public relations. Sharing program results with stakeholders, documenting school counseling activities, and communicating results of program efforts are all included in good public relations within the management component. When practicing school counselors were asked the extent to which they provided documentation of school activities to stakeholders, only 19.2% indicated they collected data continually, approximately 27% reported they did so on a frequent basis, and approximately 38% responded that they did so to a moderate extent. Approximately 12% indicated they did not share any data with stakeholders (Oberman & Studer, 2008). These results are discouraging in that school counselors who do not share information with stakeholders may be placing themselves at risk. When others are unaware of the school counselor's responsibilities it may be assumed that the counselor is able to take on additional unrelated school responsibilities.

If you are working as a school counselor-in-training in a school in which your site supervisor is not involved in data collection and engaged in numerous indirect activities, your training is being jeopardized in that you are not provided with the opportunity to recognize the value of gathering essential information. However, as a part of your clinical experiences, this is an opportune time to learn data collection strategies. Chapter 10 provides you with ideas for data collection and assessment that are recommended for you to attempt while training under supervision.

Data sharing is one method of communicating program effectiveness. Other strategies include planning, scheduling, and implementing events that meet the needs of the teachers and students. Word-of-mouth information sharing occurs regardless of whether you intend for it to occur. The word gets out, sometimes very quickly, when you conduct quality and meaningful events. For example, during her internship class one intern noted the following situation with her peer interns and instructor:

> While interning at my K–12 school, I attended a session at a counseling conference and I obtained an idea to develop a "Career Day on Wheels" at my school. Business representatives

from the local town were invited to bring a vehicle related to their business, park it in the school parking lot, and at the appointed time, share information about their career with K–6 students. The event created so much excitement that before lunch even started, the junior and senior high school teachers were asking if their students could participate in the event—of course, I consented.

There are numerous ways to publicize your activities and events. Several other public relations ideas are offered next for you to consider while you are learning about the school counselor's role:

- Write a column about school counseling issues for the local newspaper
- Write an informational advertisement for the morning public address announcements
- Post flyers in hallways, near bathrooms, and in other gathering spots
- Provide a table of information at parent conferences
- Share information learned at a conference through a brief brown bag lunch presentation with the principal or others who would be interested
- Design a T-shirt or other apparel with a school counseling logo; students can enter a contest to design the best logo
- Put information about upcoming counseling information in teachers' mailboxes
- Make yourself visible and accessible to students, especially during classroom changes
- Volunteer for specific assignments or responsibilities that do not jeopardize the effectiveness of the counseling position

ACTIVITY 8.9

Ask your supervising counselor to share examples of public relations strategies that have been or are currently being used at your school site. In collaboration with your site supervisor, create a public relations idea that you can implement to leave a lasting legacy for the school counseling program to continue after you have left the clinical experience.

_____

_____

_____

Action Plans

In the contract you have developed for practicum or internship, you and your supervisors have identified various activities in which you will be involved. Using this information, develop a plan of action that includes your contract activities and the school counseling program activities, including individuals who are involved, and when and where the activity will occur. As you are developing plans for your contract, or as you begin a new counseling position, you will be called upon to perform tasks that may require a lot of preparation time. It is not unusual for you to experience anxiety as you anticipate your role in implementing this task. For instance, as stated by a former intern

> When completing my school counseling internship, my supervisor placed me in charge of a financial aid night presentation. Fear mixed with trembling, and great consternation immediately overcame me! However, this forced me to learn as much about financial aid as possible in preparation for the presentation. Not only did I learn about a subject to which I previously had little knowledge, a secondary benefit was the invaluable relationships (business and personal) that I developed with various financial aid directors at postsecondary institutions.

TABLE 8.3 Action Plan Example

ASCA/State Domain, Standard, Competency, Indicator	Summary of Activity	Data to Support Competency	When and Where Activity Is to Begin and End	Person(s) Responsible	Evaluation(s)	Expected Result(s)
Social Skills	"Learning to Agreeably Disagree"— a guidance lesson provided to all fourth graders	24 different disciplinary reports from January through February (8-week period; average of 3/week) focused on student-to-student arguments	2 guidance lesson sessions: March 18 (room 214) & 19 (room 129); Begins at start of 2nd period; Ends 10 minutes before 2nd period finishes (50 minutes)	School counselor (lead); Assistant principal (support); 2 preidentified and solicited students to role-play (one female and one male)	(1) Pre- and posttest format: student-generated list of solution focused ways to disagree; (2) Compare preguidance activity number of disciplinary reports with postguidance activity number of disciplinary reports	Decrease baseline of 3/week average of student-to-student argument disciplinary reports to an average of 1/week or less

However, this intern also provided words of caution: "If you are new to a school community, enlist trusted individuals to join you in providing information. You need to foster a sense of trust as you talk with parents/guardians. The reputable partners you to choose to join you in your presentation will assist in fostering an impression of expertise."

ASCA (2008) reminds us that, for every desired competency and outcome, a plan needs to be outlined that includes the competencies to be addressed, a summary of the activity, the data that indicates a need to address the competency, when the activity is to begin and to be completed, who is responsible for the activity, how it will be evaluated, and the expected student results. A template that can be used is found in Table 8.3.

ACTIVITY 8.10

As you plan your contract, develop an action plan similar to that in Table 8.3, and track your activities accordingly. What was difficult for you? How did this action plan facilitate your planning? How did your plan compare with those of your peers?

_____

_____

_____

Conclusion

The Management component provides you with an organizational structure for determining the types of activities and the amount of time that is spent on these services based on needs assessment results, the process of providing services, stakeholder perceptions, and data-based results. In addition, the individual responsible for carrying out these activities, when the various activities are to occur, and the effectiveness of these activities are also integral elements within this program component. As you train for the profession of school counseling, pay attention to the school climate and how your office location and atmosphere can detract or facilitate your work with individuals. Furthermore, help the school counselor publicize the activities. Sharing information is essential to assisting others' understanding of your school counseling program as well as your education and training. There is no such thing as not communicating enough in order to share how your role in the school is essential to the academic, career, and personal/social growth of students.

Web Sites

- This Web site provides numerous documents pertaining to the Management component such as needs assessments, action plans, surveys, and checklists: http://www.schoolcounselor.org/resources_list.asp?c=73&i=16. You must be an ASCA member to access this site.
- This link contains information about the various components of the ASCA National Model, a download for the Executive Summary of the National Model, and a download for RAMP (Recognized ASCA Model Program): http://www.ascanationalmodel.org/. You must be an ASCA member to access this site.

References

American School Counselor Association (ASCA). (2008). *Management.* Retrieved April 1, 2009, from http://www.ascanationalmodel.org/content.asp?contentid=21

Oberman, A. H., & Studer, J. R. (2008). The professional school counselor and performance standards: How is time spent? *Tennessee Counseling Association Journal, 1,* 36–50.

Studer, J. R. (2005). *The professional school counselor: An advocate for students.* Belmont, CA: Brooks/Cole.

The Delivery System Component

Jeannine R. Studer
Joel F. Diambra

The purpose of this chapter is to:

- Provide information on activities within the Delivery System component for counselors-in-training to consider during clinical experiences
- Introduce strategies and interventions within each of the elements in the Delivery System component

As stated in Chapter 6, the Delivery System component provides numerous options for imparting the goals of the program through the curriculum, student planning, responsive services, and system support. This component answers the question of *how* students will acquire the knowledge, attitudes, and skills described in the American School Counselor Association (ASCA) Standards (2003).

Guidance Curriculum

Through the guidance curriculum, the school counselor and teachers can provide classroom instruction by introducing activities that relate to academic, career, and personal/social concerns. School counselors may provide workshops and presentations for students and parents/guardians on issues related to the student's growth (e.g., improving study skills, investigating college scholarship opportunities, practicing job interviewing skills, etc.).

At one time, the majority of states required school counselors to have an education background with teaching experience prior to becoming a school counselor. Today, most states have dropped the teaching requirement. When the teaching requirement was dropped, many beginning school counselors felt ill-prepared to conduct classroom instruction, construct lesson plans, engage in effective classroom management, and teach study skills. Some states have replaced this requisite with a mandate that preservice school counselors participate in designated activities in a school environment with opportunities to understand the school environment, policies, and procedures. To help you acquire more confidence in being prepared for classroom presentations, information and strategies regarding lesson plan development, classroom management, and study skills that school counselors find helpful in delivering services are included in this chapter. Consider these as you perform activities that are integral to the Delivery System.

Developing a Lesson Plan

At times we hear our students express surprise that one school counselor task is to instruct in the classroom, yet this is an essential school counselor duty. Identifying teaching goals and objectives can be a difficult task in addition to the discomfort that is felt when school counselors enter the classroom not prepared to teach. The ASCA National Standards provide guidance and assistance to address instructional preparation. The National Standards divide the teaching–learning process into three domains: academic, career, and personal/social domains. These domains provide a structure by which lessons can be organized to enhance the teaching–learning process. Each of these domains includes three standards that provide a road map for growth and learning, a competency, and an indicator that identifies student outcomes. Desired outcomes are expected changes in student knowledge, affect, and behavior.

The school counselor curriculum needs to be integrated with student needs, identified school outcomes, and ASCA National Standards. For example, suppose your school counselor supervisor indicates to you that a number of seventh-grade students at the middle school need assistance developing conflict-resolution skills. This need would complement the ASCA Personal/Social (PS) Domain. After interviewing each student and assessing the situation, you determine that each student would benefit from conflict-resolution training and setting short- and long-term goals. You choose Standard B: *Students will make decisions, set goals, and take necessary action to achieve goals*, and student competency PS:B.1 *Self-knowledge and application*. (Be sure to review the ASCA Standards that are available on the ASCA Web site, www.schoolcounselor.org.) By determining the area in which you want to track change, you decide on changing behavior, specifically social interaction; and, as a result the specific indicator chosen in this example is PS:B.1.4 *Develop effective coping skills for dealing with problems*. Now that you have determined the student outcome, there are other parts that need to be considered when designing a lesson. These include the audience, materials needed, time considerations, instructional directions, and an evaluation component.

When introducing the lesson, be sure to modify activities based on the age and developmental level of the students. It is helpful to announce the purpose of the lesson at the beginning so that students will have an idea of what to expect and how they can be actively engaged in their own learning.

ACTIVITY 9.1

With a partner, look at the ASCA National Standards and select a domain, standard, competency, and indicator. Choose a grade level and design a lesson that could be used with this group of students.

_____

_____

_____

Large Group or Classroom Management

Classroom management is one area that creates the most difficulty for school counselors-in-training due to the discomfort people often feel in facilitating large groups or a classroom of students (Geltner & Clark, 2005). There is a difference between classroom management and discipline in that discipline plans have rules that temporarily stop unwanted behavior, whereas classroom management plans have procedures that teach students responsible skills that can be adapted throughout lifetime situations (Wong & Wong, 2009). For novices, it is easy to lose control of a large group or classroom, and, once this occurs, it is equally easy to become punitive in an attempt to regain group control. If this type of reaction becomes a form of group management, students lose the desire to be led by this type of group leader. Punishment alone typically deconstructs, rather than constructs, relationships.

Understanding various and effective strategies will help put you on the road to successful large group or classroom facilitation. The key is to begin applying and practicing these proactive strategies to become more proficient at these skills. The following ideas and strategies are provided to help you begin to think about facilitating a large group or managing a classroom:

- Demonstrate respect to students and other group members. Be prepared, address others using respectful language and tone, expect students/group members to contribute to the learning process, and provide opportunities for them to contribute.
- Give students important and active roles in the group. Meaningful roles keep students involved and engaged in the process. Students can be recorders/secretaries, summarizers, critical thinkers, timekeepers, cofacilitators, demonstrators, observers/monitors, evaluators, clarifiers, and so forth. Clearly explain each role and its responsibilities.
- Involve students in making rules and norms. Establish rules and consequences and follow them consistently and predictably. Most teachers post classroom rules and involve students in making the rules; as counselors-in-training, follow their example. Post the rules and consequences and review them from time to time as you remind students that they were instrumentally involved in establishing the rules and consequences. Be willing to revise rules and consequences when circumstances deem it appropriate.
- When possible, arrange seating in a U-shape, circle, or other configuration so that you can see all students and students can see one another. When students sit in rows, discipline problems often occur in the back. Sitting in front helps everyone feel equally engaged and accountable.
- Explain, rehearse, and reinforce procedures. Give clear, concise, step-by-step instructions before involving students in an activity and then rehearse these procedures. Just as coaches have their players rehearse skills, effective classroom instructors introduce concepts, teach, model, and rehearse procedures. Reinforce students when correct procedures are demonstrated, and reteach the desired skill if the rehearsal is improper (Wong & Wong, 2009).
- When you are teaching or facilitating, physically move around the room. If students are acting in a distracting manner, use physical closeness and approach them silently. You can do this even if you are listening or talking to other students across the room. Oftentimes, your presence and the students' awareness that you are attending to them are enough of a prompt for them to change behavior.
- Develop transition rituals with time warnings that help students move from active to quieter learning activities. For example, you can flick the lights and verbally state, "We'll be shifting to from large to small group activity in 5 minutes," or "Small group reading time starts in 3 minutes so please rearrange your chairs for small group."
- Avoid "dead man rules." Dead man rules are rules that a dead man can follow: don't run, be still, don't talk, and so forth. State what action or behavior you desire rather than the behavior you do not want. For instance, instead of saying, "Don't talk when someone else is talking," say, "Raise your hand and wait until you are called on before you talk." Using strategies from solution-focused brief therapy accentuate what you want so that students develop a picture of acceptable behavior.
- Address the situation rather than the student (e.g., rather than, "You were rude when I asked you to be quiet," say, "This is a time to pay attention"). Remain focused on behavior and the situation. This objectivity helps to depersonalize the message, making it less threatening, belittling, or insulting to the student.
- Point out choices and consequences. For example, "Choosing to work on this assignment in class will likely provide more free time when you are home."
- Use the Premack principle or "Grandma's rule." You have probably heard the statement, "If you eat all of your dinner, then you can have dessert." By providing an incentive as a result of performing something that may not be viewed favorably, the student is more likely to follow through on what is expected. For example, write lightly, or by using dashes, the words *EXTRA RECESS* on the board. Each time a student responds correctly to a question, boldly write over a letter until the entire phrase is written boldly: ***EXTRA RECESS***. When all of the letters are boldly written, immediately send the students out for extra recess, or another fun activity. This

procedure works for various other words such as *PARTY, FREE TIME, SNACK, COMPUTER TIME*; activities the students enjoy.

- Lip-sync, speak in a quiet voice, or mime directions to get students' attention. A common mistake is to raise your voice over the combined talking and noise generated within a group or classroom, which typically creates more noise indistinguishable from the already existing sounds.
- If the students are engaged in a loud activity and you want to get their attention, use a cue such as blinking the lights or teaching the students that when you raise your hand each student is to raise his or her hand to alert others that attention is needed.
- Find or create humor in situations and use this humor to connect with students. By incorporating humor, the activity can be more enjoyable and motivating. Laugh with your students. Poking fun at yourself, admitting mistakes, and laughing at your errors provides powerful messages to students.
- Use your basic counseling skills such as attentive listening, summarizing, and open-ended questions.

Providing classroom lessons and facilitating large groups are professional activities conducted by school counselors and school counselors-in-training at all settings. Although managing groups of students can be challenging, implementing positive and consistent group strategies can make classroom instruction fun and productive. A list of classroom management resources that you may find helpful is included at the end of this chapter.

ACTIVITY 9.2

Read the following scenarios and decide on the classroom management strategy you would use in response to the situation.

> You are conducting a classroom guidance lesson on study skills in a fourth-grade classroom and you notice that Christina seems disengaged and uninterested despite the other students being actively involved in the lesson. When you quietly walk to her desk to prompt her to stay focused on the activity, she immediately starts to sob loudly and uncontrollably.

What would you do?

_____

_____

> Roberto is a ninth grader with whom you have developed rapport during the short period of time you have been interning in the high school. You are scheduled to talk about career planning in his social studies class, and as you are providing directions to the class, you notice Roberto talking to one of his peers. When you politely remind the class to pay attention to the instructions, Roberto yells, "I think this is a stupid lesson and you don't know what you are even talking about." After this outburst the class starts snickering at his comments.

How do you handle this?

_____

_____

Study Skills Strategies

School counselors, like other members of the school community, are under pressure to provide evidence of their contributions to the educational objectives of the schools (Sink & Stroh, 2006). In fact, there are some individuals who believe that documenting how school counselors assist in increasing academic performance is the key to showing our contributions to the school mission, and possibly eliminating unrelated school functions (Carey, Harrity, & Dimmitt, 2005). One way this can be accomplished is to employ a study skills curriculum that introduces and reinforces such topics as note taking, the use of mnemonic memory tools, tackling different types of test items, and time-management strategies. The school counselor, or you as a supervisee, can teach these functional examples in that they foster academic outcomes. Due to your efforts, teachers may have a greater appreciation for the school counselor through improved student performance, greater collaboration, and cooperation in releasing students from class. Note taking, memory aids, and test-taking strategies are discussed next for you to consider adapting in facilitating academic achievement during your clinical experiences.

Note Taking

The Cornell method of note taking is often called the "T-note system" because it involves sectioning a piece of notebook paper into an upside-down T. Notes are taken in the first, largest section; to the left of the notes is the cue column, a 2-inch section in which questions or words are written. The final section is another 2-inch border at the bottom in which review notes are summarized. An example is in Table 9.1.

Memory Aids

Sorting information associated with familiar information in a clever way can help students recall information. Mnemonic devices are memory aids that pair information that is associated with something you are learning (Carter, Bishop, & Kravits, 2006). For example, a picture-association technique helps students learn vocabulary by associating unknown words with something that is known. For instance, if students are learning the Spanish word for flower, or *flor*, you may ask students to connect this word to something that they can identify. For instance, students may visualize a floor (to represent *flor*) with a rose on it. To strengthen the memory, have students imagine a color on the rose such as red, then have them to close their eyes, think of the red rose, and repeat the Spanish word *flor* for flower. Repeat this exercise until students create a strong connection (Wyman, 2001).

TABLE 9.1   **T-Note System**

O (Key words are written here as a study guide.) O	(Notes are written in this space.)
O (A summary paragraph is written here.)	

Creating an acronym or acrostic can also be a useful memory technique. Making an acronym involves looking at a list of words that the student is trying to commit to memory and taking the first letter of each word to form a new word or list of letters. A very common acronym is USA (United States of America). An acrostic is similar to an acronym, but instead of making a new word the letters are used to make a sentence. One popular acrostic is *My Dear Aunt Sally* (order of mathematical operations: Multiply and Divide before you Add and Subtract).

Test Questions

Teaching students strategies for taking various types of tests often helps students figure out correct answers or how to respond effectively to various question formats. Multiple choice, true/false, matching, short-answer, and essay questions are common formats used on tests. Oftentimes, carefully reading the question and looking for clues can give an idea of what the answer might be. Eliminating responses as implausible reduces the likelihood of choosing an incorrect response. For instance, some responses do not include key components within the question. When you can narrow the possible responses (e.g., to two likely choices from four original responses, where there is a 50-50 chance rather than a 25% chance of getting the correct answer), your odds of getting the correct answer increase.

ACTIVITY 9.3

To help you teach some of these study skills strategies to the pre-K–12 students with whom you are working, you can adapt the following examples. Answer the following questions.

> 1. A frugalem is an
>   a. soccer ball
>   b. instrument, but only if it has been molded
>   c. yellow, organic mineral
>   d. tool that was used in the Stone Age

To narrow answers consider the following:

- Are there any qualifiers? Absolutes are generally correct. For instance, words like *always, never, all*, and *every* are all-inclusive and leave no room for exceptions.
- Answers that are different from the others in terms of length are often the correct answers.
- Look for grammatical agreement ("... is *an*...") implies the next word begins with a vowel or vowel sound.
- Look for a choice that is in the middle (b or c).

Using these strategies the probable answer is (b) instrument, but only if it has been molded. This answer is due to the grammatical article *an*.

You can incorporate these study skills strategies in your clinical experiences by working with individual students or through instruction in guidance classes. You may also want to consider developing a peer-tutoring group in which a group of students are trained to teach these strategies to their peers.

Individual Student Planning

Professional school counselors also work individually with students in identifying and developing their personal, professional, and lifestyle goals (VanZandt & Hayslip, 2001). Within the ASCA National Model® the areas of individual appraisal, advisement, and placement are elements within this component.

Appraisal

Generally, appraisal refers to the selection of a test or assessment instrument, orientation to the instrument's purpose, administration procedures, monitoring/proctoring practices, and interpretation of the test or instrument results. Based on test outcomes, and in conjunction with additional information from various sources, students can begin to more accurately assess their abilities and interests, and determine areas in which improvement is needed (Cobia & Henderson, 2003).

Students will be more apt to understand and take a test instrument more seriously when they are told the purpose of the test or inventory in advance, and how the results will assist them. When students are involved in assessment processes, they are better able to make effective decisions specific to their needs (Stiggins, 2005). Furthermore, conducting a meeting to explain test results to parents and guardians may also provide an informational forum to answer questions about career and educational planning (Cobia & Henderson, 2003).

As a school counselor-in-training, you also need to be aware of students with disabilities who struggle with traditional testing formats and may need unique test accommodations. The Individuals with Disabilities Education Act (IDEA) amendments of 1997 and Individuals with Disabilities Education Improvement Act amendments (IDEIA, 2004) mandate that reasonable adaptations and accommodations are available for optimal test-taking conditions. Additional information on working with students with special needs is found in Chapter 12.

ACTIVITY 9.4

Observe your site supervisor as he or she orients students to a particular test, monitors/proctors the test, and interprets test results. What are some of the strategies that you feel are most useful in explaining test scores? Were there some areas that you think could have been explained differently?

_____

_____

ACTIVITY 9.5

Take an opportunity to orient, administer, or interpret test results to one of your counselees. What were some of the particular challenges in performing this activity? Is there anything that you feel may have assisted you in this task?

_____

_____

Advisement

School counselors and school counselors-in-training often find themselves providing information to students, parents/guardians, teachers, and so forth to assist with academic, career, or personal/social decision making. Helping students and parents/guardians plan for the future while keeping an open mind to different options, finding postsecondary schools well matched to the student's interests and skills, and applying to college or vocational programs are all common advising activities for school counselors, especially those at the high school level. Advisement activities can be conducted individually or in small groups, and it is wise to include school personnel and parents/guardians in the process.

ACTIVITY 9.6

Read and respond to the following scenario and discuss your answers with your peers.

> Mario is a struggling 18-year-old who has not earned the appropriate credits to be considered an 11th grader. He has only earned enough credits equivalent to those of a 9th grader and he comes to you for career information. He recently spent some time with his cousin who is studying to be an electrical engineer, and Mario is now motivated to pursue this career opportunity. You discuss the requirements that electrical engineers need to be successful, and you also point out to him that he needs to not only improve his math grades, but also that advanced math and computer skills are needed in this profession. You also point out to him that he has not yet passed his algebra class despite taking the class twice. He thanks you as he leaves your office with a printout of the description of the electrical engineer job requirements. The next day Mario's mother calls you and expresses her displeasure in discouraging her son from pursuing this career.

Placement and Follow-Up

As students shift to higher-education settings or careers, counselors who have worked with them in assessment and advisement often continue to assist them as they transition to other settings (Cobia & Henderson, 2003). Follow-up studies are conducted to gather information on how well the various school programs assisted in making these transitions, and whether programs or the curriculum need to be revised to meet the needs of graduates who enter the workforce or higher educational settings.

ACTIVITY 9.7

Ask your supervisor to share a follow-up study that has been conducted of past graduates and his or her reactions to the study outcomes. How was the follow-up study conducted? What trends do you notice? Were there any changes that were made as a result of the results? Share and discuss what you found with your peers.

Responsive Services

Helping students overcome obstacles that stand in the way of growth is the primary purpose of responsive services (Gysbers & Henderson, 2000). A continuum of services such as small group and individual counseling, crisis counseling, referrals, consultation, and peer facilitation are within this component (ASCA, 2003). Because of the many school counselor responsibilities, providing counseling services for a student with more serious disorders that require in-depth, long-term counseling is difficult. It may be more appropriate to make a referral. When making a referral, consider the following questions (Ehly & Dustin, 1989, as cited in Cobia & Henderson, 2003): Am I competent to deal with this concern? Do I have enough time and energy to work with this concern? Is reasonable progress being made related to my counseling? Be sure to seek advice from your supervisor as to the protocol in making referrals.

Small Group and Individual Counseling

Small group counseling is a more time-effective method in reaching more students who may be experiencing similar concerns. Arranging for small groups (and individual counseling, for that matter) in the schools can be problematic since some teachers are reluctant to release students from classes due to the pressure to show academic achievement in subject areas. School counselors can facilitate student dismissal through such means as

- Attaching the group to a classroom period so that only one subject is missed
- Scheduling the group during a grading period to coincide with the beginning and end of the term
- Explaining the purpose of groups with teachers and administrators, and how the outcomes may result in positive classroom performance
- Meeting with the group before or after school, or during lunch, study hall, and so forth
- Sending a schedule of the group meeting to teachers in advance and sending reminders the day of the meeting
- Rotating the schedule each week so that the same subject is not missed repeatedly
- Discussing the best time and day with the student's teacher(s); for younger children, consistent meeting times are recommended due to their developmental level

Crisis Counseling

Crisis counseling is similar to medical triage when the most seriously hurting students or most significant and pressing issue is addressed first, and basic treatment is provided. This short-term counseling is generally considered as a therapeutic intervention with the purpose of restoring the individual to at least the same level of functioning that existed before the crisis. This may last one single session or the crisis may last 4 to 6 weeks (Aguilera, 1998) before it is resolved. In addition

ACTIVITY 9.8

Discuss with your supervisor the various types of crises that have occurred in the school and how these situations were handled. What was his or her role in these crises? Ask to see a copy of the crisis intervention plan.

ACTIVITY 9.9

To practice mediation skills, get in groups of three to role-play the following scenario. Identify one person as the mediator, one person as the girl, and one person as the boy.

> Two students, Alysia, an eighth-grade girl, and Marcus, a seventh-grade boy, are involved in a physical altercation in the middle school cafeteria during lunch period. You come into the cafeteria and observe Alysia hitting Marcus repeatedly over the head with her lunch tray. Marcus is swinging, kicking, and swearing at Alysia while she repeatedly strikes him. A moderately sized group of bystanders are gathered around the pair and are chanting, "Hit him again, harder, harder!" You quickly intervene by stepping through the crowd and between Alysia and Marcus. Once Alysia and Marcus see you step between them, they stop physically fighting. Marcus continues to sling verbal assaults, which Alysia returns as they glare at each other. You summon a nearby female faculty member and instruct her to escort Alysia to the main office and stay with her until you arrive. You escort Marcus to your school counseling office where you find another school counselor, inform her of the incident, and request she monitor Marcus while he sits in your office on one side of your desk to cool down. You retrieve Alysia and escort her to your office, have her sit in a chair on the opposite side of your desk from Marcus, and position yourself between the two students. You leave your door open and request that the other school counselor remain nearby in case you need her assistance. You begin mediation using the steps outlined earlier.

How did the process work? Were there any instances where you were stuck? What would have helped make this process easier?

_____

_____

to providing the type of counseling that is necessary, the school counselor is often a leader in mitigating critical incidents, situations that may create long-term distress and sometimes lead to post-traumatic stress disorder (PTSD). School situations that are likely to elicit crisis counseling include a school shooting, the death of a student or staff/faculty member, a national terrorist tragedy, or a natural disaster that impacts the school or surrounding community. Although it is nearly impossible to predict what tragedy will impact a school, prevention is key to intervening and debriefing. School counselors have the skills and training to teach preventive strategies so that students will be better prepared to cope when tragedy does strike.

Peer mediation and conflict resolution programs are additional essential components that are often included in school prevention programs.

Peer Facilitation Programs

When students are trained to work proactively with their peers, a healthier school culture may develop. In most cases the school counselor is the individual who directs this program and trains the students. Training may include such things as basic helping skills, communication skills, problem solving, role-plays, identifying feelings, and mediating conflicts. Appropriate peer selection, training, and supervision are necessary for the program to be successful. Students are effective at learning and following prescribed courses of action or mediation. Typical steps for peer mediation include (adapted from Kittrell, Comiskey, & Carroll, 2006)

1. Getting acquainted and comfortable, and establishing the rules
2. Identifying the issues from all perspectives and the people directly involved
3. Brainstorming all possible solution ideas without eliminating any options
4. Discussing all ideas, finding commonality among ideas, and eliminating implausible or ineffective options
5. Democratically choosing the best option or options
6. Making an agreement or written contract among all parties to include a follow-up schedule
7. Carrying out the agreement
8. Following up with all involved parties and celebrating success or beginning the process again

System Support

Although school counselors are leaders in a school counseling program, they do not constitute the entire program. School counseling programs exist because of students, parents, administrators, and teachers who support attaining school goals with the school counselor as the program leader. Professional development, consultation and teamwork, and program management are included as activities within the system support component.

Professional Development

New issues are constantly confronting school counselors due to societal, economic, political, or social changes. As stated in the ASCA Ethical Standards for School Counselors, F.2. Contribution to the Profession (ASCA, 2004), to learn more about the concerns facing our youth it is also necessary to be knowledgeable of professional development opportunities that are available at the local, state, and national level. The American Counseling Association (ACA) and ASCA have an annual conference that rotates throughout the various regions in the United States. The ACA generally holds its conference in the spring and the ASCA holds its conference at the end of June, when most schools are recessed for the summer, so that school counselors are able to attend without interfering with work responsibilities.

ACTIVITY 9.10

Using the Internet, search the local, state, and national counseling associations to identify the following information: upcoming conference theme, date, and location, as well as the association membership application. Both ACA and ASCA provide liability insurance with membership, and as a student this is a requirement for working in schools. Check out the insurance coverage that is available.

_____

_____

In some cases volunteer opportunities are available to assist with the conference in which registration cost is deferred or exchanged for a specified number of hours at the conference. Check to see if volunteer opportunities are available. If none are posted, contact the conference planner to ask if volunteer opportunities exist in exchange for registration, lodging, travel, and so forth. You may even notice that some association officers are students. Although this is more likely at the local or state levels, it is possible at all professional levels. You should also note the significantly reduced cost for student association membership and conference registration fees. These reductions are offered as an incentive to encourage student involvement. Conferences provide one of the best professional opportunities to learn more about the school counseling profession and to contribute to the profession through volunteerism, officer service, or conference presentations.

Consultation and Teamwork

Consultation often occurs when the school counselor interacts with peripheral adults and professionals related to the student. Consultation occurs with parents, custodial caregivers, guardians, coaches, teachers, administration, community professionals, and so forth.

School counselors probably spend more time in consultation than any other activity, and in most cases they are not even aware that what they are doing is consultation because of the difficulty in

---

ACTIVITY 9.11

The following are leadership skills that are effective for successful leading and management. Using the following scale, indicate where you believe each of these skills apply to you, and, if you identify any skills that you would like to improve, identify some strategies for developing this proficiency.

1 = Need to improve this skill
2 = Below average
3 = Average ability
4 = Above average
5 = Successful use of skill

Trait	Rating	Strategies to Improve This Skill
Creative problem solving		
Approaches challenges positively		
Willingness to compromise		
Ability to take risks		
Fair		
Responsible		
Nurtures effective relationships		
Respectful of others		
Appreciation of diversity		
Ability to listen to others		
Empathic		
Able to effectively communicate		
Uses time effectively		
Able to delegate responsibilities		
Keeps updated on new trends		
Shows appreciation for others' work		

Source: International Training and Education Center. Retrieved October 7, 2007, from www.go2itech.org/HTML/TT06/toolkit.

defining this process (Davis, 2005). Generally, school counselors assist two groups of people: students and those who work with students (Gysbers & Henderson, 2000).

An effective collaborative process includes components such as shared leadership responsibilities, a well-defined purpose, accountability strategies, time for interaction, time to celebrate successes, effective monitoring of the process, clear rules, reasonable goals, and evaluation (Johnson & Johnson, 2000, as cited in DeVoss & Andrews, 2006). School counselors have skills and training to provide a leadership role in the school within the school counseling program and in other educational initiatives. Many leadership skills have been identified as those that are vital to effective counselor relationships.

Conclusion

The Delivery System component identifies how the school counseling program is to be conveyed to students and other stakeholders, and includes the guidance curriculum, individual planning, responsive services, and system support. The school guidance curriculum includes classroom instruction, which involves classroom management and lesson plan development, areas that often create difficulty for novice school counselors without a teaching background. As a school counselor-in-training, your clinical experiences provide an opportune time for practicing these skills while under supervision. Furthermore, within the guidance curriculum, school counselors often assist student academic growth through teaching study skills strategies such as note taking, test-taking strategies, and memorization tactics.

Individual planning includes advisement and assessment so that students may make informed decisions regarding their goals based on information from assessment results and other sources that help students understand themselves better. In addition, the element of responsive services encompasses those areas that assist students who need immediate help, such as group and individual counseling, crisis counseling, and peer facilitation. Finally, the system support includes professional development, consultation, and collaboration under the leadership of the school counselor. As a supervisee, learning how a school counselor operates within each of these elements is essential to learning about the school counselor's role.

Web Sites

- The Teachers' Guide provides many useful links to techniques that can be used for better classroom discipline and commonly used techniques that are not helpful for teachers: http://www.theteachersguide.com/ClassManagement.htm
- TeacherVision.com is a Web site offering organized topics that can be used in lesson planning and activities, and many are in a printable format: http://www.teachervision.fen.com/classroom-management/behavioral-problems/26200.html
- The Really Big List of Classroom Management Resources contains a collection of classroom discipline strategies that can be utilized from elementary through secondary grades. Additional topics include classroom rules and room arrangements, as well as working with students with learning disabilities: http://drwilliampmartin.tripod.com/classm.html

References

Aguilera, D. C. (1998). *Crisis intervention: Theory and methodology* (8th ed.). St. Louis, MO: Mosby.

American School Counselor Association (ASCA). (2003). *The ASCA national model workbook.* Alexandria, VA: Author.

American School Counselor Association (ASCA). (2004). *Ethical standards for school counselors.* Alexandria, VA: Author.

Carey, M., Harrity, J., & Dimmitt, C. (2005). The development of a self-assessment instrument to measure a school district's readiness to implement the ASCA national model. *Professional School Counseling, 8,* 305–312.

Carter, C., Bishop, J., & Kravits, S. L. (2006). *Keys to success: Building successful intelligence for college, career, and life* (5th ed.). Upper Saddle River, NJ: Pearson.

Cobia, D. C., & Henderson, D. A. (2003). *Handbook of school counseling.* Upper Saddle River, NJ: Pearson.

Davis, T. (2005). *Exploring school counseling: Professional practices and perspectives.* Boston: Lakasha Press.

DeVoss, J. A., & Andrews, M. F. (2006). *School counselors as educational leaders.* Boston: Lakasha Press.

Geltner, J. A., & Clark, M. A. (2005). Engaging students in classroom guidance: Management strategies for middle school counselors. *Professional School Counseling, 9,* 164–166.

Gysbers, N. C., & Henderson, P. (2000). *Developing and managing your school guidance program* (3rd ed.). Alexandria, VA: American Counseling Association.

Individuals with Disabilities Education Act (IDEA), 20 U.S.C.A. §1401 (25) (1997).

Individuals with Disabilities Education Improvement Act (IDEIA), 20 U.S.C.A. §1401 et. seq. (2004).

Kittrell, J., Comiskey, J., & Carroll, L. (2006, February). *Establishing peer mediation in middle and high schools.* Presentation at the University of Tennessee, Knoxville.

Sink, C. A., & Stroh, H. R. (2006). Practical significance: The use of effect sizes in school counseling research. *Professional School Counseling, 9,* 401–411.

Stiggins, R. J. (2005). *Student-involved assessment FOR learning* (4th ed.). Upper Saddle River, NJ: Pearson.

VanZandt, Z., & Hayslip, J. (2001). *Developing your school counseling program: A handbook for systemic planning.* Belmont, CA: Wadsworth.

Wong, H., & Wong, R. (2009, June). *Successful teaching for teachers who want to be effective.* Paper presented at the American School Counselor Association Conference, Dallas, TX.

Wyman, P. (2001). *Learning vs testing: Strategies that bridge the gap.* Tucson, AZ: Zephyr Press.

10

The Accountability Component
and the School Counselor-in-Training

Aaron H. Oberman

The purpose of this chapter is to:

- Introduce the importance of program and personal accountability for school counselors
- Review quantitative and qualitative data
- Provide different strategies for collecting program effectiveness data
- Offer techniques for analyzing data

Accountability is multifaceted in that documentation of program activities reveals where time and effort is expended, quality of activities are self-evaluated, and data are collected that documents performance success. Tracking activities in a regular, ongoing fashion is crucial for professional school counselors and counselors-in-training. This documentation is especially critical in a time when a struggling economy and resulting budget cuts may cause programs to be negatively impacted. Programs that lack proof of progress or effectiveness are more likely to be seen as lacking value and therefore more vulnerable to budget cuts. School counseling programs may be considered as one of the areas targeted for reduction, resource reallocation, or elimination when education finances are tight (Gibson & Mitchell, 1999). Despite these potential threats to school counseling programs, some school counselors still resist the need to be accountable to those they serve (Stone & Dahir, 2004). As a counselor-in-training, you can establish a regular routine of collecting and analyzing data so that it becomes a regular part of your activities now and later when you transition to a full member of the school counseling profession.

Tracking, as an activity itself, can be time consuming. However, a time-efficient way to do this may be to keep a daily or weekly written schedule that consists of tasks accomplished. Using preestablished task categories (e.g., individual counseling, group counseling, guidance lessons, family meetings, student progress evaluation/testing, etc.) or broader categories like those offered within the American School Counselor Association (ASCA) National Model® (e.g., school guidance curriculum, individual student planning, responsive services, system support, management, and accountability) and rounding off the time to the quarter hour (15 minutes) are useful techniques that can be easily adapted. See Chapter 8 for a chart that can be adapted to track time spent on various tasks. Of course, tracking your activities does not inform you as to how successful or effective you are in performing these tasks.

Another way accountability is defined is how you evaluate the effectiveness of yourself as a school counselor or school counselor-in-training, as well as the changes that take place as a result of your efforts. School counselors benefit, as does the school, when documentation reveals how you achieved the goals you have established (Brown & Trusty, 2005; Myrick, 2003). Studying for 2 to 3 years and earning your graduate degree does not demonstrate your competence as a school counselor (Loesch, 2000); graduating signifies that you have met the minimum standards to begin working as a professional school counselor. Being able to provide outcome evidence to your stakeholders (parents, students, teachers, administrators, community members, etc.) that you are positively impacting the student body displays your value to the educational community.

Stop and reflect on your reasons for entering the school counseling profession. These may include such reasons as wanting to work with students through individual and group counseling, wanting to help students like the school counselor who helped you, or hoping to improve upon the impact of your school counselor when you were a student. It is unlikely that you envisioned sitting down, operationally defining goals and objectives, tracking progress and "crunching the numbers," or analyzing the data as part of the job description. Did any of your reasons for entering the school counseling profession include an aspect of school counselor accountability? If so, accountability may be an easier task for you. If not, accountability may be a more challenging aspect for you as a school counselor-in-training and later as a professional school counselor. Regardless of your level of affinity toward accountability and regardless of your educational experience, you are still professionally responsible for being accountable. In the remainder of this chapter, practical strategies and techniques are offered to help you consider collecting data and analyzing your program effectiveness without becoming a full-time statistician.

Types of Data

Before introducing accountability strategies, a brief review of quantitative and qualitative data will help you consider different types of information-gathering and assessment tools that are commonly used by school counselors. Simply put, quantitative data are expressed using numbers. Examples are to rank order 10 items from least desired (ranked 10) to most desired (ranked 1), or to choose a point on a Likert scale from 1 to 6, or to assign a categorized number (e.g., 1–3, weak; 4–6, moderate; 7–10, strong). Relatively simple quantitative analysis such as measures of central tendency can be done relatively quickly. Computing means (i.e., averages), modes (i.e., most frequently occurring scores), and medians (i.e., scores equidistant from the center or midscore) are popular ways to summarize data. There are more sophisticated ways to analyze quantitative data to identify strength, relationships, cause and effect, and so forth that can provide useful outcome information regarding program effectiveness, but these concepts are beyond the scope of this chapter. Should you want to further investigate or review these quantitative data and analysis, refer to the texts that are used in your educational research and assessment classes.

Quantitative data have an advantage in that numbers can be easily compared to determine if change has occurred; however, expressing complicated concepts or subtle distinctions involved in change with just numbers is not always enough. Qualitative data can often lead you to answers that may not be attainable through the use of numbers.

Qualitative data are expressed typically through words. An open-ended written summary of a student expressing how individual counseling helped her improve her school work, a third-party observer's feedback critiquing your guidance lesson, or a parent's handwritten note thanking you for your input in developing her son's Individualized Education Plan (IEP), are a few examples of qualitative data. An example of a qualitative observation form that your supervisor or classroom teacher can use to evaluate your performance in teaching a guidance lesson is found in Figure 10.1.

Information such as that found in Figure 10.1 can provide valuable insight into how others perceive your counseling activities. Allowing others to more openly respond can elicit information otherwise missed in preconstructed quantitative formats. Suffice it to say, there are advantages to both quantitative and qualitative data collection and analysis. Consider both these methods and types of data when evaluating your performance in the clinical setting and later in your professional career. Now let us look at a few specific methods by which school counselors can show evidence of progress or effectiveness.

Counseling Assessment Techniques

This section addresses strategies that school counselors can use to demonstrate their accountability to the stakeholders at the school. The following strategies include pre- and posttest data, surveys, retrospective assessment, experimental action research, and the MEASURE system.

OBSERVATION FORM

School Counselor-in-Training Trainee: _____

Date: _____

Lesson (Topic): _____

Classroom and Grade Level: _____

Rating Scale: 1 (poor) to 5 (excellent)

Counselor-in-training provided an adequate explanation of the topic to students.

          1   2   3   4   5

Counselor-in-training established goals for the session that were integral to the classroom objectives.

          1   2   3   4   5

Counselor-in-training was able to instruct students in a developmentally appropriate manner.

          1   2   3   4   5

Counselor-in-training was well prepared and transitioned activities appropriately.

          1   2   3   4   5

Counselor-in-training appropriately managed the classroom and students.

          1   2   3   4   5

What were the strengths of the counselor-in-training during the lesson?

What areas could the counselor-in-training improve during future lessons?

FIGURE 10.1 Example of qualitative observation form.

Pre- and Posttest

One strategy is to conduct a pretest assessment prior to completing an activity and a similar posttest assessment after a task or intervention has been completed. The information gathered from this form of pre- and posttest assessment can be compared to determine if the activity was successful. An example of this assessment approach would be to conduct a six-session counseling group focused on helping middle school students build social skills and friendships. You could give a pretest to the group participants at the beginning of the first session to determine knowledge, skills, or attitudes toward social skills and friendship. You may consider creating your own paper-and-pencil assessment, or you may consider finding an already established assessment. After conducting the subsequent six sessions to assist in an understanding and practicing of social skills and friendship building, you would give the same assessment as a posttest to the students during the last group session. Posttest data would be compared to the pretest data. Data comparisons could determine if the information and activities provided to the students resulted in an increase in the students' knowledge, skills, or attitudes related to social skills and building friendships with peers at school. See Figure 10.2 for an example of a pretest–posttest.

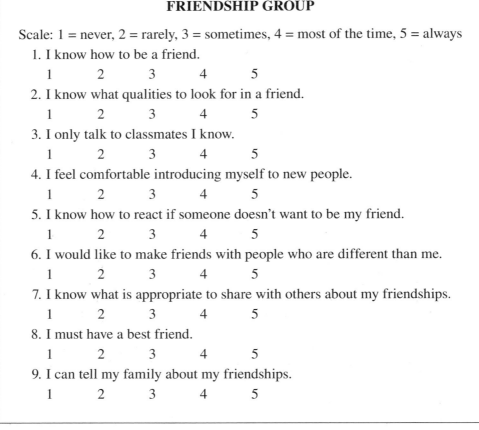

FRIENDSHIP GROUP

Scale: 1 = never, 2 = rarely, 3 = sometimes, 4 = most of the time, 5 = always

1. I know how to be a friend.

   1   2   3   4   5

2. I know what qualities to look for in a friend.

   1   2   3   4   5

3. I only talk to classmates I know.

   1   2   3   4   5

4. I feel comfortable introducing myself to new people.

   1   2   3   4   5

5. I know how to react if someone doesn't want to be my friend.

   1   2   3   4   5

6. I would like to make friends with people who are different than me.

   1   2   3   4   5

7. I know what is appropriate to share with others about my friendships.

   1   2   3   4   5

8. I must have a best friend.

   1   2   3   4   5

9. I can tell my family about my friendships.

   1   2   3   4   5

FIGURE 10.2

ACTIVITY 10.1

Talk with your site supervisor about implementing an upcoming school counseling activity concerning an identified school counseling program competency. Design a pre- and posttest that allows you to assess a change in student knowledge, attitudes, or behavior. Compare your activity and assessment with those developed by your peers. Discuss the successes and challenges in performing this activity assessment.

_____

_____

_____

Surveys

Another technique is to conduct surveys of students, teachers, parents, and administrators. Surveys can be oral or written, and can be distributed by surface mail, e-mail, online, or in person. As an example, suppose you wanted to find out what your stakeholders believe is important about your school counseling program and its impact on the school. Survey items often include open- and closed-ended questions, multiple choice, rank order, and short-answer items. Open-ended items

---

SAMPLE SURVEY QUESTIONS

Open Questions

1. This year I would like to learn more about …
2. The school counselor should focus his/her time on …

Closed Questions

1. Do students need more help with study skills?   Yes or No
2. Does the school counselor meet your needs?   Yes or No

Multiple-Choice Items

1. Which of the following groups would you be most likely to participate in?
   a. anger management
   b. friendship
   c. bullying
   d. divorce
   e. study skills
2. Which of the following guidance lessons are most needed in your class?
   a. time management
   b. stress
   c. career development
   d. anger management
   e. other _____

FIGURE 10.3   Example of pretest–posttest.

allow for a greater amount of comments from your stakeholders, while close-ended or multiple choice questions can be used to target feedback for a specific issue. See Figure 10.3 for examples of each type of question.

ACTIVITY 10.2

Ask your site supervisor about surveys he or she has designed, adapted, borrowed, or purchased. Bring this survey to class to compare with those of your peers, and talk about the advantages and disadvantages of each of the formats.

_____

_____

_____

Retrospective Assessment

A retrospective assessment strategy is similar to the pretest–posttest methodology; however, the counselor asks the student to refer or reflect back to a previous time. For example, a teacher may refer a student to you who seemed engaged and interested in class, but is now very quiet and does not like to participate. Using a retrospective assessment method, you would ask the student to think back to how he or she felt, thought, or behaved in this class at the beginning of the school year. You could instruct this student to place an *X* on a scale from 1 to 5 indicating his or her recollections of specified feelings, thoughts, or behaviors in the class. Then, you could prompt the student to rate how he or she is currently feeling, thinking, or behaving according to the same identifiers, and to place an *O* on the same scale. These two notations are then evaluated to see if a positive, negative, or no change has taken place (Studer, 2005). Any discrepancy between the two scales could then serve as a place to begin counseling. Refer to Figure 10.4 for an example.

Feelings at First Counseling Session

	1	2	3	4	5
Frustrated	X				
Stressful			X		
Angry			X		
Nervous				X	
Happy			X		
Worried			X		

Feelings at Fifth Counseling Session

	1	2	3	4	5
Frustrated	O				
Stressful				O	
Angry			O		
Nervous			O		
Happy			O		
Worried		O			

1 = I never have this feeling.
2 = I rarely have this feeling.
3 = I sometimes have this feeling.
4 = I usually have this feeling.
5 = I almost always have this feeling.

Trends

Frustrated, no change
Stressful, negative change
Angry, no change
Nervous, positive change
Happy, no change
Worried, positive change

FIGURE 10.4   Example of retrospective assessment.

ACTIVITY 10.3

Work with your site supervisor to design a retrospective assessment that can be used in your counseling duties. Share your assessment with your peers and discuss the challenges and successes you had in designing this assessment.

_____

_____

_____

Experimental Action Research

An experimental action research approach can be used to measure the effectiveness of an intervention on two similar groups of students, using one as a treatment/experimental group and the other as a control group. The treatment/experimental group receives the treatment or intervention while the control group does not receive the treatment/intervention (or is delayed in receiving the treatment/intervention). For this approach to be most effective, students should be randomly assigned to each group (each student should have an equal chance of being selected into either group).

For example, you may want to determine if the study skills you are teaching students are improving their test-taking abilities. To determine if the study skill-building sessions are benefiting students, you could collect data from teachers of two fifth-grade classes. (These would be convenience groupings, but not randomly assigned groups.) Ideally, you would collect preintervention data on both groups to establish a baseline average test score for each group. Following the pretest, one class would receive a series of four classroom guidance lessons on study skills, while the other class would receive no guidance lessons during a 4-week period. The group receiving the study skills guidance lesson is considered the treatment/experimental group, while the class not receiving guidance lessons is the control group. After the 4 weeks of sessions are completed, you would assess the posttreatment/intervention test scores of both groups and compare these scores to their pretest scores to see if there was any improvement and differences between the two groups' test scores. If the change between pretest and posttest scores for the treatment/intervention group improved more than did the control group, you have an indicator that your study skills guidance lessons may have had a positive impact on test score improvement. When evidence suggests a strategy was effective, you have an ethical responsibility to provide this treatment to all students. In this case, the fifth graders who did not receive the study skills intervention should now have the opportunity to receive the same guidance lessons.

ACTIVITY 10.4

Ask your supervisor to assist you in developing an experimental action-based assessment in which you can collect data to compare groups. Discuss your assessment and intervention with your peers and discuss the pros and cons of developing this type of intervention and assessment.

_____

_____

_____

MEASURE

The MEASURE program was developed by Stone and Dahir (2004) and is an acronym for a method developed to help counselors document their accountability in the schools. MEASURE stands for mission, elements, analyze, stakeholders-unite, reanalyze, and educate.

Stone and Dahir (2004) purport that school counselors should first align their role in the school with the school's mission. Second, they need to determine the "current critical data elements" (p. 59) that they are trying to impact or change. Next, the school counselors are to examine and analyze the data to establish goals for the counseling program. Then, they are to collaborate with the school's stakeholders and unite to create an action plan that will affect the student body. Fifth, they reanalyze the data to see whether any changes have taken place and make modification as needed. Last, they educate school and community members through a report card that shows where the counselors have made a difference in the school and where improvement is still required. MEASURE provides a fairly comprehensive method to help school counselors document their activities and progress within the school.

ACTIVITY 10.5

With the help of your site supervisor, look at the school's report card where you are doing your internship. Use the MEASURE accountability system to target an identified area and determine strategies for changing this target area. Compare your system with those of your peers.

_____

_____

_____

Performance assessments are another type of evaluation that provides meaningful feedback based on the tasks you perform. As a supervisee, the evaluative criteria is outlined prior to beginning your clinical experiences, and it should be discussed with your supervisors in advance so that you and your supervisor are aware of the criteria that will be used for this evaluation.

Counselor Performance Assessment Techniques

When a supervisor evaluates a school counselor, there is the likelihood that they rely on assessment instruments designed for teacher performance rather than those that more accurately reflect the tasks and duties of a professional school counselor. This mismatch creates an invalid performance evaluation, one that does not accurately represent the professional responsibilities of the school counselor. Talk with your supervisor about the evaluation instrument that is used to evaluate his or her performance.

The following section describes peer, student, self, and portfolio assessment strategies that are commonly used to evaluate the school counselor and school counselor-in-training. As a supervisee, you can become acquainted with these methods and adapt them once you enter the school counseling profession.

Peer Assessment

Peer assessment may be used for determining how you are performing as a supervisee and later as a professional school counselor. As a counselor-in-training, your site and faculty supervisor will evaluate you, and in some instances your school counseling peers may provide you with personal feedback. More likely than not, while you are a student training for the counseling profession, this will be the last time that you will be provided feedback on your clinical skills. As a school counselor, it is most likely that a school administrator will evaluate you, and in many cases this individual will not have a background in counseling. Therefore, it will be up to you to have an open dialogue as to your training and education, and how your counseling skills can be utilized to improve student growth. To help you improve these skills, you may wish to seek other evaluators such as the district school counselor director, school counselors within the district, or local counselor educators. Seeking someone who is considered an expert to observe and evaluate your clinical skills will help to improve your counseling strategies and techniques. For a more comprehensive understanding of some of the performance competencies that have been adapted by the ASCA in the School Counselor Performance Standards, refer to Chapters 6 and 14.

Student Assessment

A student assessment is another useful form of evaluation. After conducting a guidance lesson or counseling session, your students can be the best reviewers of your work because they experience your performance firsthand. One straightforward method for requesting student feedback is through creating different evaluation items or creating a rating scale. Incorporating a basic rating scale from 1 (poor) to 5 (excellent) is a simple technique for tracking how the students experienced the counseling or group guidance session. Although this method can give you a basic understanding of how students felt about the sessions, other methods need to be implemented to determine the extent to which thoughts, feelings, or behavior changed. For instance, case notes provide a means for school counselors and school counselors-in-training to refresh their memory on what occurred in counseling so that future counseling sessions may continue seamlessly.

Although confidentiality is a cornerstone of the profession, as a supervisee, confidentiality in counseling sessions cannot be guaranteed, because it is generally a program requirement to videotape or audiotape sessions and to keep case notes on counselees for supervision purposes. However, once you become a professional school counselor, there is debate as to the wisdom of keeping case notes. Two cautionary suggestions in keeping these records are (a) any information that is shared is no longer private and becomes part of the student records, and (b) the school counselor's personal notes (and yours, as a supervisee) can be subpoenaed. Although your school counseling training program has probably provided you with forms to use in conjunction with the taping requirement, a sample form is provided in Figure 10.5 and an easy-to-follow format for documentation is in Figure 10.6.

In addition to these tape review forms, you may want to familiarize yourself with the SOAP (subjective, objective, analysis, plan) method of writing case notes to assist in remembering the specific concerns each counselee brings to counseling (Cameron & turtle-song, 2002). Figure 10.6 provides an outline of the SOAP method that can be adapted for your personal needs.

Self-Assessment

Identifying and setting goals for yourself at the beginning of the school year, and self-evaluating if you failed to meet, met, or exceeded your goals at the end of the year, is another method of determining your effectiveness to the educational system. Although personal goals are helpful for improving your role and function within the school, they are often not objective, and therefore do not have the same evaluative weight as assessments conducted by a third-party stakeholder. Your clinical training program may require you to journal your weekly thoughts, feelings, and behaviors to track and assess progress from the beginning of the clinical experience until you are completed with the program requirements. Figure 10.7 provides an example of prompts that may assist you with this process.

COUNSELOR-IN-TRAINING TAPE REVIEW FORM

Counselor-in-Training: _____

Date: _____

Counselee Initials and Grade Level: _____

Session #: _____

Counselee's presenting problem:

Session goals:

What were your feelings regarding the counselee?

What detracted from working most effectively with the student?

What was your theoretical approach in working with this student?

What techniques did you implement in the session? Why?

What strategies did you use to evaluate the session?

What were your strengths in the session?

What were your areas for improvement?

Plans for next session:

Rate yourself on an overall rating from 1 (poor) to 5 (excellent) and briefly explain.

_____

_____

FIGURE 10.5   Counselor-in-training tape review form.

Portfolio

As a school counselor-in-training, you may be required to submit a portfolio that will be reviewed by your faculty members before graduation. A portfolio is a working document that typically includes an accumulation of documents or media that demonstrate the knowledge, attitudes, and behaviors you acquired during your graduate school counselor training. A portfolio may be a large binder filled with information, or it may be in an electronic format that is considered a capstone assignment summarizing the school counselor-in-training experience. The portfolio is much like a comprehensive resume or vita that you should begin early, and regularly update with various assignments that you have completed throughout the curriculum. Artifacts you might include in your portfolio include your philosophy of school counseling, current resume, samples of guidance lessons or group plans, an outline of a CDSC (comprehensive, developmental school counseling) program you developed as a class assignment, and other types of data that document your progress as a school counselor-in-training. If you are interviewing for a position, you can either drop the portfolio off at the interviewer's office or provide a link in advance to access your electronic portfolio before the interview.

CONFIDENTIAL

Student Counselor-in-Training _____

Student Counselee (First Name or Initials): _____

Date of Session (Day of Week, Month/Day/Year): _____

Session #: _____ Type of Session: _____

Start Time: _____ Stop Time: _____

Subjective Impressions

How did the counselee present self (e.g., affect, behavior, nervousness, lethargic, etc.)?
What were your subjective reactions to the counselee?

Objective Impressions

What are the factual items that were discussed in the session?
What did you say?
What did the counselee say?
What was the presenting issue?

Analysis

How did the session relate to the counseling goals?

Plan

What are your goals for the next session?
What do you need to prepare?
What aspect of the problem is most essential?

FIGURE 10.6   Case notes.

Developing an Assessment Instrument to Measure Effectiveness

Similar to the concept of being accountable to your stakeholders, creating an assessment instrument can seem like a daunting task for school counselors. As a school counselor-in-training, you do not receive extensive training in data collection and analysis; therefore, you may feel like you do not have the training required to conduct sophisticated assessments or research (Gladding, 2000), or you may worry that the data you collect will not show a positive change in the student body (Myrick, 1990).

To develop an effective assessment instrument, you need to determine what is being assessed and how the results will be used. It is also important to consider where and when the assessment will happen. Certain times during the academic year may be better than others to conduct various lessons and evaluate your counseling program (Studer, Oberman, & Womack, 2006). Moreover, it is important to constantly revise the instrument to make sure the data being collected is in line with your school counseling program's established goals.

Since there are very few ready-made instruments that will meet all of your programmatic needs, it is likely that you will need to design the instrument. Some of the questions to consider when designing your instrument include the type of data to collect, how to collect the data, the types of questions or items that will yield accurate and meaningful results, analysis methods, and the manner in which to share the information with stakeholders. Refer to Figure 10.8 for a sample assessment instrument checklist.

Name: _____ Date: _____

Total number of hours for week: _____ (Total) _____ (Direct) _____ (Indirect)

Discuss your weekly activities:

On a scale of 1 to 10, with 1 indicating a stressful, anxiety-filled week, and 10 indicating a productive, successful week, what number would you use to indicate your weekly experience? Explain.

What were some of the most difficult challenges you faced this week? Explain.

What were some of your accomplishments and successes? Explain

What do you need from supervision this week?

What are your goals for next week?

Any questions or concerns?

Student's Signature: _____ Date: _____

FIGURE 10.7   Practicum and internship weekly journal reflection.

1. Why is the assessment being done?

2. Who will be surveyed?

3. What is the best method for data collection?

4. When is the best time to conduct this assessment?

5. Where and when will the assessment take place?

6. How will you the share the information in an easy-to-understand format?

FIGURE 10.8   Sample checklist to create an assessment tool.

Conclusion

As a professional school counselor in the twenty-first century, it is imperative that you demonstrate how your program impacts the student body and other stakeholders. Keeping a running tally of all of your activities is no longer sufficient to prove that you are making a positive difference within the school. You need to plan and carry out pre- and postassessments, administer surveys, or conduct action research, and so forth, to demonstrate how counseling activities benefit the students. As a school counselor, it is not enough to rely on positive reports that demonstrate that you are a critical and valuable asset to your school; you must demonstrate your importance and impact through planned, thorough, and ongoing performance and program assessment.

Web Site

This link will take you to the school counselor performance appraisal form that is based on the ASCA National Model. This form can be adapted to integrate with your job description: www.vsca. org/PSC Manual/School Counselor Performance AppraisalForm.doc

References

Brown, D., & Trusty, J. (2005). The ASCA national model, accountability, and establishing causal links between school counselors' activities and student outcomes: A reply to Sink. *Professional School Counseling, 9,* 13–27.

Cameron, S., & turtle-song, i. (2002). Learning to write case notes using the SOAP format. *Journal of Counseling and Development, 80,* 286–292.

Gibson, R. I., & Mitchell, M. H. (1999). *Introduction to counseling and guidance* (5th ed.). Upper Saddle River, NJ: Merrill Prentice-Hall.

Gladding, S. T. (2000). *Counseling: A comprehensive profession* (4th ed.). Upper Saddle River, NJ: Merrill Prentice-Hall.

Loesch, L. C. (2000). *Assessing counselor performance. Highlights: An ERIC/CAPS Digest.* Ann Arbor, MI: Clearinghouse on Counseling and Personnel Services (ERIC/CAPS Digest No. ED304635).

Myrick, R. D. (1990). Retrospective measurement: An accountability tool. *Elementary School Guidance & Counseling, 25,* 21–29.

Myrick, R. D. (2003). Accountability: Counselors count. *Professional School Counseling, 6,* 174–189.

Stone, C. B., & Dahir, C. A. (2004). *School counselor accountability: A MEASURE of student success.* Upper Saddle River, NJ: Merrill Prentice-Hall.

Studer, J. R. (2005). *The professional school counselor: An advocate for students.* Belmont, CA: Thomson/Brooks Cole.

Studer, J. R., Oberman, A. H., & Womack, R. H. (2006). Producing evidence to show counseling effectiveness in the schools. *Professional School Counseling, 9,* 385–391.

11

Applying the American School Counselor Association (ASCA) Ethical Standards

Melinda M. Gibbons
Shawn L. Spurgeon

The purpose of this chapter is to:

- Describe the ethical principles used in counseling
- Review an ethical decision-making model
- Demonstrate the application of the ethical decision-making model to school counseling issues
- Illustrate the American School Counselor Association (ASCA) Ethical Standards
- Apply the ASCA Ethical Standards to various case examples

Professional counselors and counselors-in-training, regardless of their work setting, are required to abide by the ethical code of their profession. As individuals training for the school counseling profession, you are constantly faced with ethical dilemmas and often have to make clinical decisions that require knowledge of ethical codes and a strong ethical decision-making model. Although you have probably already taken a class in ethical/legal standards, this chapter reviews the principles on which ethical codes are based, and outlines common ethical decision-making models used by professional counselors. This discussion will be followed by a highlighting of the current ethical decision-making model adopted by the American Counseling Association (ACA). Following this model, a summary of the ASCA Ethical Standards will be provided along with case examples and activities for you to consider. Finally, general discussion questions on ethics in school counseling are included.

Ethical Principles

School counselors-in-training need strong ethical decision-making skills for the dilemmas they will face in the education setting. Ethical guidelines do not provide a definitive answer for every dilemma a school counselor will face, but instead serve as a guide to meet the challenges these situations may create. The cornerstone of ethical guidelines is Kitchener's (1984) moral principles, which serve as a foundation to help clarify difficult dilemmas. The principles are autonomy, justice, beneficence, nonmaleficence, fidelity, and veracity.

Autonomy is the principle that allows clients the freedom to choose their own paths without criticism of their choices. Kitchener (1984) stated that the essence of this principle is that counselors encourage counselees to act on their values in making sound, appropriate decisions related to their well-being. The key considerations for counselors are the counselee's ability to make rational, sound decisions, and the counselor's need to help the counselee understand the consequences related to those decisions. Counselees should not be allowed to make decisions that will cause harm to themselves or that may harm others.

Kitchener (1984) defined *justice* as "treating equals equally and treating unequals unequally but in proportion to their relative differences" (p. 49). Justice takes into consideration the unique nature of problems individuals face, and counselors who demonstrate this principle must consider the individual and the unique nature of his or her problem. To this end, you need to be able to provide a sound rationale for treating the individual differently and need to be able to articulate this difference to the individual. The treatment must be both appropriate and necessary.

Beneficence requires that counselors strive to "do good" when working with counselees. Often considered the cornerstone of ethical principles, counselors should consider the welfare of their counselees in all situations. Counselors and supervisees maintain a proactive stance when considering treatment options for their counselees and advocate for them when it is in their best interest to do so. An important aspect of this principle is that counselors need to be willing to prevent counselees from harming themselves and from harmful situations when necessary.

Nonmaleficence is a medical concept that requires counselors to not cause harm to others. Though all the principles are valued and important, researchers consider this principle to be one of the most important (Forester-Miller & Rubenstein, 1992; Remley & Herlihy, 2007; Stadler, 1986). Kitchener (1984) simplified this principle as the "above-all-do-no-harm" principle. Counselors are expected to avoid things that inflict harm on their counselees and to not engage in actions that risk harming others.

Fidelity highlights the idea that counselees need to be able to trust their counselors, and counselors need to be able to help counselees see the value in the therapeutic relationship. Counselors should honor commitments with their counselees and maintain a sense of loyalty, transparency, and honesty. Counselors work to fulfill all obligations with counselees to the best of their abilities, without using their power to threaten the therapeutic relationship.

Veracity refers to truthfulness when working with individuals. For professional counselors, this means that you have an obligation to be honest with your counselees. This serves as a vital part of developing a strong, therapeutic relationship with your client; the more honest you are, the more likely your counselee will respect you as a professional. It includes the counselor's ability to provide honest feedback to a counselee who is not living optimally. Honesty must also be extended to other professionals with whom the counselor works.

ACTIVITY 10.1

Discuss Kitchener's ethical principles with your site supervisor and how to apply them to your counseling sessions. Ask your supervisor to share with you instances in which he or she used them to make an ethical decision.

Ethical Decision-Making Models

Kitchener's (1984) moral principles serve as the foundation for exploration of the ethical dilemmas you will face in training and practice. When making decisions, you are expected to relate these principles to specific situations to clarify the issues involved, which may create even more complex problems for the counselor. In challenging cases that require complex decision making, you can employ an ethical decision-making model to sift through the confusion to help resolve the dilemma. Some of the more commonly used ethical decision-making models include Forester-Miller and Rubenstein (1992), Remley and Herlihy (2001), and Tarvydas (2003). You may wish to research these models and determine that which best fits your values. Or, you may decide to use the ACA ethical decision-making model that incorporates aspects of these models or others.

The ACA has adopted an ethical decision-making model that highlights the principles espoused by Kitchener (1984) and incorporates the work of Van Hoose and Paradise (1979), Stadler (1986), Haas and Malouf (1989), Forester-Miller and Rubenstein (1992), and Sileo and Kopala (1993). The model provides a seven-step, sequential approach to addressing any ethical dilemma. The model is very practical in nature and you will find that it serves as a useful approach to resolving ethical issues. We have modified the model to include the ASCA Ethical Standards rather than the ACA Code of Ethics. The steps are as follows:

1. Identify the problem.
2. Apply the ASCA Ethical Standards for School Counselors.
3. Determine the nature and dimensions of the dilemma.
4. Generate potential courses of action.
5. Consider the potential consequences of all options and choose a course of action.
6. Evaluate the selected course of action.
7. Implement the course of action.

Identify the Problem

Try to gather as much information about the situation as possible so that you can develop a snapshot of the dilemma. It is important to be as specific and objective as possible and to separate the facts from innuendos, assumptions, and suspicions. This fact-checking process serves as a critical step in the decision-making process. First, you need to determine if the problem is one concerning ethics, laws, the profession, a clinical situation, or a combination of two or more of these. Check with your site supervisor if you believe the situation is a legal issue, and, if a legal consultation is necessary, have your supervisor accompany you to the attorney who represents the school district for consultation. Oftentimes the problem can be resolved by implementing a policy developed by the school, and you may be the instrumental person in bringing about this adaptation. Remember to examine the problem from different perspectives and avoid a simplistic solution because ethical situations can be very complex (Remley & Herlihy, 2007).

Apply the ASCA Ethical Standards

After you have clarified the problem, refer to the Ethical Standards (ASCA, 2004) to determine if the issue is addressed. Sometimes there is a standard that directly addresses the situation, or several standards that are applicable, specific, and clear. Follow the course of action indicated. This often leads to a resolution of the problem. Read the ethical codes carefully so that you can effectively apply them to the situation, but if the problem seems more complex and a resolution does not seem apparent, then you probably have a true ethical dilemma. Further steps will be needed to proceed in making an ethical decision.

Determine the Nature and Dimensions of the Dilemma

Be sure to examine the problem and all its various dimensions. There are different strategies to ensure you have considered all dimensions of the problem. You may start by considering Kitchener's (1984) moral principles and deciding which principles apply to the specific situation, determine those principles that take priority, and review the relevant literature to ensure you are using the most current professional thinking in reaching a decision. Consultation is a key part of this step. You can connect with your supervisors, and former or current professors to help you review the information you have gathered. Oftentimes, they present a perspective you may or may not have considered or that you are not considering objectively. You also can consult your state or national professional associations for help with the dilemma.

Generate Potential Courses of Action

After you have determined the nature and dimensions of the dilemma, you need to brainstorm as many possible courses of action as possible. Your creativity and openness to exploration are critical aspects in this process (Kitchener, 1984). Consider all options in your exploration, write down the courses of action you generate, and be sure to consult with your site and faculty supervisor. It is not uncommon for practicing school counselors to seek help from colleagues in generating options for consideration.

Consider the Potential Consequences of All Options and Determine a Course of Action

Analyze the courses of action you have generated by evaluating each option and assessing the potential consequences for everyone involved. You need to consider who will be affected by the course of action as well as the consequences for you. Options that will not produce the desired results or that may produce more problematic consequences need to be eliminated. After you have eliminated these options, review the remaining options to determine those that provide the most effective resolution to the situation. The selected course of action will need to address the priorities you identified in Step 1 and the best fit for the situation.

Evaluate the Selected Course of Action

Be sure to review the selected course of action to see if it presents any new ethical considerations. If it does, then you will need to go back to the beginning and reevaluate each step of the process. It may be that you chose the wrong option or incorrectly identified the problem. Stadler (1986) stated a selected course of action can be tested for appropriateness by asking three simple questions:

- For the test of publicity, ask yourself, "Would I want my behavior reported in the press?"
- In applying the test of justice, ask yourself, "Would I treat others similarly in this situation?"
- To determine universality, ask yourself, "Would I recommend the same course of action to another counselor in the same situation?"

If you can answer each question in the affirmative and you are satisfied that you have selected an appropriate course of action, then you are ready to move on to the next step of implementation.

Implement the Course of Action

The implementation stage sometimes presents a challenging dilemma for school counselors-in-training. Appropriate action can often have devastating consequences for the individual involved as well as for you. Your ego strength and the values you place on the importance of ethical and professional behavior will be critical in helping you carry out the plan you have developed (Remley & Herlihy, 2007). Once you have completed this step, you should follow-up and assess the effectiveness and consequences of your actions for future ethical dilemmas you could face.

Van Hoose and Paradise (1979) suggested that a counselor "is probably acting in an ethically responsible way concerning a client if: (1) he or she has maintained personal and professional honesty, coupled with (2) the best interests of the client, (3) without malice or personal gain, and (4) can justify his or her actions as the best judgment of what should be done based upon the current state of the profession" (p. 58). Ethical decision making requires you to apply ethical codes and to examine your own values in dealing with complex problems. Each professional will have a unique perspective when assessing an ethical dilemma; there is rarely one right answer to a complex ethical dilemma.

The use of a systematic ethical decision making will help you adhere to the ethical standards developed by the counseling profession.

The ASCA Ethical Standards

To reiterate, this chapter is based on the belief that you have fully explored the ACA Code of Ethics. As school counselors-in-training, however, you are required to understand the ASCA Ethical Standards for School Counselors, heretofore referred to as the Standards (ASCA, 2004), as well. Therefore, this section reviews each piece of the Standards and provides examples for better understanding.

ASCA views the Standards as a guide for professional school counseling practice regardless of whether the school counselor is a member of the organization or a supervisee. It is assumed that all school counselors abide by these Standards in order to maintain an acceptable standard of practice. The Standards are divided into responsibilities to the various stakeholders: students, parents/guardians, colleagues/other professionals, school and community, self, and the school counseling profession. Specific issues are detailed under each stakeholder section.

Responsibilities to Students

The Standards clearly state that school counselors have a primary obligation to their students. Counselors are reminded to focus on career, personal/social, and academic issues with all students, to respect the beliefs of their students, and to know the laws and policies applicable to working with students. These responsibilities are discussed next.

Confidentiality

School counselors are reminded that informed consent and an explanation of confidentiality are required before counseling can begin. Issues related to communicable diseases, court requests, student records, and parental/guardian rights are considerations related to confidentiality. Consider the following ethical situations in the remaining activities in this chapter. Use the ethical decision-making model described earlier to determine the correct course of action to be taken in each situation. The section of the Standards that helps address each ethical dilemma is in parentheses.

Counseling Plans, Dual Relationships, Referrals

The next three sections focus on other professional responsibilities of counselors and school counselors-in-training as related to their work with students. The counselor and supervisee are ethically required to implement a comprehensive school counseling program and to advocate for students regarding their postsecondary plans. School counselors and supervisees also are required to avoid dual relationships if at all possible. Finally, referrals must be made when it is necessary.

Group Work and Danger to Self or Others

These next sections of the Standards discuss policies related to counseling work with counselees. In particular, informing students about the limits of confidentiality and the purposes of counseling are covered extensively in these sections. For example, school counselors and school counselors-in-training are ethically bound to screen group members, inform them that confidentiality cannot be guaranteed in a group setting, notify parents/guardians of group participation if appropriate, and follow-up with group members following initial meetings. In addition, you must break confidentiality when there is imminent risk to the student or others by the student.

ACTIVITY 10.2

Read and respond to the following scenarios.

A middle school supervisee discusses the limits of confidentiality during her first class-room guidance visits each year. She further explains her role as a school counselor-in-training and encourages students to come see her if they have academic, career, or personal/social concerns. Her rationale for explaining confidentiality in classroom guidance is that when a student comes for counseling, she will not have to spend their limited time together discussing the issue of confidentiality. (A.2.a, A.2.b)

A male high school student tells you that he has syphilis. The student further mentions that he has had unprotected sex with three partners in the last 6 months. When you suggest he tell the partners about the disease, he refuses because he fears his parents will find out. You discuss this situation with your supervisor and the decision is made that you must inform the sexual partners about the potential of disease. (A.2.c)

A fourth-grade boy has been seeing you about feelings of sadness and anger related to his parent's recent divorce. His mother calls you and wants to know what her son has been discussing in counseling. After discussing this situation with your site supervisor you explain the concept of confidentiality and refuse to divulge any information. (A.2.g)

What are your concerns about each example? Have you acted ethically in each case? How would you respond in each situation? Review the Standards and then reconsider your response if needed.

_____

_____

_____

ACTIVITY 10.3

Read and respond to the following scenario.

A high school supervisee suspects a student has an eating disorder. She has spoken with the student, who acknowledges losing a lot of weight in a short period of time. In consultation with the site supervisor, the supervisee contacts this student's parents and provides the parents with three possible referrals for mental health professionals who specialize in this disorder. (A.5)

Was the counselor ethically appropriate? What would you have done in this situation?

_____

_____

_____

ACTIVITY 10.4

Read and respond to the following scenario.

> As a counselor-in-training, you have been asked to lead a small group on anger management with seventh-grade boys. Your site supervisor gives you the names of six boys she believes would benefit from the group (A.6).

What are your next steps? What might be some ethical considerations related to running this type of group?

_____

_____

_____

Student Records, Evaluation and Assessment, Technology, Peer Support

The final sections of the Standards focus on ethical responsibilities to students and include various issues. School counselors and supervisees should create and secure written records on students, keep these records separate from the cumulative record, understand the legal limits of keeping written records, and destroy records after an appropriate length of time. Regarding evaluation and assessment, you should understand how to select, administer, and interpret assessments that you are trained to use, and use these assessments with caution and to close educational gaps as appropriate. When using technology, school counselors and supervisees should advocate for equal access, attempt to maintain confidentiality of student records, protect students from inappropriate online material, and generally protect students from harm. Finally, if you engage in peer support programs, you assume responsibility for all students participating in the program.

ACTIVITY 10.5

Read and respond to the following scenario.

> Jim is a counselor-in-training at Happy Days Elementary School, and he is fortunate to have a veteran counselor serve as his supervisor. This experienced counselor explains that it is best not to keep case notes on students because many students are from families of divorce and the records can be subpoenaed if they exist. (A.8)

What are the ethical dilemmas posed in this scenario? How can you apply the decision-making model to help determine the best course of action?

_____

_____

_____

Responsibilities to Parents/Guardians

Two main ethical responsibilities are covered in this section of the Standards. First, school counselors and school counselors-in-training are responsible for recognizing and respecting parental/

ACTIVITY 10.6

Read and respond to the following scenarios.

Josie, a fifth-grade student, is having difficulty completing her homework. You believe that Josie lacks organizational skills and that keeping a daily planner and separate homework folder will help greatly. You call Josie's mom and ask her to buy a planner for Josie and review it every day for homework assignments. Josie's mom becomes frustrated and explains that she works until 9 p.m. and when she comes home, Josie is already up in her room. You discuss this situation with your supervisor who believes that Mom is part of the reason why Josie is not doing her homework. (B.1 and B.2)

Sam's mother and father have recently divorced. His mom has custody and his dad has weekend visitation. Because Sam lives with his mom, his report cards and progress reports are mailed to that address. Sam's father calls and requests that copies of all academic information be sent to his home as well. (B.2.d)

Consider your reactions to each case. What would you do in each situation? What are the ethical issues involved?

---

guardian rights. These include viewing the parent/guardian as a collaborative partner, understanding the legal rights of parents/guardians, respecting confidentiality with parents/guardians, and demonstrating sensitivity to diverse populations. Second, school counselors and supervisees should recognize parental/guardian rights related to confidential information. This includes working to inform parents/guardians about confidentiality with students, acknowledging the importance of parents/guardians in the counseling relationship, providing pertinent information to parents/guardians, and attempting to keep parents/guardians informed regarding student progress.

Responsibilities to Colleagues and Professional Associates

Professional relationships and information sharing are addressed in this section of the Standards. Under the topic of professional relationships, the Standards include the importance of creating professional relationships with school staff, treating all colleagues with respect and equality, and understanding referral sources. Regarding information sharing, the Standards discuss the importance of understanding and following confidentiality guidelines and providing school staff with necessary and objective information. Also discussed is the need for the release of information forms and knowledge of what is appropriate information to share with parents/guardians.

Responsibilities to School and Community

The school personnel as a whole and the local community members are other stakeholders with whom school counselors and counselors-in-training work. School counselors must examine the educational program of the school to ensure that it works in the best interests of all students. Relatedly, school counselors and supervisees should understand the school's mission and work to support that mission by connecting their counseling program to the total school philosophy. If counselors or

ACTIVITY 10.7

Read and respond to the following scenarios.

> You are working with a seventh-grade girl who has been physically abused by a parent. She has been having outbursts in class and recently was sent to in-school suspension for shouting at a teacher. While you know that maintaining confidentiality is vital, you also believe that sharing information about the student's home life with her teachers would be helpful to both the teachers and the student.

What steps would you take to ensure confidentiality for the student while also respecting professional relationships with school staff? (C.1 and C.2)

_____
_____
_____

> Jon is working with a 10th-grade student on academic issues when the student reports that she has begun seeing a mental health counselor for anxiety and depression. Jon decides that, since he is solely focusing on academic concerns, it is appropriate for him to continue counseling the student while she sees the outside therapist as well.

Is this the correct course of action? (C.2)

_____
_____
_____

ACTIVITY 10.8

Read and respond to the following scenario.

> You are interviewing for a job as a school counselor for a rural K–12 school. Although you are certified as a pre-K–12 counselor, your fieldwork was with K–8 students in a suburban area serving mostly middle-income families. The principal informs you that your primary duties will include classroom guidance for the lower grades, and career and college planning for the high school students. In addition, she would like for you to coordinate a peer helper program and to develop a program designed to better connect with the many low-income families in the community.

What might you need to address to remain ethical and still have the chance of obtaining the job? (D.1)

_____
_____
_____

supervisees learn of behavior that goes against the school mission, they must inform the administration while still upholding confidentiality of counseling relationships. Additionally, school counselors should only accept a position for which they meet the qualifications, and work to create a developmental and comprehensive counseling program in the school. Finally, school counselors and school counselors-in-training should work to collaborate with outside agencies and organizations from the local community to enhance student services. This collaboration includes structuring programs to include community resources that add to the comprehensive nature of the program.

Responsibilities to Self

School counselors as well as supervisees must demonstrate professional competence and honor diversity as part of their job. As such, they should know the limits of their abilities and work within those boundaries. In addition, school counselors and counselors-in-training should avoid activities where they are unable to provide adequate services and engage in personal and professional growth activities to broaden and increase their knowledge of the counseling profession. School counselors and supervisees have an obligation to honor diversity in their constituents, and to constantly evaluate their own beliefs and actions to ensure they are doing so. In addition, the establishment of a knowledge base on the various diverse groups they may encounter in the schools is an essential component. For a full list of these diverse populations, consult section E.2.d of the Standards.

ACTIVITY 10.9
Read and respond to the following scenario.

A 12th-grade student whose parents are illegal immigrants comes to you to discuss his plans after high school. He has average grades and wants to discuss the possibility of continuing his education.

What do you need to know to work effectively with this student? What personal values and beliefs might you need to consider? (E.2)

_____

_____

Responsibilities to Profession

The last section of the Standards focuses on the school counseling profession as a stakeholder. It stresses the importance of following the Standards, advocating for the profession, and generally recognizing that each school counselor and you, as a school counselor-in-training, are representatives of the school counseling profession. Participation in research, professional organizations, and formal and informal mentoring relationships are all mentioned as ways to support the school counseling profession.

Conclusion

Understanding the ethical codes for the profession is a vital part of being an effective school counselor. The ASCA Ethical Standards for School Counselors (2004) can be used within the framework of a comprehensive ethical decision-making model to help school counselors-in-training be prepared for and able to effectively address ethical dilemmas faced daily in their profession. Being familiar with both the Standards and the decision-making model add to a school counselor's ability to successfully serve his or her constituents.

ACTIVITY 10.10

Read and respond to the following discussion questions:

1. It is impossible for school counselors-in-training to anticipate all the potential ethical dilemmas they will face in their career, so how can you best prepare yourself for these potential situations?
2. As a school counselor-in-training, what can you do when you see another school counselor acting in what you consider to be an unethical manner?
3. What ethical dilemmas are you most concerned about, and why?

Web Sites

- This Web page titled "Dual Relationships & Other Boundary Dilemmas" by Ken Pope shares information regarding decision making about crossing identified boundaries. Ethical scenarios and questions are provided: http://www.kspope.com/dual/dual.php
- To test your ethical knowledge, this link will take you to a quiz on ethical issues in school counseling: http://findarticles.com/p/articles/mi_m0KOC/is_1_6/ai_93700934/

References

American School Counseling Association (ASCA). (2004). *Ethical standards for school counselors*. Alexandria, VA: Author.

Forester-Miller, H., & Rubenstein, R. L. (1992). Group counseling: Ethical and professional issues. In D. Capuzzi & D. R. Gross (Eds.), *Introduction to group counseling* (pp. 307–323). Denver, CO: Love Publishing Co.

Haas, L. J., & Malouf, J. L. (1989). *Keeping up the good work: A practitioner's guide to mental health ethics*. Sarasota, FL: Professional Resource Exchange, Inc.

Kitchener, K. S. (1984). Intuition, critical evaluation and ethical principles: The foundation for ethical decisions in counseling psychology. *Counseling Psychologist, 12*, 43–55.

Remley, T. P., & Herlihy, B. (2001). *Ethical, legal, and professional issues in counseling*. Upper Saddle River, NJ: Prentice-Hall.

Remley, T. P., & Herlihy, B. (2007). *Ethical, legal, and professional issues in counseling* (Updated 2nd ed.). Upper Saddle River, NJ: Pearson Prentice Hall.

Sileo, F., & Kopala, M. (1993). An A-B-C-D-E worksheet for promoting beneficence when considering ethical issues. *Counseling and Values, 37*, 89–95.

Stadler, H. A. (1986). Making hard choices: Clarifying controversial ethical issues. *Counseling & Human Development, 19*, 1–10.

Tarvydas, V. M. (2003). The ethical imperative for culturally competent practice. *Rehabilitation Education, 17*(2), 117–123.

Van Hoose, W. H., & Paradise, L. V. (1979). *Ethics in counseling and psychotherapy: Perspectives in issues and decision-making*. Cranston, RI: Carroll Press.

SECTION III:

*GUIDELINES FOR WORKING
WITH SPECIAL POPULATIONS*

Understanding Differences in the Schools

Jolie Ziomek-Daigle
Michael Jay Manalo

The purpose of this chapter is to:

- Assess school counselor-in-training awareness, knowledge, and skills in regard to counseling diverse student populations
- Gain experience with creating a school profile to help identify the needs of the school, students, and gaps related to achievement, attainment, and opportunities
- Expand knowledge and skills around student cultural and ethnic diversity issues
- Increase knowledge and skills to counsel students with special needs
- Add knowledge and skills to counsel gifted students
- Gain knowledge and skills to counsel and advocate for students in regard to sexual orientation and gender expression

In this chapter, you will assess your diversity competency (i.e., awareness, knowledge, and skills), consider a school profile to better understand your school's students, review differences among people in your school (e.g., multicultural, special needs students, gifted students, students with various sexual orientations), and use various scenarios and activities to practice developing your counseling competence.

Introduction

Understanding differences in the schools begins with understanding ourselves in relation to others and our student populations. The population of the United States can be described as multiethnic, multicultural, and multilingual (Holcomb-McCoy & Chen-Hayes, 2007; Sue, 1990). The diversity that is represented in the United States and most likely represented in the schools can be broadly defined to include (a) race/ethnicity, (b) gender, (c) physical or mental ability, (d) sexual orientation/gender expression, (e) socioeconomic status, and (f) other characteristics of background or group membership (Lee & Hipolito-Delgado, 2007). Moreover, it is estimated that the United States will become majority-minority in the next few decades in which the Latino, Asian American, and African American populations will represent more than half of the United States (Wasow, 2005). With the knowledge in hand that student populations will be as diverse as ever, school counselors-in-training can begin with an assessment of their own awareness, knowledge, and skills in relation to working with diverse populations.

Assessment of School Counselor-in-Training Awareness, Knowledge, and Skills

In terms of assessing multicultural competence, faculty members and your supervisors will examine if you have gained awareness, knowledge, and skills to work with diverse student populations in the school setting. At this juncture in your graduate training, you most likely have gained multicultural awareness and knowledge through foundational courses. These skills will be further assessed during clinical placements. Therefore, you should graduate with an increased awareness and knowledge related to issues of diversity as well as advanced skills that are consistently in a state of refinement.

Holcomb-McCoy and Chen-Hayes (2007) suggest ways that you can increase your multicultural competence including (a) investigate your own cultural or ethnic heritage; (b) attend workshops and events on multicultural and diversity issues; (c) join counseling organizations focused on cultural and diversity issues such as Counselors for Social Justice (CSJ), the Association for Multicultural Counseling and Development (AMCD), and the Association for Lesbian, Gay, Bisexual, Transgender Issues in Counseling (ALGBTIC); (d) read literature by culturally diverse authors; and (e) become immersed in multicultural and diversity-focused literature such as journals from the aforementioned associations. It is important for you to realize that professional development extends throughout the career of a school counselor and does not stop at graduation. By utilizing the ways mentioned earlier, you can further develop your diversity awareness and multicultural competence to remain lifelong, reflective practitioners.

This section is intended to advance your competence as you embark on practicum and internship experiences. Holcomb-McCoy (2004) created a multicultural checklist containing nine sections (i.e., multicultural counseling, multicultural consultation, understanding racism and student resistance, understanding racial and/or ethnic identity development, multicultural assessment, multicultural family counseling, social advocacy, developing school–family–community partnerships, and understanding cross-cultural interpersonal interactions) with 51 items in total. To provide you with a better understanding of your multicultural competence and areas in which you need to address complete the School Counselor Multicultural Competence Checklist in Table 12.1.

ACTIVITY 12.1

Using the Multicultural Checklist (Table 12.1), respond to the following questions and process your answers in small groups with your peers.

1. What are my strengths and stated competencies?

   _____

   _____

2. In what areas do I need to gain competence?

   _____

   _____

3. In using my strengths and competencies, how can I help other professionals in gaining competence?

   _____

   _____

4. In reviewing the areas in which I need to gain competence, how can I work with other professionals to get there?

   _____

   _____

TABLE 12.1   School Counselor Multicultural Competence Checklist

Competence	Met	Unmet
I. Multicultural Counseling		
1. I can recognize when my attitudes, beliefs, and values are interfering with providing the best services to my students.		
2. I can identify the cultural bases of my communication style.		
3. I can discuss how culture affects the help-seeking behaviors of students.		
4. I can describe the degree to which a counseling approach is culturally inappropriate for a specific student.		
5. I use culturally appropriate interventions and counseling approaches (e.g., indigenous practices) with students.		
6. I can list at least three barriers that prevent ethnic minority students from using counseling services.		
7. I can anticipate when my helping style is inappropriate for a culturally different student.		
8. I can give examples of how stereotypical beliefs about culturally different persons impact the counseling relationship.		
II. Multicultural Consultation		
9. I am aware of how culture affects traditional models of consultation.		
10. I can discuss at least one model of multicultural consultation.		
11. I recognize when racial and cultural issues are impacting the consultation process.		
12. I can identify when the race and/or culture of the client is a problem for the consultee.		
13. I discuss issues related to race/ethnicity/culture during the consultation process, when applicable.		
III. Understanding Racism and Student Resistance		
14. I can define and discuss White privilege.		
15. I can discuss how I (if European American/White) am privileged based on my race.		
16. I can identify racist aspects of educational institutions.		
17. I can define and discuss prejudice.		
18. I recognize and challenge colleagues about discrimination and discriminatory practices in schools.		
19. I can define and discuss racism and its impact on the counseling process.		
20. I can help students determine whether a problem stems from racism or biases in others.		
21. I understand the relationship between student resistance and racism.		
22. I include topics related to race and racism in my classroom guidance units.		
IV. Understanding Racial and/or Ethnic Identity Development		
23. I am able to discuss at least two theories of racial and/or ethnic identity development.		
24. I use racial/ethnic identity development theories to understand my students' problems and concerns.		
25. I have assessed my own racial/ethnic development in order to enhance my counseling.		
V. Multicultural Assessment		
26. I can discuss the potential bias of two assessment instruments frequently used in the schools.		
27. I can evaluate instruments that may be biased against certain groups of students.		
28. I am able to use test information appropriately with culturally diverse parents.		

(continued on next page)

TABLE 12.1 (continued)   School Counselor Multicultural Competence Checklist

Competence	Met	Unmet
29. I view myself as an advocate for fair testing and the appropriate use of testing of children from diverse backgrounds.		
30. I can identify whether or not the assessment process is culturally sensitive.		
31. I can discuss how the identification of the assessment process might be biased against minority populations.		
VI. Multicultural Family Counseling		
32. I can discuss family counseling from a cultural/ethnic perspective.		
33. I can discuss at least two ethnic group's traditional gender role expectations and rituals.		
34. I anticipate when my helping style is inappropriate for an ethnically different parent or guardian.		
35. I can discuss culturally diverse methods of parenting and discipline.		
VII. Social Advocacy		
36. I am knowledgeable of the psychological and societal issues that affect the development of ethnic minority students.		
37. When counseling, I consider the psychological and societal issues that affect the development of ethnic minority students.		
38. I work with families and community members in order to reintegrate them with the school.		
39. I can define "social change agent."		
40. I perceive myself as being a "social change agent."		
41. I can discuss what it means to take an "activist counseling" approach.		
42. I intervene with students at the individual and systemic levels.		
43. I can discuss how factors such as poverty and powerlessness have influenced the current conditions of at least two ethnic groups.		
VIII. Developing School–Family–Community Partnerships		
44. I have developed a school–family–community partnership team or some similar type of group that consists of community members, parents, and school personnel.		
45. I am aware of community resources that are available for students and their families.		
46. I work with community leaders and other resources in the community to assist with student (and family) concerns.		
IX. Understanding Cross-Cultural Interpersonal Interactions		
47. I am able to discuss interaction patterns that might influence ethnic minority students' perceptions of inclusion in the school community.		
48. I solicit feedback from students regarding my interactions with them.		
49. I verbally communicate my acceptance of culturally different students.		
50. I nonverbally communicate my acceptance of culturally different students.		
51. I am mindful of the manner in which I speak and the emotional tone of my interactions with culturally diverse students.		

Source: From *Developing & Managing Your School Guidance Program* (3rd ed.), by N. C. Gysbers and P. Henderson, 1999, Alexandria, VA: American Counseling Association. Reprinted with permission.

Assessment of School Site and Developing a School Profile

You can assess a school site to help better understand not only the needs of the individual students but the student body as well. School profiles provide a backdrop of the school and are based on accessible, existing data. Information that is revealed from a school profile may include gaps in achievement, attainment, funding and opportunities, and certain student groups that may be isolated and not receiving the full range of services from the school. School profiles provide the data for school counselors-in-training and school counselors to take action in terms of better defining their school counseling program and the services that are offered. Barr and Parrett (2000) recommend collecting baseline data on an ongoing basis to monitor the progress of student groups and emerging needs. Some baseline data needs to determine potential areas of discrimination could include

- Percent of students enrolled in the free or reduced lunch program
- Percent of students who have passed or failed state standardized tests
- Percent of students who scored at or above the national averages on the ACT and SAT
- Percent of students who are homeless
- Percent of students enrolled in the special education program
- Percent of students enrolled in the gifted education program
- Percent of students who are bilingual and enrolled in the English for Speakers of Other Languages (ESOL) program
- School's daily and weekly attendance rate
- School's daily and weekly suspension rate
- School's daily and weekly behavior referrals rate
- School's dropout rate
- Student pregnancy/teenage parent rate

ACTIVITY 12.2

Look at the demographic profile of the school in which you are completing your practicum or internship experience and determine the numbers of students who fit into the baseline data categories. Compare your list with those of your peers.

_____

_____

_____

Culturally and Ethnically Diverse Students

We, as well as all students, are different from one another. We also share similarities. In an attempt to categorize these differences and similarities, key aspects of who we are have been identified and used to help people understand one another culturally. Race, ethnicity, age, gender, sexual orientation, gender expression, disability, socioeconomic status, and disability are some aspects of culture. Culture, however, incorporates much more than these variables. Culture considerations also include, but are not limited to, views and practices related to individualism versus collectivism, masculinity and feminism, communication practices, physical proximity and closeness, religion/spirituality, language(s) spoken, structure and predictability, work ethic, political views, holidays recognized and celebrated, geographic region in which one is reared or lives, food and music preferences, value

ACTIVITY 12.3

Read the following scenarios, answer the questions that appear at the end of each scenario, and then discuss your answers in small groups with your peers.

Sara is a first-year professional school counselor in an inner-city setting. The student population consists of the following: 82% African American, 12% Latino/a, and 6% biracial. Ninety-five percent of the students are enrolled in the free or reduced lunch program. Sara is White and from a middle- to upper-class background. Her dad worked while her mom stayed at home. She does not speak a second language because her parents did not "like the idea" of her taking a foreign language while she was in school. Her school did not have a free or reduced lunch program that she knew of and, generally, she socialized with people who looked and acted similar to the way she did. While in graduate school, Sara took one course on multicultural counseling and completed her practicum and internship at a rural, White, working-class high school.

In regard to Sara's new position, how can she assess her multicultural competence?

_____

_____

Where and how can she begin this work?

_____

_____

What could be her goals in this area as a professional school counselor?

_____

_____

What could be her specific outreach strategies to students, parents, administrators, teachers, and community members?

_____

_____

Veronica is a first-year school counseling student. She is African American, grew up in a rural and poor area in a Southern state, and was raised by her aunt. Because of her aunt's influence and many determined teachers and school counselors, Veronica was committed to her school work and rose to the top of her class in high school. She was enrolled in the gifted education program and knew the program would help her to reach her educational goals, but she did not like being the only student of color with others who grew up in very different circumstances. Veronica is now deciding on practicum and internship placements and has this awareness in mind. She is considering interning at a middle-/upper-class high school because she feels that she has biases against upper-class families and does not really think "those families" have problems. Veronica knows that all families do have problems and that all students struggle at some point, so she wants to push herself to experience something different than what she already knows.

ACTIVITY 12.3 (continued)

How should Veronica proceed in identifying her clinical placements?

_____

_____

With whom should she consult on a consistent basis?

_____

_____

How can she become familiar with the school culture and in the lives of her students and families?

_____

_____

placed on education, and so on. Our focus in this section will remain on increasing your awareness of cultural and diverse student populations. As discussed earlier, the development or review of an existing school profile will help you understand the backdrop and unique needs of the school and certain student groups. Understandably, a school profile may also reveal equity gaps that a multiculturally competent school counselor will need to work toward reconciling. These gaps are usually most noticeable in achievement, attainment, funding, and other opportunities (Holcomb-McCoy & Chen-Hayes, 2007).

Though universities are doing a better job in the recruitment and retention of diverse students, many school counseling graduates continue to be white, female, and middle class. Given that people of European descent have been the dominant group throughout the years of formalized education in the United States, it would behoove you to gain an understanding of oppression and privilege. An extension of Activity 12.2 can be spent on further understanding the influences of power and prejudice as they relate to oppression. In addition, you can begin with interviewing your own family members to better understand their histories. Holcomb-McCoy and Chen-Hayes (2007) suggest that school counselors-in-training read Howard Zinn's *A People's History of the United States* or excerpts from the book so that they can analyze the information and messages they received in school or within the family while growing up.

Students With Special Needs

Until the 1960s and 1970s, students with special needs such as mental illness or mental disability were commonly institutionalized and held separate from the rest of society (Hallahan & Kauffman, 2006). It was not until more recently that these students were integrated into mainstream classrooms and schools. Additionally, there have been several legislative movements such as Section 504 of the Rehabilitation Act of 1973, the Education for All Handicapped Children Act (PL 94-142) in 1975, the Individuals with Disabilities Education Act (IDEA) in 1990, the Americans with Disabilities Act (ADA) in 1990, and the reauthorized and renamed Individuals with Disabilities Education Improvement Act (IDEIA) in 2004. These directives have greatly shaped the role and function of school personnel (including school counselors and school counselors-in-training) in working with students with special needs. Though these legislative acts have been helpful in providing accommodations to students, school counselors must also recognize where legislation for disabilities may or

TABLE 12.2   Disabilities Present in School Settings

Common Disabilities	Possible Accommodations and Interventions
• Mental retardation (MR)	• Resourced (pull-out) specialized instruction
• Learning disabilities (LD)	• Teaching everyday adaptive skills (making change, reading newspapers, etc.)
• Attention-deficit hyperactivity disorder (ADHD)	• Community-based instruction in real-life settings
• Emotional or behavioral disorders	• One-on-one instruction
• Communication disorders	• Tutoring
• Deaf/hearing impaired	• Extra time on testing
• Blindness/low vision	• Preferential seating in classroom (near teacher or away from hallway)
• Autism spectrum disorders	• Providing supplemental outline of class lecture material
• Traumatic brain injury (TBI)	• Allowing student to audio record class lecture
• Physical disabilities	• Giving exam orally (read aloud)
	• Providing materials in Braille

Source: Adapted from *Exceptional Learners: Introduction to Special Education* (10th ed.), by D. P. Hallahan and J. M. Kauffman, 2006, Boston: Pearson/Allyn & Bacon; and *Accommodations Checklist,* by Nebraska Department of Education, 2008, http://www.nde.state.ne.us/sped/iepproj/appc/acc.html.

may not overlap. For example, a student with attention-deficit hyperactivity disorder (ADHD) may qualify for accommodations either under IDEA, under Section 504, or under neither act depending upon the nature of student's disability and other health conditions (Lockhart, 2003).

Disabilities that may be present in school settings are listed in Table 12.2. These terms can be used as a reference as you work with various school-aged children, as it is important for you to realize that the terminology used for certain disabilities or disorders in schools may be different from the terminology used by nonschool mental health professionals; for example, depression is commonly classified in schools as an emotional or behavioral disorder (EBD; Hallahan & Kauffman, 2006). Furthermore, some states use different terminology to describe the same syndrome.

Although much research to date in working with students with special needs has focused on a deficit or pathology-based model, other researchers have suggested that a strengths-based approach may also be in order. Dykens (2006) cites research that families with children who have mental retardation may have stressors related to raising such a child, but may also find the experience of having a special needs child in the family one that leads to a more fulfilling life. For example, the family of a child with a disability may find that they are better able to accept differences in other people, are more socially and politically active and aware, and are connected emotionally (Hallahan & Kauffman, 2006).

The American School Counselor Association (ASCA, 2004) has provided a position statement on working with special needs students. In addition to providing direct counseling services to students with disabilities, the ASCA calls school counselors to also take part in the interdisciplinary teams of special education teachers, administrators, school psychologists, and others to assess and serve these students. The work of these teams typically results in written Individualized Education Programs (IEPs), 504 plans, and other documentation. The statement also urges school counselors to be aware of community support resources for referrals, both while the student is in school as well as for post-secondary employment options. The ASCA's statement also advises school counselors to not serve in certain supervisory or administrative roles in the planning for students with special needs, roles that would better be served by school administrators or special education coordinators. Such inappropriate roles include the school counselor making the sole determination as to a student's placement or retention, coordinating a 504 team, or supervising the actual implementation of the student's plan.

Students Who Are Gifted

Oftentimes, school counselors will not be required to identify gifted students, but may need to help facilitate the process for parents and teachers. Consultation with the gifted education teacher or the district office in terms of how you can partner in servicing this student group would be

ACTIVITY 12.4

Read and respond to the following questions and then process the questions with your peers in small groups.

1. From your clinical placement experiences, how closely do school counselors work with the special education coordinator? How involved are the school counselors in working with the special education population in general? What are the specific practices that you have observed?

   _____

   _____

2. What unique issues would students face with comorbid disabilities or disabilities that also overlap with other identities discussed in this chapter (e.g., a student with both a learning disability [LD] and ADHD, a student with mental retardation [MR] who is Hispanic, a student with a reading disorder who is a lesbian, etc.)?

   _____

   _____

3. What considerations should you, as a school counselor-in-training, think about in terms of a special needs student's transition to college, the workforce, or adulthood?

   _____

   _____

4. Do you think that all students with disabilities or other special needs require accommodations? Why or why not?

   _____

   _____

5. Many students with special needs have a significant physical health component of their condition. As a school counselor-in-training, how could you make yourself more aware of the physical and medical needs of these students?

   _____

   _____

helpful to you as a school counselor-in-training. School counselors often work with these students through such means as connecting parents to the gifted education teacher or school district office, counseling students individually or in small groups, conducting a classroom guidance unit for the gifted, facilitating curriculum changes, and discussing postsecondary options based on student academic strengths.

According to the National Association for Gifted Children (2008), gifted children may have characteristics that include general intellectual ability, specific academic aptitude, creative thinking and production, leadership, psychomotor ability, and visual and performing arts. Conversely, according to Delisle and Galbraith (2002), some misconceptions of gifted students may include that all are White and from middle- to upper-class families, are loved by teachers, excel in all subjects, enjoy school and learning, and will succeed no matter the circumstances. Further, Wood (2008) suggests

ACTIVITY 12.5

Read and respond to the question at the end of the following scenario, and in small groups process your answer with your peers.

Mr. Stevens is a social studies teacher at Anytown High School. He is also the father of Greg, a 15-year-old freshman who just started at Anytown this school year. Mr. Stevens has been good friends with one of the school counselors, Mr. Sheetz, for several years since the two started working together at the high school. Mr. Stevens and Mr. Sheetz work out at the local gym together and share their love of adventure sports through their frequent rock climbing and whitewater kayaking trips. As luck would have it, Greg happens to be one of the students with whom Mr. Sheetz is assigned to counsel. Mr. Sheetz was concerned about this at first, but since he feels he already knew Greg and Mr. Stevens fairly well, he did not anticipate Greg to be a frequent visitor to his office. He knew Greg to have had a few disciplinary problems in middle school and that Greg was a somewhat sensitive and emotional teenager in general, but Mr. Stevens had always said that Greg had persevered and done well in school. One afternoon while Mr. Sheetz and Mr. Stevens are on bus duty together, Mr. Stevens has a concerned look on his face. "You know, ever since Greg started high school here, he just hasn't been quite the same," Mr. Stevens tells Mr. Sheetz. "Mrs. Park in math said that Greg has been having some strange emotional outbursts in class and that his grades on his past few quizzes have been very low. Some days when we get home he just locks himself in his room and I think I hear him crying. Other times, he stays up all night working on homework and fixing his skateboard." Before Mr. Sheetz can respond, Mr. Stevens adds, "You know, I saw this TV special on kids with bipolar disorder, and I hate to say it but Greg sounds an awful lot like some of the kids on that show. Do you think he might be bipolar? I just get scared thinking of him being in that EBD classroom with all those crazy kids." Mr. Stevens' walkie-talkie buzzes and he gets called into the building. "Well, I've got to run, but I'll tell you more about it later at the gym, OK?" says Mr. Stevens. As Mr. Sheetz watches Mr. Stevens walk away, he sighs, anticipating what their conversation will be about at the gym that night.

What should Mr. Sheetz do?

_____

_____

_____

_____

_____

_____

that asynchronous development, affective regulation, and being from an already challenged population (e.g., a student of color, LGBTQ [lesbian, gay, bisexual, transgender, and queer], or lower socioeconomic status) can present additional unique challenges for the gifted student population.

School counselors should be monitoring the total development of gifted students in the personal/social domain, not just in academics. An example would be the development of characteristics related to the happiness, well-being, life satisfaction, self-regulation (Peterson, 2006), and peer relations of gifted students. Additionally, school counselors need to be aware of and actively engage in updated identification and retention practices so that all students from diverse gender, racial, ethnic,

ACTIVITY 12.6

Read and respond to the question at the end of each of the following scenarios and discuss your answers in small groups with your peers.

> Karl is a 10th grader and enrolled in the gifted education program. He is African American and from a middle-class family. Karl did not want to enroll in the gifted program and have to make new friends in the classes, but his parents insisted, stating, "If you got it, use it." Karl is one of two students of color and has to sit by himself during lunch because all of his old friends eat lunch at a different time. He is having trouble with the accelerated pace in his new classes and does not finish all of his nightly homework. Karl's grades have slipped slightly and he is not used to receiving B's. He volunteers after school and helps the technology teacher update the school computers and has aspirations to become a computer technician. You are providing career counseling to him during your internship and Karl's parents called and want you to get him more motivated to succeed.

How would you proceed?

_____

_____

> Delia is in ninth grade and is classified as twice exceptional. She has cerebral palsy and uses an electric wheelchair at school. Delia is also enrolled in the gifted education program and her talents are in math and science. It has been a hard semester for her and she has not liked the transition to high school. Delia has to leave the ninth-grade hall twice a day to rush across campus to the gifted classes. She runs into other students and has to use ramps that take time to maneuver around the corners. She is late to all of her classes almost every day. Delia also gets self-conscious when she interrupts the class. She loves being in the gifted classes because she is learning new things, making friends, feels inspired, and knows she wants to be an civil engineer. As a counselor-in-training, you are also learning about the school culture and want to help Delia.

How can you assist her?

_____

_____

socioeconomic, and disability backgrounds benefit from the services a gifted education program can offer.

The following illustrates ways of working with students who are gifted within the academic, career, and personal/social domains (Wood, 2008).

Academic counseling domain
- Facilitate gifted identification, placement, and allow for flexible plans
- Assess for decision-making, organization, and time-management skills
- Provide inventories that help students understand learning styles, learning preferences, and personality characteristics and personal/social domains

Career counseling domain
- Explore possible careers as an extension of talents through inventories and the Internet
- Help connect students to job shadowing, apprenticeships, and internships

- Explore leisure and free-time activities
- Encourage contribution to society via service learning or volunteering

Personal/social counseling domain

- Normalize student feelings, experiences, and the unique characteristics of giftedness
- Validate feelings of loneliness, uniqueness, being different than others
- Work on regulation of emotions and negative thinking
- Consider stress-reducing activities and relaxation techniques
- Include expressive arts such as play, music, bibliotherapy, journaling, and drama

Students Who Are Lesbian, Gay, Bisexual, Transgender, and Queer

In January 2005, White County High School junior Kerry Pacer made national headlines from the small town of Cleveland, Georgia. She asked the administration of her high school if she could form a Gay-Straight Alliance club. The organization, named Peers Rising in Diverse Education (PRIDE), was initially allowed to meet but quickly drew controversy and protests (Yoo, 2005). Soon afterward, the county school board passed a ruling that all nonacademically related clubs, including Pacer's, would not be allowed to meet, although other nonacademic clubs such as a dance club and a shooting club were still permitted to meet at the school. The American Civil Liberties Union (ACLU) represented Pacer and other students in a lawsuit against the school board that stated that the students' rights had been violated and that the club should be allowed to meet (Ghezzi, 2006). In July 2006, a federal district judge ruled in the ACLU and Pacer's favor, allowing the organization to meet (Scott, 2006).

The preceding example from recent news headlines illustrates how lesbian, gay, bisexual, transgender, and queer (LGBTQ) students can experience institutionalized discrimination in the schools. The Gay, Lesbian and Straight Education Network (GLSEN, 2008a) in a report noted that 73.6% of LGBTQ students often or frequently heard homophobic remarks at school. The majority of the students expressed being verbally harassed due to their sexual orientation (86.2%) or gender expression (66.5%). Unfortunately, the report also stated that 22.1% of the students reported being physically assaulted due to sexual orientation, and 14.2% due to gender expression. Even more disturbing is that the report found that even after such students reported incidents of harassment or assault to school staff, almost one third said that staff did nothing to respond to their report. The report also found among LGBTQ students higher levels of school absenteeism and lowered pursuit of postsecondary education as compared to a national sample of students.

There is a reluctance for school counselors to work with this population of students (Pollock, 2006), and training in counseling programs is sparse to nonexistent (Pearson, 2003). Even with a higher rate for victimization, mental health disorders, suicide, and dropping out (Callahan, 2001; Varjas et al., 2007), school counselors are in a unique position to provide services to LGBTQ students but often recoil from the opportunities (Callahan, 2001). Some explanations may include (a) incongruence with personal, religious, and political beliefs; (b) concerns with legal age, parental notification, and consent; and (c) lack of professional development (Ziomek-Daigle & Singh, 2008). Moreover, the ethics, professionalism, and efficacy of school counselors might be called into question if they are not advocating for and providing services for all youth, including those identified as LGBTQ.

You should be aware of the discrimination and difficulties that face LGBTQ youth in schools, and discuss this issue with your site supervisor. Such issues may present themselves in terms of difficulty with "coming out," increased class absences, negative self-esteem, increased bullying, and issues related to school disengagement and dropping out. The ASCA's position statement on working with LGBT youth (ASCA, 2007) calls for professional school counselors to support students of all sexual orientations and gender identities as well as to recognize how their own views of these subjects may affect their work with students. In addition to working with individual students, the position statement describes the role of professional school counselors as advocates against discriminatory policies (such as those presented in the introduction of this section) as well as educators for faculty and staff in schools about the importance of diversity in schools including that of LGBTQ students. The statement also supports these students by stating that sexual orientation and gender identity are not areas that are indicative of any underlying mental illness or pathology, nor are they indicative of a student being sexually active.

Legal Implications of Working (or Not Working) With LGBTQ Students
(Adapted from McFarland & Dupuis, 2003)

As noted in the introduction to this section, several instances of legal action have taken place against administrators and schools that have failed to protect the rights of LGBTQ students. Legal precedent has shown that school administrators must provide equal access and protection to students regardless of gender or sexual orientation. For example, in the 1996 case of *Nabozny v. Podlesny*, a student named Jamie Nabozny was subjected to verbal and severe physical abuse by other students and sued the principals and school district. In his suit, Nabozny stated that the school had treated

---

ACTIVITY 12.7

Answer the following questions and discuss your responses with your peers in small groups.

1. In light of the introductory story of a high school student trying to start a Gay-Straight Alliance at her school, what would be your reaction if one of your students approached you about starting such an organization at your school?

   _____

   _____

2. What unique concerns do you think LGBTQ students of color face in terms of their multiple identities (e.g., a Black lesbian or a person with a disability who identifies as transgender)?

   _____

   _____

3. How do you think the coming out experience of a transgender student would differ from the coming out experience of a gay student?

   _____

   _____

4. How appropriate do you think it is for a school counselor to self-disclose his or her own sexual orientation or gender expression to an LGBTQ student he or she is counseling?

   _____

   _____

him differently from other students who had been sexually harassed by failing to take action against the perpetrators of the abuse. The principals settled the suit, costing them nearly $1 million. In 1997, the Office of Civil Rights of the Department of Education specified under its Title IX guidelines that gay and lesbian students should be protected from sexual harassment. The guidelines were used in the 1998 court case of *Wagner v. Fayetteville Public Schools*, in which the school district was mandated by the Department of Education to integrate policies around sexual harassment related to sexual orientation. These and many other cases are monitored by the Lambda Legal Defense and Education Fund, an organization dedicated to legal issues for LGBTQ persons. (A link to its Web site is provided at the end of this chapter.) School counselors, then, must be aware of the legal implications for unfair treatment of and failure to protect LGBTQ students, particularly with regard to sexual harassment in schools.

Language and terms are important as they help people communicate complex ideas in mutually understood words and phrases. Within the LGBTQ community there are a number of terms and acronyms used to communicate aspects unique to that subculture. As a school counselor-in-training, it would be beneficial to familiarize yourself with some of these terms. Table 12.3 provides an alphabetical list of terms and definitions that may help you get started.

TABLE 12.3   Commonly Used Terms in LGBTQ Community

Term	Definition
Ally	A person who advocates for or supports LGBTQ people; many allies often identify themselves as straight/heterosexual
Biological sex	Sex as determined by chromosomes, hormones, internal/external genitalia
Bisexual	A person who is attracted to both men and women
Coming out	A lifelong process of declaring one's identity to another individual, to a group of people, or in a public setting
Gay	A person who is attracted only to people of the same sex; this term can be used for both men and women, although the term *lesbian* is typically used for gay women and the term *gay* by itself typically refers to gay men
Gender identity	How we perceive or call ourselves as "male" or "female"; gender identity may or may not correspond with a person's biological sex
Genderqueer	A person who identifies their gender to be either between or outside of the male/female dichotomy
Intersexual	A person born with biological aspects of both male and female; about 1.7% of the population can be defined as intersexual
Lesbian	A woman who is only attracted to other women
LGBTQ	An acronym for lesbian, gay, bisexual, transgender, and queer
LGBTQQI	An acronym for lesbian, gay, bisexual, transgender, queer, questioning, and intersexual
Queer	Although this term was historically considered a negative used against LGBTQ people, it has been reclaimed as an umbrella term to refer to people who do not conform to traditional gender or sexual identities or roles; this term frequently appears in a political context
Questioning	Refers to people who are questioning or unsure of their sexual orientation or gender identity
Sexual identity	What we call ourselves or how we perceive ourselves to be; may include gay, lesbian, bisexual, bi, queer, etc.
Sexual orientation	A person's orientation as related to their sexual and emotional attraction; may include homosexual, bisexual, heterosexual
Transgender	A person who expresses their gender differently from the way that society would traditionally identify that person; transgender is an umbrella term for several other terms which may include transsexuals, drag kings, drag queens, cross-dressers, etc.
Transsexual	A person who surgically/hormonally changes their sex to match their gender identity

Source: Adapted from *The 2007 National School Climate Survey: Executive Summary*, by Gay, Lesbian and Straight Education Network, 2008, New York: GLSEN; and *LGBT Definitions* by Gay, Lesbian, and Straight Education Network, 2008, http://www.glsen.org/cgi-bin/iowa/all/library/record/2335.html?state=media.

ACTIVITY 12.8

Read and respond to the following scenario and discuss your answers with your peers in small groups.

> Ms. Johnson is a second-semester school counseling intern at Anytown Middle School. She has recently attended a diversity training seminar at her university that focused on LGBTQ issues among university students. The seminar is part of the university's Safe Space program in which participants identify themselves as LGBTQ allies by placing a rainbow-colored sticker in their rooms or offices. Ms. Johnson is very excited about the program and decides to put one of the stickers in the window to her office at Anytown Middle. Her supervisor, Mr. Hood, says that he is supportive of this decision. Ms. Johnson is pleased that several of her students who come in for individual counseling appointments notice the new sticker and ask her what it means. One day, Ms. Johnson arrives at school and finds a note on her door from the principal, Dr. Smith. In the note, the Dr. Smith requests that Ms. Johnson remove the sticker from her window, stating that the parents of some students had called the office saying that "the school is no such place for controversial displays." As she finishes reading the note, Dr. Smith enters the counseling suite. What should Ms. Johnson do?

_____

_____

Conclusion

In this chapter you explored student differences. Although the focus of this chapter was specifically students, it is important to remember that many of these differences can apply to administrators, staff, faculty, parents, and other stakeholders in the school. You assessed your diversity competency, looked at components of a school profile to better understand your school's students, reviewed differences among students in your school, and used various scenarios and activities to practice developing your counseling competence. Multicultural competence begins with understanding that there is always more to learn, understand, and respect when considering all your counselees, those who share similarities and those who are different from you.

Web Sites

Multicultural Differences

- "Diversity and Complexity in the Classroom: Considerations of Race, Ethnicity, and Gender." Strategies are provided to help work with the wide range of students present in today's schools: http://teaching.berkeley.edu/bgd/diversity.html

Students With Special Needs

- "Teaching Special Kids: Online Resources for Teachers." This link will take you to online information about resources that can help you better understand students with special needs: http://www.education-world.com/a_curr/curr139.shtml
- "Adaptations and Modifications for Students with Special Needs." This link provides easy modifications to incorporate into the curriculum for students with special needs: http://www.teachervision.fen.com/special-education/resource/5347.html

Students Who Are Gifted

- "Working with Gifted & Talented Students." This Web page provides a list of traits that are frequent indicators of students who are gifted, strategies and ideas that can be utilized to ensure students who are gifted use their abilities to the greatest potential, and a list of resources: http://www.teachersfirst.com/gifted.cfm
- "Who are the "Gifted" Children—and How Should Schools Handle Them?" This article discusses considerations for working with students who are gifted and includes resources that are available on the Web: http://www.education-world.com/a_curr/curr101.shtml

Students Who Are Gay, Lesbian, Bisexual, Transgender, and Queer

- The Gay, Lesbian and Straight Education Network (GLSEN) provides research and statistics on LGBTQ students: http://www.glsen.org
- PFLAG (Parents, Families, and Friends of Lesbians and Gays): http://www.pflag.org
- ASCA Position Statement on Gay, Lesbian, Bisexual, Transgender, and Questioning Youth: http://www.schoolcounselor.org/content.asp?contentid=217. You must be an ASCA member to access this site.
- The Human Rights Campaign is an organization dedicated to political advocacy for LGBTQ people: http://www.hrc.org/
- Lambda Legal is an organization dedicated to LGBTQ legal issues: http://www.lambdalegal.org/

References

American School Counselor Association (ASCA). (2004). *Position statement: Special-needs students.* Retrieved November 22, 2008, from http://www.schoolcounselor.org/content.asp?contentid=218

American School Counselor Association (ASCA). (2007). *Position statement: Gay, lesbian, bisexual, transgendered and questioning youth.* Retrieved November 14, 2008, from http://www.schoolcounselor.org/content.asp?contentid=217

Barr, R. D., & Parrett, W. H. (2000). *Hope fulfilled for at-risk and violent youth: K–12 programs that work* (2nd ed.). Boston: Allyn & Bacon.

Callahan, C. (2001). Protecting and counseling gay and lesbian students. *Journal of Humanistic Counseling, 40*(1), 5–10.

Delisle, J., & Gailbrath, J. (2002). *When gifted kids don't have all the answers: How to meet their social & emotional needs.* Minneapolis, MN: Free Spirit Publishing.

Dykens, E. M. (2006). Toward a positive psychology of mental retardation. *American Journal of Orthopsychiatry, 76*(2), 185–193.

Gay, Lesbian, and Straight Education Network (GLSEN). *GLSEN safe space: A how-to guide for starting an allies program.* New York: GLSEN. Retrieved from http://www.glsen.org/binary-data/GLSEN_ATTACHMENTS/file/000/000/294-3.PDF

Gay, Lesbian, and Straight Education Network (GLSEN). (2008a). *The 2007 national school climate survey: Executive summary.* New York: The Gay, Lesbian and Straight Education Network. Retrieved from http://www.glsen.org/binary-data/GLSEN_ATTACHMENTS/file/000/001/1306-1.pdf

Gay, Lesbian, and Straight Education Network (GLSEN). (2008b). *LGBT definitions.* Retrieved November 25, 2008, from http://www.glsen.org/cgi-bin/iowa/all/library/record/2335.html?-state=media

Ghezzi, P. (2006, February 28). ACLU files suit vs. district over school clubs rule; gay support group seeks right to meet. *The Atlanta Journal-Constitution,* p. 3B.

Hallahan, D. P., & Kauffman, J. M. (2006). *Exceptional learners: Introduction to special education* (10th ed.). Boston: Pearson/Allyn & Bacon.

Holcomb-McCoy, C. (2004). Assessing the multicultural competence of school counselors: A checklist. *Professional School Counseling, 7*, 178–186.

Holcomb-McCoy, C., & Chen-Hayes, S. F. (2007). Multiculturally competent school counselors: Affirming diversity through challenging oppression. In B. T. Erford (Ed.), *Transforming the school counseling profession* (2nd ed., pp. 98–120). Upper Saddle River, NJ: Pearson Merrill Prentice Hall.

Lee, C. C., & Hipolito-Delgado, C. (2007). Counselors as agents of social justice. In C. C. Lee (Ed.), *Counseling for social justice* (pp. xiii–xxviii). Alexandria, VA: American Counseling Association.

Lockhart, E. J. (2003). Students with disabilities. In B. T. Erford (Ed.), *Transforming the school counseling profession* (pp. 357–409). Upper Saddle River, NJ: Merrill Education/Prentice Hall.

McFarland, W. P., & Dupuis, M. (2003). The legal duty to protect gay and lesbian students from violence in school. In T. P. Remley, M. A. Hermann, & W. C. Huey (Eds.), *Ethical & legal issues in school counseling* (2nd ed., pp. 341–357). Alexandria, VA: American School Counselor Association.

National Association for Gifted Children. (2008). *Characteristics checklists for gifted children.* Retrieved October 1, 2008, from http://www.austega.com/gifted/characteristics.htm

Nebraska Department of Education. (2008). *Accommodations checklist.* Retrieved November 22, 2008, from http://www.nde.state.ne.us/sped/iepproj/appc/acc.html

Pearson, Q. M. (2003). Breaking the silence in the counselor education classroom: A training seminar on counseling sexual minority clients. *Journal of Counseling and Development, 81*, 292–300.

Peterson, C. (2006). *A primer in positive psychology.* New York: Oxford University Press.

Pollock, S. L. (2006). Counselor roles in dealing with bullies and their LGBT victims. *Middle School Journal, 38*(2), 94–102.

Scott, J. (2006, July 15). Judge rules gay group can use school. *The Atlanta Journal-Constitution,* p. 3E.

Sue, D. W. (1990). *Counseling the culturally different: Theory and practice.* New York: John Wiley and Sons.

Varjas, K., Graybill, E., Mahan, W., Meyers, J., Dew, B., Marshall, M., et al. (2007). Urban service providers' perspectives on school responses to gay, lesbian, and questioning students: An exploratory study. *Professional School Counseling, 11*(2), 113–119.

Wasow, B. (2005). *Majority minority.* Retrieved November 20, 2008, from http://www.tcf.org/list.asp?type=NC&pubid=1072

Wood, S. (2008, March). *Counseling gifted students.* Paper presented at the meeting of the American Counseling Association, Honolulu, Hawaii.

Yoo, C. (2005, May 8). Gay teens seek support and safety; White county has become center of emotional clash over equal rights. *The Atlanta Journal-Constitution,* p. 1C.

Ziomek-Daigle, J., & Singh, A. A. (2008, June). *Beyond safe zones: Setting new standards by making schools safer for LGBTQ youth.* Paper presented at the meeting of the American School Counselor Association, Atlanta.

Developmental Issues of Students

Robin Wilbourn Lee
Jennifer Jordan
Lydia Turner Archibald
Angela Cahill

The purpose of this chapter is to:

- Review human development as it relates to school counseling
- Introduce developmental themes and concepts
- Discuss major developmental theories
- Consider the impact of basic forces in human development
- Provide scenarios to help the reader consider strategies for working with counselees in the schools

Concepts surrounding human growth and development are required in school counselor training programs. Although you have probably taken a course that highlights life span developmental issues, this chapter is intended not only as a review of conceptual considerations, but also to present ideas to consider while assisting school-aged youth with issues that they bring to your counseling setting.

Developmental Themes and Concepts

Because human development addresses every aspect of the life span, the concepts and themes discussed in the literature play a particularly important role in understanding those with whom school counselors work. The themes of nature versus nurture, continuity versus discontinuity, universal versus context specific, and normative influences are a few developmental concepts for you to review as you apply these concepts during your practicum and internship experiences.

Nature Versus Nurture

Nature versus nurture involves the degree to which genetic or hereditary influences (nature) and/or environmental influences (nurture) determine personal attributes and characteristics. For years, a multitude of research has been conducted to determine which of these influences most directly impacts development. It has been consistently found that development is not due exclusively to either; rather, it is shaped by both, and therefore both are considered interactive influences. For example, a student may be predisposed to heart disease based on heredity and genetics (nature), but with healthy lifestyle choices, proper diet, and exercise, heart disease may be prevented.

Continuity Versus Discontinuity

Continuity is a concept indicating that development is a smooth progression throughout the life span. Continuity indicates that if a person develops certain characteristics early in life (e.g., a student who is shy or timid), these characteristics will continue throughout life (e.g., student becomes a shy and timid adult). Discontinuity indicates that development has a series of abrupt shifts, which influence changes that may occur. For example, a shy, timid child is taught social skills by parents and provided opportunities to utilize these skills. As a result, changes can occur to the child's personality and he or she may become more social and outgoing.

Universal Versus Context Specific

The field of human growth and development considers the path of development as either universal (one similar path for all people) or context specific (different paths related to environmental factors). Many developmental tasks occur similarly and in the same timeframe (e.g., language development across different cultures); however, context or environment still can have an impact (e.g., the fact that the child learns the language(s) to which she is exposed) on development.

Normative Influences

Many developmental tasks are normative, or what are considered typical or average. However, developmental tasks can be affected by age, history, and atypical occurrences. When considering age-graded normative influences, developmental tasks are affected by events that are related to particular age groups, generations, or cohorts (i.e., birth group). Living generations and cohorts include GIs, Baby Boomers, Generation Xers, Millennials, and a yet-to-be-identified generational group (suggestions include the Homelanders or Generation Z). Normative history-graded influences describe the impact that historical events can have on development. For example, the tragic events of September 11, 2001, will have a major impact on the development of future generations.

Keep these developmental themes and concepts in mind when you work with students. They provide constructs from which to view and understand student temperament, behavior, and characteristics. They can also be used as reframing tools when counseling students; counselees can be taught these development ideas to better understand their own journey and the journey of their peers.

Theories of Development

From a human growth and development perspective, a theory is defined as "an organized set of ideas that is designed to explain development" (Kail & Cavanaugh, 2007, p. 11). Theories of development can be divided according to perspectives. Some of the broader perspectives include psychodynamic, learning, cognitive, and systems theories. Although there are numerous additional developmental theories, each of the aforementioned perspectives is briefly reviewed next.

Psychodynamic Theory

According to Kail and Cavanaugh (2007), psychodynamic theories describe behavior as scientifically impacted by motives, drives, and unconscious forces. Psychodynamic theories are typically stage based, in that development is based on sequences of stages. Erikson (1950, 1968) developed a theory that explained human development in terms of the impact of social demands on the person. Erikson's psychosocial theory is composed of eight stages with each stage merging at a particular age. Within these stages, the person is met with a developmental task or interpersonal challenge with the outcome dependent on whether the person meets the challenge successfully. If the person is successful at each stage, there is a positive outcome; if they are not successful, then there is a negative outcome (see Table 13.1 and Table 13.2).

TABLE 13.1　Erikson's Eight Stages of Psychosocial Development

Developmental Task/ Interpersonal Challenge	Age	Positive Outcome	Negative Outcome
Trust vs. mistrust	Birth to 1 year	Hope	Fear and mistrust of others
Autonomy vs. shame and doubt	1–3 years	Self-sufficiency if exploration encouraged	Doubts about self, lack of independence
Initiative vs. guilt	3–6 years	Discovery of ways to initiate actions	Guilt from actions and thoughts
Industry vs. inferiority	6 years to adolescence	Development of sense of competence	Feelings of inferiority, no sense of mastery
Identity vs. role confusion	Adolescence	Awareness of uniqueness of self, knowledge of role to be followed	Inability to identify appropriate roles in life
Intimacy vs. isolation	Early adulthood	Development of loving, sexual relationships and close friendships	Fear of relationships with others
Generativity vs. stagnation	Middle adulthood	Sense of contribution to continuity of life	Trivialization of one's activities
Ego-integrity vs. despair	Late adulthood	Sense of unity in life's accomplishments	Regret over lost opportunities of life

ACTIVITY 13.1

Consider some of the students you have met and counseled in your practicum or internship. Identify which of Erikson's stages best fits each student. Describe the student and the stage you chose, and discuss your reasoning with your peers. How might you use this information when counseling these students?

_____

_____

_____

TABLE 13.2 Various Developmental Aspects

Life Span	Cognitive Development	Social Development	Early Childhood			Gender Roles and Concerns
			Moral Development	Emotional Development	Play	
Stage characteristics	Preoperational: Egocentric, lack ability to be empathic, have difficulty following rules.	Shame and doubt: Begin to understand they are autonomous. Initiative vs. guilt: Work on gaining autonomy, develop intentionality, begin to understand they are responsible for their own behavior.	Preconventional: Child's view is based on the outcome of pain or pleasure in the consequences.	Emotions are not socialized. Children need to learn how to interpret emotions, control them, and learn how and when they are appropriate.	Pretend play helps with problem solving, and cognitive and social development. Daydreaming is normal at this stage. Solitary play, parallel play, onlooker play, associative play, and cooperative play.	Understand gender and begin to conform to sex-appropriate patterns. Those who differ are often rejected by peers.
Implications for school counselors	Do not assume children know why they have done something. They look at things from one point of view; this causes difficulty understanding what teacher wants. Children now have a new tool for making sense of the world through questioning.	Important to allow for exploration and independence. Do not overprotect.	Authority figures are seen as the ones who determine the consequences; therefore, children react primarily to them. Understand the motivation for misbehavior using Dinkmeyer's theory: Undue attention, power, revenge, and assumed inadequacy.	Children who are a product of insecure attachment to parents or caregivers in the first years of life may show signs of manipulation, aggression, disrespect, and deceitfulness. Help teachers to understand where the behavior stems from, encourage empathy and understanding, know children will push the envelope as far as possible to test for trust. Do not give up on these children.	Play is the child's language; there are short-term play techniques that can be much more effective than talk therapy to solve school problems.	Gender differences in bullying. Boys tend to be more physically aggressive to solve conflict; girls tend to use more relational aggression.
Age-appropriate actions	Make age-appropriate contracts and give children a prize for completion.	Allow children to create their own games and rules; allow them to create rewards and consequences; use strategic games like checkers, Sorry, Trouble, or Connect Four; you can let the kids win because it is about the process of learning self-regulation by taking turns.	Talk with the teacher; understand the reaction and consequences given to the child. Explore the child's perception of the teacher's consequences to see where they fit into the theory above. Work with teacher to change consequences if they are not getting the reaction that they want.	Play the feeling word game. Play a game to show you can have more than one feeling at a time (put each emotion on a separate piece of paper to tell a story that involves several emotions, have the child identify them and put the appropriate amount of poker chips on the feelings chosen to show the different intensity levels of each feeling). Self-control techniques can be taught with the games Pickup Sticks and Operation.	Use fun games that allow laughter and silliness to build rapport, like catching bubbles before they hit the floor, or using bubbles to teach breathing techniques to calm themselves. (Show how to blow very large bubbles: it takes a deep breath that must be exhaled slowly.) Use ask-the-expert game: pretend the child is the expert and you are interviewing them with pretend questions from other children who have similar issues as them; this is great for developing problem-solving skills.	Develop an antibullying school policy. Intervene immediately. Increase adult supervision at key times.

Middle Childhood

Life Span	Cognitive Development	Social Development	Moral Development	Emotional Development	Friends and Peers	Gender Differences
Stage characteristics	Concrete operational: Have a more logical thought process, base knowledge on things they have seen or can imagine easily.	Industry vs. inferiority: Need to feel successful in school; failure results in feeling insecure and inferior. Self-worth and esteem come from acknowledging how others act toward them, how they perceive themselves in comparison to others, and how closely they feel they are who they want to be. Emotions are often strongly tied to feelings of worth. Happy children express more happiness than sad children. Friendships become very important and selective.	Conventional: Progress from obeying rules of others to understanding others' perspectives to wanting to maintain social order.	Parental authority is questioned, emotions become regulated.	Friendships become very important and selective. Reciprocity is key. Social skills determine the ability to make friends.	Relational regression peaks in middle school girls. Relationships become more intimate and are used to gain power. Boys gain power through physical means.
Implications for school counselors	Conversation has advanced; children's primary mode of expression is no longer through play. Cognitive behavioral, solution-focused, and choice theories become applicable. Play can still be incorporated to help process from the preoperational stage to the concrete stage.	This is time for children to be given every chance to be successful. They need to be exposed to many activities to find their niche.	Intentions matter more than consequences. They know not all negative behavior will be immediately punished or even detected.	Regulation of feeling often masks true feelings. Shame may be associated with negative feelings; fear for self or those who have been emotionally abusive are hidden. Societal taboo limits expression of emotion regarding sexual abuse. Emotional issues become a hidden secret that affects socializing, trusting, self-worth, and many other aspects of emotional development.	Many children in middle childhood do not have friends. Friends influence behaviors of other in their peer group (peer pressure).	Interpersonal relationships differ between boys and girls. Children are developing physically at different rates, causing more awareness of body image and potential self-esteem issues related to body image. Be aware of subtle relational exclusion from girls.
Age-appropriate actions	Use groups to focus on the here and now, which leads to the development of empathy for others. Use creative activities that are age-appropriate. Apply short-term objectives to academic and behavioral objectives.	Encourage students to find a niche in school as well as outside school. Run groups that include social skills training. For those with developmental disorders, it is especially needed in the middle school years. Guidance lessons can concentrate more heavily on issues that children are going to face this now or in the future. Smoking, drinking, drug use, and sex are some examples of topics needed for guidance or group activities.	Punishments must fit the crime or these children become angry. They depend on a fair consequence, which shows that wrongs need to be righted.	Activities that promote self-worth and self-esteem are important. Programs include Girls on the Run.	Implement social skills training; have a plan set up for new children to adjust to school and meet other children. Peer mediation applications are successful with this population.	Incorporating gender roles into your lessons becomes important. The issues the sexes face are now more complicated and diverse. Guidance lessons including sexuality should be split between the sexes. Friendships with the opposite sex are explored including dating rituals.

(continued on next page)

TABLE 13.2 (continued)   Various Developmental Aspects

Life Span	Adolescence					
	Cognitive Development	Social Development	Moral Development	Emotional Development	Self-Worth	Friends and Peers
Stage characteristics	Formal operational stage: Can now understand hypothetical concepts; they begin to ponder the meaning of life, feel others are always passing judgment, and at the same time feel they are special and are not susceptible to the same risks as others: "It won't happen to me."	Identity vs. role confusion: Need to develop a strong sense of self-understanding; what one's own beliefs and values are. Staying closely in line with this creates a strong sense of self. Whereas those that stray from this struggle with themselves have a low sense of worth and are more susceptible to peer pressure. Social learning theory suggests suicide is linked to the child's social system.	Postconventional: Can understand moral versus legal implications and can take perspective of mankind as a collective whole.	Emotional distancing from caregivers. Suicide rates soar. Isolation leading to depression.	With independence comes the ability to make their own decisions.	Freedom is a primary value. More independence. Relationships with more intense intimacy are coveted. For some, becoming more comfortable with self, showing more of the values they believe instead of those from parents or others in their lives. Being shunned from a peer group can cause many psychological stressors.
Implications for school counselors	High-risk behavior is more prevalent.	Understanding how one differentiates from others is important. Those with a lack of clarity in themselves will struggle with career choices and experimentation of the choices available to them.	Fictitious dilemmas are not very powerful. Often students do not progress past a stage two orientation without guidance.	Be aware of isolated students, who do not display outward problems, as they may be more at risk for depression.	Those without social groups feel isolated and think, "If I weren't here no one would even notice."	Peer interactions are imperative.
Age-appropriate actions	Plan events such as bringing in a wrecked car to campus, bringing in speakers whom the kids can relate to, programs to show the impact of pregnancy and parenthood.	Use more group activities to foster the need for socialization.	Encourage debates using real moral dilemmas. Challenge the students by incorporating thoughts consistent with next developmental level.	Help identify goals, create a sense of belonging.	Help others get kids connected.	Volunteer and become part of the greater whole.

Source: Adapted from *The Lifespan*, 1996, by G. L. Lefrancois, Belmont, CA: Wadsworth.

Learning Theory

Whereas psychodynamic theories focus on the influence of motives and drives, learning theories focus on the influence of learning on the person's development. According to social learning theory, the focus includes the importance of modeling, or the person's ability to learn from others. Albert Bandura's (1977, 1986) social cognitive theory integrates both cognitive and social influences. Bandura believed that people attempt to understand the world around them, as well as their place in the world (cognitive). In addition, Bandura considered the influence of others an important force of development (social). For instance, consider the influences of parents/guardians on the social process to better understand the students with whom you are working.

ACTIVITY 13.2

Read and respond to the following scenarios and discuss your answers with your peers.

> Angela is a second grader at a local elementary school. Over the years, she has shown tremendous anxiety whenever a thunderstorm occurs, often crying uncontrollably and demanding her mother be called to take her home. Her teachers and the school counselor are very puzzled by her behavior. Angela is upset by her reaction and does not understand why she reacts this way. After a brief meeting with the school counselor to discuss Angela's situation, Angela's mother reports that as a child, her family home was destroyed by a tornado, and whenever there is a report of inclement weather, Angela's mother insists they all get in the closet to protect themselves. How may have Angela's mother's previous experience affected Angela's thinking (cognitive) and reaction (behavior) to thunderstorms?

How might you work with Angela to calm her fears?

_____

_____

_____

> Kim is a sixth grader at a local middle school. She tells the school counselor she would like to meet with her. During the visit, Kim reveals she has recently been diagnosed with diabetes and is having to take daily shots for her condition. With Kim's permission, the school counselor schedules a consultation with the school nurse to learn what she can do to help Kim. The school nurse reports that Kim has not been diagnosed with the condition. After meeting with Kim again, the school counselor learns that Kim's parents were recently divorced. Kim attended a school assembly where an eighth grader recently diagnosed with diabetes was joined by her parents on stage to help the school understand how to deal diabetes. Kim believes that by having an illness, her parents will reconcile.

How did the eighth grader's condition and the assembly influence Kim's beliefs about her parents divorce? How can you assist Kim?

_____

_____

_____

Parent/Guardians and Other Social Influences

Parents or primary caregivers are the most influential social models for children. Working alongside and supporting parents or primary caregivers is one way you, as a school counselor, can greatly impact a student. Parenting style has a deep impact on the social and emotional well-being of children. Positive parenting styles have been linked to high self-esteem, self-regulation of emotions, academic achievement, prosocial skills, and friendship development, as well as low levels of aggressive behavior and negative social skills (Jackson, Pratt, Hunsberger, & Prancer, 2005; Maccoby & Martin, 1983). Negative parenting styles have been linked to low self-esteem, aggressive behavior, anxiety, anger, poor social skills, and possibly being more susceptible to bullying.

Baumrind (1971) developed four parenting styles based on the quality of parenting: (a) authoritative, (b) authoritarian, (c) permissive, and (d) rejecting–neglecting. Authoritative parents are considered the most positive form of parenting. Authoritative parents provide both nurturing and discipline, and children are given freedom, while adhering to consistent rules and limits. Authoritarian parents are inflexible, rigid, and often cold, establishing rules which require unquestionable obedience. Children of authoritarian parents may have difficulty expressing emotions due to the fact that a negative emotional environment is the norm. Permissive parents are the exact opposite of authoritarian parents. They are typically very loving but provide few rules. Discipline is not a priority with these parents. Children of permissive parents may have high self-esteem but may be

---

ACTIVITY 13.3

Two scenarios are offered in the following. Read each scenario and respond to the questions. Compare your answers with your peers.

> Jackson has recently been getting in trouble with other classmates. He is easily frustrated and takes out his frustration on the other students. When talking to you as the school counselor-in-training, he reveals that his father beats him almost every day and never lets him make decisions for himself. He also says that he is criticized for everything he does and is often threatened to be sent away if he does not do what his father says.

What kind of parenting style is Jackson's father using? How would you intervene in this situation?

_____

_____

_____

> Tonya's parents recently divorced after her mother caught her father cheating. Tonya and her two younger brothers are in her mother's custody, but Mom does not take the time to care for the three children because she has lost the initiative and ability to do so. Mom often sits in her room, depressed because of how her life has turned out. When Tonya and her brothers try to spend time with her, she tells them to go away. What might Tonya be experiencing and what kind of parenting style is Tonya using? How is this impacting Tonya and her two brothers? How might you respond to Tonya and the family?

_____

_____

_____

less self-reliant than other children. These children may exhibit impulsive and aggressive behavior. Rejecting–neglecting parents, the most flawed type of parenting style, provide little nurturing and discipline. These parents spend little time with their children and tend to be less affectionate. Children of rejecting–neglecting parents are neglected and ignored, often leading to significant aggression and depression.

Although awareness of parenting styles can help school counselors understand the dynamics between children they encounter and their parents, we must acknowledge that other factors may affect children's development, including genetics, gender, different beliefs of mother and father, culture, and child temperament. It should be expected that school counselors will encounter each of these parenting styles in their careers. Parent education may be an appropriate activity for you to consider during your clinical experiences while learning about the school counselor's role in working with parents/guardians.

Cognitive Theories

Cognitive theories focus on the influence of thought processes on development, particularly on how people think and how their thinking changes over time. Piaget (1926, 1929, 1972; Piaget & Inhelder, 1969) developed one of the most influential cognitive theories known as cognitive development theory. Piaget's theory focused on cognitive development in childhood and adolescence, focusing primarily on the construction of knowledge and changes that occur over time. Piaget believed that it is the natural inclination of children to try to understand their world, and that significant cognitive changes occur three times in a person's life: at 2 years old, at 7 years old, and right before adolescence. Each change is based on children's ability to understand and organize their environment as cognition becomes increasingly more sophisticated. Piaget's theory is based on four stages—sensorimotor, preoperational thought, concrete operational thought, and formal operational thought (see Table 13.3).

ACTIVITY 13.4

Read and respond to the following situation. Compare your answers with those of your peers.

> Cassie, a high school freshman, is shown a glass of water by her teacher. The teacher then pours the water into a shorter wider container and asks which glass had the most water in it. Cassie responds that both glasses contain the same amount of water, but that it appears to be different amounts only because the glasses are shaped differently. She is asked to arrange sticks on her desk from shortest to tallest, a task she completes without difficulty. She can also give the teacher directions from her classroom to the lunchroom.

What stage of Piaget's cognitive development is Cassie likely in?

_____

Consider some strategies school counselors can use to engage students who are in this stage of development?

_____

_____

_____

TABLE 13.3   Piaget's Four Stages of Cognitive Development

Stage	Age	Description
Sensorimotor	Birth to 2 years	Infant knows the world through their senses and through their actions. For example, they learn what dogs look like and what petting them feels like.
Preoperational	2–7 years	Toddlers and young children acquire the ability to internally represent the world through language and mental imagery. They also begin to be able to see the world from other people's perspectives, not just from their own.
Concrete operational	7–12 years	Children become able to think logically, not just intuitively. They now can classify objects into coherent categories and understand that events are often influenced by multiple factors, not just one.
Formal operational	12 years on	Adolescents can think systematically and reason about what might be as well as what is. This allows them to understand politics, ethics, and science fictions, as well as to engage in scientific reasoning.

A Russian psychologist and theorist, Lev Vygotsky (1934/1986), developed several important concepts helpful to understanding how children learn. Vygotsky's concept of *scaffolding* is used quite frequently by parents and school personnel. Scaffolding is the process by which a more accomplished learner (parent, teacher, or peer) provides direct instruction via prompts and cues to assist learning, and then slowly provides less instruction as the child's knowledge increases. Scaffolding requires the advanced learner to enter the child's *zone of proximal development*, defined as the difference between the child's ability to solve problems and the ability to be taught by another person. These two concepts can be particularly significant for you to remember as a school counselor-in-training since you are involved in the direct instruction of social/emotional knowledge and problem-solving skills related to personal situations. You can enter the child's zone of proximal development and use scaffolding to help the child learn how to deal with peers, adjust emotional reactions, and deal with problems such as attention-deficit hyperactivity disorder (ADHD). Or, as a supervisee, you may consider applying this concept by creating a mentorship program in which older students who understand and can model concepts are paired with younger students to enhance academic and social skills.

ACTIVITY 13.5

As a school counselor-in-training, what are some other strategies that can be used to apply the concepts of scaffolding in your school setting?

_____

_____

_____

Systems Theories

Systems theories are often referred to as ecological theories due to the environmental focus on development. Bronfenbrenner's (1979) ecological systems theory is based on the fact that development is based on the interaction of various systems in the person's life. According to Bronfenbrenner's theory, the environment is divided into four systems: microsystem, mesosystem, exosystem, macrosystem. The microsystem is defined as the person's immediate environment (e.g., parents, children, daycare, schools, church), which has significant influence on development. The mesosystem refers to the interaction between the person's microsystem and any modification that can occur based on this interaction. The exosystem is defined as the social settings that influence the person, either directly

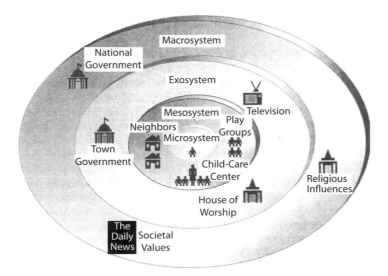

FIGURE 13.1   Four systems, according to Bronfenbrenner's theory.

or indirectly (e.g., extended family, media, job/work environment, neighbors). The macrosystem is considered the broadest of the systems and involves cultural influences (see Figure 13.1).

In working with students at various age and grade levels, consider how each of the developmental theories and concepts impact students and how change occurs. Further considerations include your values and perspective in relation to those values and perspectives of the individuals you are counseling. For instance, consider Lawrence Kohlberg's (1976) theory of moral development adapted from Piaget's work, to explain the development of moral reasoning as you work with children and adolescents.

ACTIVITY 13.6

Lydia is an 8-year-old girl who lives with her mother and grandmother. She and her mother moved in with her grandmother after Lydia's father died. Lydia's father was a soldier who was killed during combat in Afghanistan. There are two cousins who live with Lydia's grandmother as well as her uncle Bob, Lydia's mother's brother. Because of the death of her father, Lydia's family has been attending church regularly to deal with their grief. Her mother also takes Lydia to a local support group for children who have lost a parent. The family recently attended a memorial service held by the community to honor soldiers from the community who died while serving in the military. Lydia is very proud of her father and believes that serving in the military is very noble. She is considering joining the military when she is older.

Which system can you, as a supervisee, access to assist in Lydia's development? How can the various systems influence how school counselors or school counselors-in-training work with their students?

_____

_____

_____

Moral Development

Kohlberg (1976) extended Piaget's theory by considering moral development as a continual process occurring throughout the life span. Whereas Piaget described a two-stage process of moral development, Kohlberg's theory of moral development outlined six stages within three different levels. Preconventional, the first level, begins with making moral choices to avoid punishment and progresses into a hedonistic stage in which moral judgment is based on self-indulgence (if it feels good, it must be the right thing to do). Conventional, the second level, begins with interpreting the reactions of others and how they would view the person as a result of decisions made. As this stage progresses, values of honor and duty motivate conduct. Postconventional, the third level, moves away from social acceptance to the rights of individuals and the societal responsibility to uphold those rights to principles of justice for everyone (see Table 13.4).

ACTIVITY 13.7

Read and respond to the following scenario. Compare your answers with those of your peers.

> Cara is an 18-year-old girl who is a senior in a private high school. Recently she has gotten a facial piercing and a visible tattoo, though both are against school rules. Her parents discouraged her from getting the piercing and tattoo because they knew it was against school policy; however, because Cara is of legal age, she went ahead and got them anyway. She is currently suspended and faces possible expulsion from school if she does not remove the piercing and cover the tattoo while at school. Cara refuses to do either and references the Constitution and its statement of "freedom of choice" as her justification.

At which stage of Kohlberg's moral development theory is Cara? How would you, as a school counselor-in-training, use Kohlberg's theory to assist you in addressing this situation?

_____

_____

_____

Basic Forces in Human Development

Developmental tasks are typically examined in terms of what is happening to the student biologically, physically, cognitively, and psychosocially. By considering and combining the effects of these variables, we can begin to better understand the development of the student. The interaction of these forces is referred to as a *biopyschosocial framework*. Biological forces are defined as aspects of development pertaining to genetics and heredity, physical development, and overall health-related issues. Psychological forces include cognitive development, as well as emotional and affective issues and personality characteristics. Social–cultural forces describe the impact of social issues and culture on the person's development. By using the biopychosocial framework, each stage of development and age group can be understood better, helping you to apply these concepts in counseling.

TABLE 13.4   Kohlberg's Three Levels of Moral Development

Level	Substage	Description
Preconventional	Punishment and obedience orientation	What is seen as right is obedience to authority. Children's conscience is fear of punishment, and their moral action is motivated by avoidance of punishment. The child does not consider the interests of others or recognize that they differ from his or her own interests.
	Instrumental and exchange orientation	What is right is what is in one's own best interests or involves equal exchange between people.
Conventional	Mutual interpersonal expectations, relationships, and interpersonal conformity	Good behavior is doing what is expected by people who are close to the person or what people generally expect of someone in a given role. Being "good" is important in itself and means having good motives, showing concern about others, and maintaining good relationships with others.
	Social system and conscience orientation	Right behavior involves fulfilling one's duties, upholding laws, and contributing to society or one's group. The individual is motivated to keep the social system going and to avoid a breakdown in its functioning.
Postconventional	Social contract or individual rights orientation	Right behavior involves upholding rules that are in the best interest of the group, are impartial, or were agreed upon by the group. However, some values and rights, such as life and liberty, are universally right and must be upheld in any society, regardless of majority opinion.
	Universal ethical principles	Right behavior is commitment to self-chosen ethical principles that reflect universal justice. When laws violate these principles, the individual should act in accordance with these universal principles rather than the law.

Elementary School-Aged Children and Developmental Issues (Grades K–5)

Biological Development

In general, elementary school-aged children are typically healthy and self-reliant. Growth is fairly steady at this age with the greatest growth occurring in the legs and trunk. Growth can be negatively affected by poor nutrition, genetic factors, and gender. Brain size development reaches adult size by age 7, and both boys' and girls' brain sizes tend to be the same, although individual differences can exist based an environmental factors. Middle childhood is a period of time when chronic illness is less common than in any other time in life. Changes in fine and gross motor development become apparent. For girls, there is a focus on fine motor skills with improvement in dexterity, flexibility, and balance. For boys, the focus is primarily on gross motor skills, with improvement in strength.

Common contemporary issues in early childhood include childhood obesity, asthma, developmental disorders, autism spectrum disorders, and ADHD. School counselors-in-training should be aware of concerns that can develop in childhood, understand treatment, and know how to discuss these issues with parents when necessary.

Childhood Obesity

Childhood obesity is an issue that the medical community is currently considering an epidemic in the United States. Children may either be overweight (20% above ideal weight for height) or obese (30% over ideal weight for height). According to the American Obesity Association (2009), the rate of overweight children has doubled over the past 30 years and it estimates that one in five children in the United States are now overweight. Overweight children may have psychological, physical, and medical problems, low self-esteem, and difficult peer relationships. Childhood obesity can occur due to genetic factors; however, it may also occur due to environmental issues such as cultural values, lack of exercise, poor-quality food, and sedentary lifestyle (e.g., watching excessive television and playing video games).

Asthma

Asthma is the most common medical problem that causes school absences and is the third leading cause of hospitalization among children under the age of 15 (American Lung Association, 2009). Asthma, three times more prevalent than 20 years ago, is defined as a chronic inflammatory disorder of the airways that affects between 10% and 20% of school-aged children in North America. The rate of asthma is expected to double again by 2020. Although school medical personnel (i.e., school nurse) will likely be the school staff member to deal directly with any medical concerns, the school counselor may be the entry point for students who are dealing with physical issues. School counselors can be aware of the early warning signs of a child who may be developing asthma or asthmatic children who are at risk of an attack. Children who appear or act differently from the norm, even with something relatively minor like asthma, may be teased or ostracized. As a school counselor-in-training, you can use the clinical experiences as an opportunity to learn more about the emotional toil a physical condition like asthma may cause.

Autism

In the *Diagnostic and Statistical Manual* (*DSM*)-IV-TR (American Psychiatric Association, 2000), autism is defined as "the presences of markedly abnormal or impaired development in social interaction and communication and a markedly restricted repertoire of activity and interest" (p. 70). Autism falls under the area of pervasive developmental disorders, which are characterized by impairment in social and communication skills, as well as by the presence of repetitive behaviors. Other developmental disorders include Asperger's syndrome, Rett's disorder, and childhood disintegrative disorder. According to the Centers for Disease Control and Prevention (CDC, 2008a), autism spectrum disorders are the second most common serious developmental disability after mental retardation/intellectual impairment. However, these disorders are still less common than other conditions such as speech and language impairments, learning disabilities, and ADHD. Early intervention is key to helping children diagnosed with autism or other related disorders. Because symptoms usually can be observed by 18 months of age, children with autism may already be diagnosed by the time they enter school. However, as a school counselor-in-training, you can learn more about this disorder and hone skills to help children diagnosed with autism improve their social and communication skills, provide information to parents, and act as a support for teachers of autistic students.

Attention-Deficit Hyperactivity Disorder (ADHD)

According to the National Institute of Mental Health (2009), ADHD is one of the most common disorders of childhood, which may continue through adolescence and even into adulthood. The *DSM-IV-TR* (American Psychiatric Association, 2000) states that the essential feature of ADHD is "a persistent pattern of inattention and/or hyperactivity-impulsivity that is more frequently displayed and more severe than is typically observed in individuals at a comparable level of development" (p. 85). In addition, the *DSM* describes three subtypes of ADHD. First, the predominantly inattentive type focuses primarily on inattentive behaviors such as not paying attention to details; poor listening and organizational skills; not following instructions; failing to complete work, chores, and so forth; avoiding tasks requiring mental effort (e.g., schoolwork, homework); losing items such as toys and school materials; and forgetting daily activities. Second, the predominantly hyperactive/impulsive type focuses on behaviors such as fidgeting, squirming, running, or climbing excessively when inappropriate; having difficulty focusing on leisure activities or playing; talking excessively; blurting out answers; difficulty awaiting turn; and often interrupting others. ADHD combined type has criteria of both inattention and hyperactivity/impulsivity types. Although the causes of ADHD are unknown, possible causes include neurological problems and genetic vulnerability. The primary treatment of ADHD includes medications such as Ritalin or Adderall. In some cases, the most appropriate treatment is a combination of medication and counseling to help the child develop coping skills for dealing with the impact the condition may have on school and learning. As a school counselor-in-training, you can learn about special accommodations that assist these individuals, provide individual and group counseling, consult with teachers, and observe and participate in an Individualized Education Plan (IEP) team.

Cognitive Development

In childhood, cognitive ability rapidly develops and is typically reflected in improved test scores including aptitude and intelligence quotient (IQ; measuring the potential to learn or achieve in the future), and achievement (measuring what the child has already learned). Although the school psychologist may be the helping professional most likely to conduct intelligence testing, school counselors are often asked to participate in the testing process. Although IQ testing is a common assessment in schools, this type of testing comes with criticism because it does not consider achievement and the influence of other environmental factors such as culture, family, strength of school, and rate of development.

One specific use of IQ testing is to determine if a student has a learning deficiency. Some students experience learning disabilities that, if identified early, can be addressed to enhance the student's ability to be successful in school. A learning disability is defined as having a marked delay in a particular area of learning that is not associated with any physical handicap, mental retardation, or any significant stress in the home environment. A common type of learning disability is dyslexia, which is typically manifested by reading difficulty. Once a student has been identified as having a learning disability, schools are legally required to provide special accommodations for those students. Refer to Chapter 12 for more information on children with exceptional needs.

Memory is another concept important to understanding the cognitive development of children. *Working memory* is defined as the part of memory that holds information currently being used or accessed at a specific time. Changes occur in early childhood through an expansion of the capacity to hold information. In addition, *executive functions*, referring to skills related to managing memory, controlling cognitions, planning behaviors, and inhibiting responses, increase significantly after age 5. *Rehearsal* is an example of an executive function that helps students remember new information through repetition. *Selective attention* is defined as the student's ability to attend to information from several areas of the brain at one time while attending to the most important elements. Although selective attention improves with age, younger children face the challenge of being distracted by irrelevant information. As you train for the school counseling profession, helping children focus on the more important aspects of information may be crucial to successfully overcoming problems. *Automatization* is defined as the process by which thoughts and actions are repeated in sequence until they become routine or automatic; therefore, *automatic* thoughts and actions require very little conscious thought. Reading is an example of automatization. Automatization affects how children maintain appropriate and desirable behaviors, whether in the classroom or with peers, and is helpful for you to remember as you work with school-aged youth.

Janet Belsky, author of *Experiencing the Lifespan* (2007), offers information processing tips that are beneficial to any adults, including school counselors. Some of her tips for students in early and middle childhood are

Early Childhood
1. Do not expect a child to remember, without considerable prompting, regular chores such as feeding a pet, the details of a movie, or the name of the person who telephoned that afternoon.
2. Expect the child to have a good deal of trouble with any situation that involves inhibiting a strong "prepotent impulse," such as not touching toys, following unpleasant rules, or keeping a secret. Instead, tell them what you want (e.g., keep your hands to yourself, raise your hand and wait to be called on before speaking).

Middle Childhood
1. Do not assume that the child knows how to best master school-related memorization tasks. Actively teach the need to rehearse information, selective attention strategies (such as underlining important points), and other studying skills.
2. Scaffold organizational strategies for school and life. For example, get the child to use a notebook for each class assignment and to keep important objects, such as eyeglasses, in a specific place.
3. Expect that problems may occur with situations that involve many different tasks, such as getting ready for school. Also, expect activities that involve ongoing inhibition to give children trouble, such as refraining from watching TV or using the Internet before finishing their homework. Try to build in a regular structure for mastering these difficult executive-functioning tasks: "The rule is that at 8 or 9 p.m., it's time to get everything ready for school for tomorrow," or "Homework must be completed by dinner time, or the first thing after you get home from school."
4. To promote selective attention (and inhibition), have a child do homework or other tasks that involve concentration, in a room away from tempting distractions such as the TV or Internet.

Psychosocial Development

The psychological and social development for elementary-aged children tends to focus primarily on establishing independence and developing stability for future emotional life. Much of psychological development and socialization begins with the parents and cultural influences. Children, who are trying to master abilities and cultural values, often judge themselves as either competent or incompetent, productive or failing, winners or losers. Competence increases are related to emotional regulation and the understanding of self and others. However, this self-awareness has consequences, which can include lower self-esteem and more self-criticism and self-consciousness. *Social comparison* among peers emerges. Social comparison is the tendency to assess abilities, achievements,

ACTIVITY 13.8
Read and respond to the following scenario. Compare your answers with those of your peers.

Andre often gets in trouble for fighting at school with his classmates. He claims they make comments to disrespect him and he is not going to let anyone run over him. Many of the students are scared of him and think he is a bully.

What types of strategies will you, as his school counselor-in-training, implement to help Andre learn more effective social skills?

_____

_____

_____

social status, and other attributes by measuring against others such as peers. Friendship building and relating to peers is the most important aspect of the psychosocial developmental tasks at this age. Children begin to develop peer groups that are usually composed of the same age, ethnicity, and socioeconomic status that play, work, or learn together. Children depend on each other for companionship, advice, and self-validation. Children who are willing to assume the best about other children are successful with friendship development and therefore are typically well-adjusted and prosocial. Well-adjusted children often have prosocial behaviors such as altruism, empathy, and sympathy. In contrast, children who have difficulty connecting with peers often feel rejected, which may lead to other psychological problems later in life.

Adolescents and Developmental Issues (Grades 6–12)

Biological Development

When discussing the biological development of adolescents, the first and most critical aspect discussed is puberty. Puberty is the time in life when children become more mature sexually, based on hormonal and physical changes. Puberty is a period of rapid physical growth and sexual maturation, and is typically completed 3 to 4 years after the first visible signs.

Puberty cannot be discussed without acknowledging the extreme emotional reactions associated with biological changes that occur in adolescents during this time. G. Stanley Hall (1904) referred to the difficulty adolescents experience during puberty as *storm and stress*. Due to the rapidly increasing hormone levels, extreme emotional shifts occur, and increased hormone levels produce visible signs of sexual maturation, which often leads adults to think of the adolescents as adultlike, with an expectation of maturity. School counselors-in-training can help the adolescent entering puberty by normalizing what is happening and recognizing that they are not alone in that it is a universal development task that happens to everyone.

Normally, body changes begin to appear between ages 8 and 14, a wide span of years. With puberty comes a growth spurt, defined as rapid changes in size, shape, and proportions of the body. There is an average increase in height of about 8 inches in boys and about 4 inches in girls. Boys may gain an average of about 40 pounds, while girls may gain an average of about 35 pounds. Facial features change dramatically, with the nose and ears growing before the skull, causing disproportional facial features that are corrected when the head growth catches up to the rest of the face. This pattern may create emotional distress for youth who are already coming to grip with self-concept in relation to their peers. For girls, the growth spurt typically begins 2 years before boys with adult height often reached by age 12.

Although puberty is considered a universal developmental task, it is also context specific. All individuals go through puberty (universal), but the timing of puberty can vary (context specific). Factors that can affect puberty include genetics, culture, ethnicity, nutrition, body weight, family stress, and socioeconomic status.

The stress experienced by most adolescents in puberty can manifest in a variety of ways. Early-maturing girls may be embarrassed by their early development. Late-maturing girls can have equal embarrassment due to their childlike appearance when their peers are becoming more adultlike. Both can be subjected to teasing. Early-maturing boys often excel in sports, making them more popular than their late-maturing counterparts. Late-maturing boys may be shunned and ostracized. Early-maturing adolescents may experience unrealistic expectations from adults who expect them to demonstrate more adultlike thoughts and feelings than they are capable. Early-maturing girls may begin to choose friends who are older, therefore exposing themselves to more risky behaviors such as sex, drugs, and alcohol. For both boys and girls, another problem that can cause stress is an overproduction of oil and sweat in the skin causing acne. Due to the tremendous changes in the physical appearance during puberty, dissatisfaction with body image can become a stressful part of adolescence. Many adolescents become very critical of their bodies, often leading to extreme measures such as dieting, exercising, or developing an eating disorder.

Helping the prepubescent adolescent rather than focusing on the adolescent already experiencing puberty is an ideal approach for you as a counselor-in-training. According to Omar, McElderry, and Zakharia (2003), adolescents reported receiving their first formal education about puberty between the ages of 13 and 15, well after puberty had begun. For schools that do provide sex education classes, the focus is typically on what not to do (avoid sexual contact, sexually transmitted diseases, teen pregnancy), rather than on having an open discussion about these issues and strategies to handle the significant changes that adolescents are, or about to, experience. Educating parents about how to deal with their prepubescent adolescent can be an important school counselor function. Parents can be encouraged to talk to their children about puberty, and, when possible, parents can be reminded about the pros and cons of talking to their same-sex child. Specifically, it is important for mothers to remember to avoid negatively discussing menstruation in front of their female children (Rembeck & Gunnarsson, 2004), and both parents can also avoid teasing their children about their changing bodies.

Cognitive Development

During adolescence, many intellectual advances occur in logical and intuitive thinking. Brain maturation continues, helping in the areas of planning, analyzing, and being able to pursue goals. Language mastery also improves. According to Piaget (1972), adolescents are in the fourth and final stage of his model—formal operations, which begins around 12 years of age. In this stage, Piaget believed that adolescents are able to think logically, abstractly, and hypothetically, and are better able to see the various aspects of a problem. Determining the cognitive level of your counselees is helpful in determining a theoretical counseling approach and techniques that would work best for each individual you counsel. For instance, a youth at the concrete cognitive level may benefit more from physical movement as opposed to theories that rely on higher-level cognition.

One of the positive aspects of this improved adolescent thinking is the ability to self-monitor and self-regulate, however with this improved thinking comes other challenges that rival only puberty in terms of difficulty. Elkind (1978) applied Piaget's theory to help understand adolescent emotional states. He developed the term *adolescent egocentrism* to describe the adolescent's focus on self to the exclusion of others and the belief that their personal thoughts, feelings, and experiences are unique. Elkind described three types of adolescent egocentrism: (a) invincibility fable, (b) personal fable, and (c) imaginary audience. The *invincibility fable* is defined as the adolescents' belief that they are immune to the laws of mortality, probability, and nature. This belief can explain why adolescents tend to engage in risky behavior without recognizing the consequences of their choices. The *personal fable* describes when adolescents imagine their own lives as unique, mythical or heroic, and destined for fame or fortune. The *imaginary audience* is characterized by adolescents fantasizing about how others will react to them. They tend to be very concerned about the opinions of onlookers, often assuming that others are judging their appearance.

Although adolescents may be able to think logically, they may often be challenged with decision making; they tend to think about possibilities, not practicalities. Because of this, they may be less likely to consider important matters rationally. This may cause parents and other involved adults to spend a great deal of time and effort trying to protect teenagers from experiencing consequences resulting from poor judgment.

School counselors can be influential when adolescents are learning to make thoughtful, wise, and healthy decisions. Adolescents will be challenged with many aspects of life. Some of these aspects that relate more closely to the school counselor include the school environment; decisions about sex, drugs, and alcohol; establishing a healthy independence; depression; and suicide.

ACTIVITY 13.9

Read and respond to the following scenarios. Compare your answers with your peers.

> While at a school-sponsored swimming party, Jody decided to jump off the roof of the nearby pool house into the pool. Despite being cautioned of the risks by some partygoers, Jody dismissed their concerns and listened to those who were encouraging his antics.

How will you, as a school counselor, work with Jody or other individuals who exhibit these types of behaviors?

_____

_____

_____

> Naomi is a talented high school basketball player. Her coaches and others encourage her to pursue playing for a college basketball team. Although Naomi accepts this encouragement to pursue college basketball, she believes she is destined to play basketball in the major leagues (WNBA). She e-mails the manager of the Los Angeles Sparks, requesting a tryout.

What are some strategies that school counselors can utilize to assist adolescents develop a realistic outlook on self and others?

_____

_____

_____

School Environment

Some of the challenges that adolescents face are decisions about school. When adolescents graduate from high school, they are exposed to many benefits including healthier lives, living longer, a likelihood of financial stability, stronger possibility of marriage, and owning a home. However, there are also numerous reasons for dropping out of high school. According to a Web site titled "The Silent Epidemic" (2007), adolescents across the country reported reasons for dropping out such as classes being uninteresting, being unmotivated to work hard, getting a job, becoming a parent, or caring for a family member. In addition, some reported failing in school as a major factor. Another important factor discovered by the survey was that 70% reported feeling confident they could have graduated, despite having lower grades. A majority of teens reported they would have stayed in school if classes had helped prepare them for real-world experiences, if higher expectations were required from school personnel and parents, and if more supervision was provided.

Another very interesting aspect of our schools today is that the school schedule may create difficulties for the adolescent. According to Berger (2007), our school structure was established in the early 1900s when only 8% of teens completed high school, and today this structure may not meet the needs of today's students. For example, despite often very large schools, there is little supervision, minimal interaction between teachers and students, and a schedule that does not match the needs of the adolescent. According to sleep researcher Mary Carskadon (1999), there are biological reasons adolescents may seem drowsy for most of the day. She found that in the preteen years, the biological clock or circadian rhythms change, making adolescents less likely to be "sleepy" at night.

Basically, the biological clock of teens is working against them with alertness coming at night rather than during the day when school is in session.

Decisions About Sex

Sexual activity is one of the most difficult decisions teens have to make. Research shows that more than one-fourth of teens are sexually active by age 14 and about one-half are active by high school graduation (Hogan, Sun, & Cronwell, 2000; Santali, Lindberg, Alma, McNeely, & Redneck, 2000). But with decisions about sex come other risks such as sexually transmitted diseases (STDs) and teen pregnancy. Sexually active teenagers have higher rates of the most common STDs (i.e., gonorrhea, genital herpes, syphilis, and chlamydia) than any other age group (CDC, 2009).

Although teen pregnancy rates have been declining for years, recent reports indicate they are rising again. Over the past few years, the definition of what teens consider sexual activity has changed because most teens do not believe being sexually active includes sexual behaviors other than penile–vaginal penetration. For example, most teens believe that oral or anal sex is not considered sex.

Drugs and Alcohol

Tobacco, alcohol, and marijuana are three drugs that are known as *gateway drugs* due to their potential to lead to abuse and addiction, as well as other socially significant problems. Tobacco, the most physically addictive of the gateway drugs, can decrease food consumption, interfere with absorption of nutrients, and reduce fertility. Alcohol is harmful in adolescence due to its affects on the teen's physical, sexual, and emotional development. Marijuana seriously slows thinking processes, especially memory and abstract reasoning, and can create a lack of motivation and indifference toward the future. According to Berger (2007), almost every teenager in the United States has experimented with at least one of the gateway drugs, with most high school graduates having tried all three.

Depression

The self-esteem of children tends to drop at around age 12, and adolescents without support from family, friends, or school are more vulnerable to self-esteem issues than others. A loss of self-esteem may push the adolescent toward depression, which can affect 1 in 5 teenage girls and 1 in 10 teenage boys. It is possible that hormonal changes can account for depression, but various stress factors experienced by adolescents also can play a part. Teens can experience internal and external emotional problems. Internalizing problems are manifested inward to inflict harm on oneself (depression or suicide), while externalizing problems are "acted out" by injuring others, destroying property, or defying authority.

Suicide

According to the CDC (2008b), approximately one-third of teen girls report feeling hopeless in the past year, with about one-fourth having seriously considered suicide. Although suicidal ideation appears to be common enough among high school teens that it can be considered the norm, the act of suicide is rare. According to Berger (2007), adolescents are less likely to commit suicide than adults. So why do we believe suicide is a common occurrence during this time? First, the rates of suicide have tripled in the last 40 years. Second, although these figures may be alarming, it is important to note that these statistics typically include young adults (ages 20 to 24), who tend to have much higher rates of suicide than adolescents. Third, when adolescents commit suicide, the media is more likely to focus attention on it than on adult suicides. Last, although suicide may not be common, suicide attempts are very common, thus affecting the perception of others.

Establishing a Healthy Independence

The antithesis of establishing a healthy independence can be adolescent rebellion. As discussed previously, adolescents do not have the cognitive ability to recognize what is considered to be risky behavior. According to the CDC (2006), "motor vehicle crashes are the leading cause of death for U.S. teens, accounting for more than one in three deaths in this age group. In 2005, twelve teens ages 16 to 19 died every day from motor vehicle injuries" (p. 1). Drinking alcohol excessively is associated with approximately 75,000 deaths per year. Youth violence (homicide, physical assaults, extreme sports injuries, exposure to guns at school, etc.) is the second leading cause of death for adolescents.

Based on these alarming statistics, it is crucial that the adults in the lives of teenagers are aware of the risks and are prepared to help them make better decisions. You can be a strong voice to encourage teens to choose wisely. According to Belsky (2007), there are certain factors that can alert school counselors and others to adolescent risk factors including emotional problems early in life, adolescents with poor family relationships, and adolescents who engage in risky behavior (drinking, doing drugs, being truant, and exhibiting aggressive behaviors) in middle school. She offers six questions to consider when working with at-risk teens (p. 285):

1. Does the child have close family relationships?
2. Does the child have nurturing relationships with other competent and caring adults?
3. Does the child live in a community with good schools and good after-school programs for teenagers?
4. Does the child have close friends who are prosocial?
5. Is the child religious?
6. Does the child have a life passion or special talent?

Answering no to any of these questions does not mean the adolescent is destined to have problems, but the responses may serve as a guide when making decisions about teens who may need some type of intervention.

Psychosocial Development

The primary focus of psychosocial development for adolescents is based on developing *self* and *identity*. The primary question they must answer is "Who am I?" According to Erikson (1968), the developmental struggle for the adolescent is identity versus role confusion. Identity can be defined as unique individual beliefs based on roles, attitudes, values, and aspirations. Erikson believed that unsuccessful teens will develop *identity confusion*, marked by an inability to develop a positive path toward adulthood. Until they are able to integrate all aspects of their identity, they may try out *multiple or possible selves*, various possibilities of who they are or who they wish to become in the future.

Through the process of engaging in multiple or possible selves, teens come closer to integrating all aspects of their identity, and they begin to reach identity achievement. This process occurs when they are successful in establishing their own identity by accepting or rejecting the values, beliefs, and goals they have been or will be exposed to through parents, community, and culture. However, this is a challenging process, with some adolescents being successful and others not. James Marcia (1966) developed four types of identities to help understand the process of identity development,

ACTIVITY 13.10

Read and respond to the following scenarios. Compare your responses with those of your peers.

Tim is a 13-year-old, late-developing boy and physically small compared to the other boys. Tim's father is a large man, who won an Olympic medal in wrestling. Tim's father has always talked about how good he was at wrestling and how disappointed he is with Tim's size. Upon entering middle school, Tim joined the middle school wrestling team. He is not successful and is often hurt during matches. He becomes withdrawn and depressed.

How will you assist Tim in reflecting on his own strengths and weaknesses to determine future sport or career choices?

_____

_____

_____

identity achievement being the first type. *Identity foreclosure* describes an adolescent who adopts values and goals of parents and culture without questioning. Basically, the process of identity development closes before it actually begins. *Identity diffusion* describes the most troubled adolescent, who lacks commitment to goals or values and is apathetic about taking on any role. *Identity moratorium,* the healthiest approach to identity, describes an adolescent who experiments with different identities, by trying them out in order to make decisions about the future.

One of the key aspects of successfully navigating adolescence is a strong support system that consists of family, friends, and positive relationships. This support system helps the adolescent through both good and bad times, and you may be a significant part of that support system.

Considering the impact of developmental issues on children and adolescents can be an important aspect of a school counselor's work. Because of the comprehensive nature of human growth and development, a tremendous amount of knowledge can be gained by understanding developmental concepts and how these can be applied in a school setting.

ACTIVITY 13.11

Read and respond to the following scenario. Compare your responses with those of your peers.

Michelle is a 16-year-old female who is failing her classes. In middle school, Michelle was a good student who reported wanting to be a doctor. She has become very withdrawn and is associating with a new peer group that is not interested in school and spends most of its time at the local mall. The school has reported to Michelle's parents that she has been absent from school multiple times for the past few weeks. Michelle appears content with following her new peer group rather than considering her future goals. She reports having no career goals or interest in her future.

How can you help Michelle develop a sense of who she is in relation to others?

_____

_____

_____

Conclusion

Throughout this chapter you have reviewed many theories and concepts related to human development. Your task is to understand how developmental constructs influence your counseling relationship with your students. Not all the students with whom you work will be at the same developmental stages biologically, cognitively, or socially. School counselors have the responsibility to work with all students in the school and to facilitate an understanding of developmental issues with other educators and parents/guardians so that each counselee will have the opportunity to develop his or her potential to be contributing members of our society.

References

American Lung Association. (2009). *Childhood asthma overview.* Retrieved March 16, 2009, from http://www.lungusa.org/site/c.dvLUK9O0E/b.22782/k.8D9C/Childhood_Asthma__Overview.htm

American Obesity Association. (2009). *Childhood overweight.* Retrieved March 14, 2009, from http://www.obesity.org/information/childhood_overweight.asp

American Psychiatric Association. (2000). *Diagnostic and statistical manual of mental disorders* (4th ed., text revision). Washington, DC: Author.

Bandura, A. (1977). *Social learning theory.* Englewood Cliffs, NJ: Prentice-Hall.

Bandura, A. (1986). *Social foundations of thought and action.* Englewood Cliffs, NJ: Prentice-Hall.

Baumrind, D. (1971). Current patterns of parental authority. *Developmental Psychology, 4*(1), 1–103.

Belsky, J. (2007). *Experiencing the lifespan.* New York: Worth.

Berger, K. S. (2007). *The developing person through the life span.* New York: Worth.

Bronfenbrenner, U. (1979). *The ecology of human development.* Cambridge, MA: Harvard University Press.

Carskadon, M. (1999). When worlds collide: Adolescent need for sleep versus societal demands. *Phi Delta Kappan, 80,* 348–353.

Centers for Disease Control and Prevention (CDC). (2006). *Teen drivers: Fact sheet.* Retrieved March 4, 2009, from http://www.cdc.gov/MotorVehicleSafety/Teen_Drivers/teendrivers_factsheet.html

Centers for Disease Control and Prevention (CDC). (2008a). *Prevalence of ASDs.* Retrieved March 4, 2009, from http://www.cdc.gov/ncbddd/autism/faq_prevalence.htm#Whatisthedifference

Centers for Disease Control and Prevention (CDC). (2008b). *Suicide prevention.* Retrieved March 4, 2009, from http://www.cdc.gov/ViolencePrevention/suicide/index.html

Centers for Disease Control and Prevention (CDC). (2009). *Sexually transmitted diseases.* Retrieved July 19, 2009, from http://www.cdc.gov/std/

Elkind, D. (1978). Understanding the young adolescent. *Adolescence, 13,* 127–134.

Erikson, E. (1950). *Childhood and society.* New York: W. W. Norton & Co.

Erikson, E. (1968). *Identity: Youth and crisis.* New York: W. W. Norton & Co.

Hall, G. S. (1904). *Adolescence.* New York: Arno Press.

Hogan, D. P., Sun, R., & Cronwell, G. T. (2000). Sexual and fertility behaviors of American females aged 15-19 years: 1985, 1990, and 1995. *American Journal of Public Health, 90,* 1421–1425.

Jackson, L. M., Pratt, M. W., Hunsberger, B., & Prancer, S. M. (2005). Optimism as a mediator of the relation between perceived parental authoritativeness and adjustment among adolescents: Finding the sunny side of the street. *Social Development, 14,* 273–304.

Kail, R. V., & Cavanaugh, J. C. (2007). *Human development: A life-span view* (4th ed.). Belmont, CA: Wadsworth.

Kohlberg, L. (1976). Moral stages and moralization: The cognitive-developmental approach. In T. Lickona (Ed.), *Moral development and behavior* (pp. 31–55). New York: Holt, Rinehart & Winston.

Lefrancois, G. L. (1996). *The lifespan.* Belmont, CA: Wadsworth.

Maccoby, E. E., & Martin, J. A. (1983). Socialization in the context of the family: Parent–child interaction. In P. H. Mussen (Ed.) & E. M. Hetherington (Vol. Ed.), *Handbook of child psychology: Vol. 4. Socialization, personality, and social development* (4th ed., pp. 1–101). New York: Wiley.

Marcia, J. (1966). Development and validation of ego-identity status. *Journal of Personality and Social Psychology, 3,* 551–558.

National Institute of Mental Health. (2009). Attention deficit hyperactivity disorder (ADHD). Retrieved April 4, 2009, from http://www.nimh.nih.gov/health/publications/attention-deficit-hyperactivity-disorder/complete-index.shtml#pub3

Omar, H., McElderry, D., & Zakharia, R. (2003). Educating adolescents about puberty: What are we missing? *International Journal of Adolescent Medicine and Health, 15*(1), 79–83.

Piaget, J. (1926). *The language and thought of the child* (M. Worden, Trans.). New York: Harcourt Brace Jovanovich.

Piaget, J. (1929). *The child's conception of the world* (J. Tomlinson & A. Tomlinson, Trans.). New York: Harcourt Brace Jovanovich.

Piaget, J. (1972). Intellectual evolution from adolescence to adulthood. *Human Development, 15,* 1–12.

Piaget, J., & Inhelder, B. (1969). *The psychology of the child.* New York: Basic Books.

Rembeck, G. I., & Gunnarsson, R. K. (2004). Improving pre- and postmenarcheal 12-year old girls' attitudes toward menstruation. *Health Care for Women International, 25,* 680–698.

Santali, J. S., Lindberg, L. D., Alma, J., McNeely, C. S., & Redneck, M. (2000). Adolescent sexual behaviors: Estimate and trends from four nationally representative surveys. *Family Planning Perspectives, 32,* 156–165.

The silent epidemic. (2007). Retrieved February 21, 2009, from http://www.pbs.org/thesilentepidemic

Vygotsky, L. S. (1986). *Thought and language* (A. Kozulin, Trans.). Cambridge, MA: MIT Press. (Original work published 1934)

SECTION IV:

COMPLETING THE CLINICAL EXPERIENCES

Transitioning Forward

Michael Bundy

The purpose of this chapter is to:

- Present ideas on how to terminate the clinical experiences
- Provide tools to self-assess your competencies as a school counselor with regard for knowledge, skills, and attitudes
- Suggest strategies for interviewing for a position as a professional school counselor
- Offer ways to enhance professional identity and to obtain professional development once employed

Practicum/Internship Closure

The time has come for you to plan how to leave your practicum or internship site. Your site supervisor has encouraged you and has provided you with positive guidance. Teachers and administrators at your clinical sites gave you support and assistance when you needed it. Many counselees were changed by the individual and small group sessions you held with them. You need to show your appreciation to them and ensure that the counselor-in-training who follows you to this school will be warmly received, too. So, give careful consideration to how you separate from your students, teachers, site supervisor, and others with whom you have worked closely.

Terminating Relationships With Students

The process of terminating a counseling relationship can be a stressful time for students, but it can also be an opportunity to affirm their growth and see ending as a new beginning. Students who have received special attention from you may become uneasy when you begin to discuss terminating their counseling sessions. They may need help considering what it will be like to function without you as part of their support system. Seeing the end of one relationship or event as a natural time to redefine and begin new relationships and activities is a healthy way to perceive change. Here are a few tips on closing your relationships with students and some examples of what you can say to implement the suggestions in a session with them:

- *Give students advance notice.* You should begin talking with students about ending their counseling at least two sessions before their last one. What to say: "Jill, in two weeks my time at Jefferson School will end because my internship training with your school counselor Ms. Jones will be completed. I would like for us to talk a bit about what we have done together to help you with the goals you wanted to work on."
- *Have students self-assess their progress.* Allow students to express the progress they think they have made as a result of their relationship with you. You should help them acknowledge their accomplishments in terms of how they changed their behaviors, their thoughts, and their emotional responses. What to say: "I'd like to hear what changes you think you have made since we have been meeting. You had some goals you wanted to accomplish. What progress do you think you have made toward them?"

- *Offer your observations.* Be prepared to provide students with your assessment of their progress. Students often need to hear what you think of what they have done. This can be an encouraging and confidence-building time for them. The more specific your observations, the more powerful and meaningful they will be to your students. What to say: "Jill, would you like for me to tell you what I think you have done these past few weeks toward achieving your counseling goals? I have noticed that you no longer say things like 'I must do what Bill tells me to do or he won't like me anymore.'"
- *Anticipate future challenges.* Help students identify potential stumbling blocks they may encounter. It is quite likely that students will continue to face challenges when their counseling sessions with you are over. Talk about those potential hurdles and how students might overcome them. This could be another confidence-builder for students as you help them realize how resourceful they have become. What to say: "Jill, what will you think if Bill says that he wants to spend time apart? What will you say to him? How will you control your emotions?"
- *Identify student resources.* Help students utilize resources within their support systems for times when they may need extra assistance to overcome difficulties. Those resources could be the adults they respect and with whom they have a good working relationship (e.g., school counselor, favorite teacher, trusted relative, youth minister). What to say: "Jill, should one of those 'stumbling blocks' begin to give you a big hassle, what can you do? Is there someone you can talk to about it?"
- *Create a picture of the future.* To help students feel confident and build resiliency to cope with the challenges to come, it is usually effective to have students think and talk about what they would like to have happen, new relationships they may want to develop, or activities they want to start. If this is too difficult, have students try to imagine how they would like things to be for them. This could give them a positive image and provide motivation to continue moving forward along the path of successful change they found in counseling with you. What to say: "Jill, where would you like to be in six months when it comes to having or not having boyfriends?"
- *Write notes to students.* Recording your goodbyes in handwritten notes can be powerful and can give meaningful messages to students. Students have been known to carry these treasured thoughts with them for months. Your note should express appreciation for what you have learned from them, and it should communicate encouragement to them to continue growing, learning, and moving forward. The following notes were written by a school counseling intern to significant people at her internship site (D. Finchum, personal communication, December 14, 2008).

Janna,

You are truly a very special person. Your mom would be so proud of where you are. That first day *you* made me feel at ease. I looked forward to seeing your smiling face every day. I will miss our talks. Remember to give your dad a break; he loves you very much and you are still his baby. Study hard in college and you will do well. People who deal with you will see that you are genuine and honest. You are great role model. Watch over Vicki and please continue your friendship with her. You will be a tremendous school counselor one day. You have already changed lives … including mine … you will always have a place in my heart.

Debbi

Terminating counseling groups should be another growth experience for students and can be a fun activity as well. Most counselors-in-training give their groups a 2-week notice so the students have ample time to process their feelings and to plan for the future. The following provides a few suggestions that counselors-in-training have found to be effective closing activities:

ACTIVITY 14.1

Think about one of your past or current students. To make this activity more challenging, think of a student with whom you had difficulty. Write a brief note to this student. In your note, review resources available and create a positive picture of the future.

_____

_____

_____

- *Have refreshments at the last group session.* Food always makes for an enjoyable time. Be sure that your refreshments are consistent with any dietary restrictions group members or school rules have. Popcorn and juice boxes are usually safe for elementary students. Older students could be responsible for bringing their own tasty treats to the final group meeting. Put some limits on what can be brought; food can become a distraction to your final group agenda. Have some group process activities planned so closure is focused and meaningful.

- *Have group members acknowledge their progress.* This would be a time for group members to proudly announce changes they have made as a result of group support. Expressive art activities or open letters written to the group provide structured approaches for sharing retrospective observations.

- *Give feedback to group members.* Upon terminating the group, give each group member your assessment of their progress in specific terms before you leave. Follow a similar approach to that which is given earlier for individual students; offer your observations to the group as a whole and to members in individual sessions.

- *Write notes to group members.* These notes should offer specific observations and encouragement. Your message could be to the whole group allowing them time to respond, or you could give notes to individual members outside the group session. If the notes are read to the whole group, it could make a powerful closing session that builds cohesiveness among group members, or assist in members seeing their peers from a different perspective. If your note contains content to a specific student, provide that student with positive pragmatic feedback to help him or her continue improving upon the growth already started in the group. Imagine how a group member would be affected upon receiving the following note.

Emilie,

How can I ever put in words how proud I am of you? You never missed a group session and always kept up with the other students. You now have the confidence to keep a smile on your face. I know how hard it is, but just remember that we talked about how we can control what we think and how we act, and as a result our feelings will follow. I have seen you do this for the past five weeks. Your teachers have noticed how much easier you are to get along with and how your anger doesn't boil over so quickly. YOU are the one who chooses these actions, you made your own decisions and you can continue on. I will miss you, but know that all the lessons we talked about are still in your head and you can pull out your group notes and use them when you feel stressed. Please don't forget to be as proud of yourself as I am of you!!!

Debbi

ACTIVITY 14.2

Consider the same student you identified in the previous activity or think of a different student. Review the student's progress and provide feedback specific to him or her. Be encouraging and be honest.

_____

_____

_____

Terminating With Colleagues

Bringing relationships with your new colleagues to a close requires a heartfelt expression of appreciation for the mentorship and collaboration they provided. Throughout your experience, your site supervisor offered you wisdom and encouragement. Teachers in your school site worked with you to meet student needs, resulting in confidence in your counseling and consulting competencies. It may seem that a simple thank-you note would be insufficient to communicate your feelings toward them, but it carries special meaning to those who receive one. Shortly, you expect to be employed as a professional school counselor, and when this dream becomes your reality, these folks who helped you during your training may now meet with you as new colleagues in professional meetings or conferences. The impression you leave them with will be carried over into new professional relationships. Give them something extraordinary to remember about you. Try writing a note similar to the following:

Bruce,

The words 'Thank you' can hardly express how I feel about all I have learned and experienced in school counseling this semester. Your training has been exemplary, and I have learned so much. Seeing CT (Choice Theory) in action is so much more powerful than just reading about it. You taught me how to teach others but never criticize them. You taught, by example, how to empower students to find the answers for themselves. You have shown me what school counselors are doing on a daily basis. You truly made a difference in so many lives; just add me to the list. Thank you so much for allowing me to be your student! I hope someday to make you proud. I will never forget this time and what a truly great mentor you are! You're really the best!

Debbi

Terminating With Administrators

You must not avoid or forget to say goodbye to administrators who approved your placement and backed up your clinical activities. Central office supervisors and building-level principals may not have worked as closely with you as your site supervisor or the teachers, but their support was certainly critical to your success. Moreover, they will be important to your future job plans. When you apply for a counselor position, the employing principal will likely call the principal where you conducted your clinical experiences to ask about your performance. You will certainly want to leave the principal at your practicum/internship site with a positive impression of your maturity, independence, and competencies as a school counselor.

Here are two things you should consider doing: (1) make an appointment to debrief the principal of the things you accomplished before you leave, and (2) send a note of thanks to the principal and any central office personnel involved in your placement. The following is a note written by a school counseling intern to her site principal after she met with him before she left her internship experience.

Mr. Schneitman:

Thank you so much for the opportunity of completing my internship at Jefferson County High School. You are a multi-talented administrator who has put together an awesome staff. I also know that I would not want your job for love or money.

Thank you for allowing me the pleasure to put together a program using the peer counselors already in place as mentors for special-needs children and helping them learn social and emotional skills. You allowed me time for group counseling during school and gave me a place in the media center to conduct my sessions. You have allowed our program to have some great successes and for that I will be forever indebted. I wish you, your staff, and your students continued success.

Debbi

ACTIVITY 14.3

Write a thank-you termination note to either a colleague or administrator. Express your sentiments and provide specific examples of how this person assisted you. Keep in mind that this person may provide a reference or recommendation letter for you or even be your future employer.

_____

_____

_____

Self-Assessment

With your clinical experiences almost finished, and as you continue your transition from student to professional school counselor, it can be both an anxious and an exciting time for you. At this point, you should reflect upon the development of your competencies as a future professional school counselor. You will want to approach this new challenge with the same intensity and determination that you exemplified during your training program. But where do you begin the process?

Because counselor preparation programs provide ample opportunities for students to examine themselves and to facilitate personal growth, most counselors-in-training know themselves fairly well at this stage of their training. The information you have accumulated from your counseling coursework should be used to help you identify your strengths and areas that may need further development. Most recently, you have (or will have) feedback from your site supervisor and from your program professor. They have objectively assessed your readiness for assuming the responsibilities that come with organizing a comprehensive school counseling program as an appropriately credentialed professional. You should take these data and develop a plan to maximize your strength and to overcome your relative weaknesses; however, a more systematic self-assessment would be most beneficial to your planning.

The American School Counselor Association (ASCA) has a long history of providing vigorous leadership in articulating a professional identity for counselors who work primarily in school settings

(Lambie & Williamson, 2004). As the needs of pre-K–12 students have changed, and as society's expectations have changed for schools, the ASCA has been at the forefront in promoting standards for counseling training and for the practice of counselors. The ASCA (2008) published its most recent report, called "School Counselor Competencies," and later announced its approval at the 2008 ASCA Convention in Atlanta. This document lists the knowledge, skills, and attitudes counselors should posses in order to implement a comprehensive school counseling program.

These competencies were formatted in Chapter 6 to assist you in identifying tasks to perform during your training. To facilitate your self-appraisal, these same competencies are also reformatted into a self-assessment instrument. The ASCA prefers the competencies be considered along a continuum rather than as an either–or dichotomy. For this reason, each competency is presented in a 5-point Likert scale, with 1 being the lowest and 5 the highest. This will allow you to set specific improvement goals and to monitor your progress as new knowledge, skills, and attitudes are gained with experience and professional development.

With the emphasis on accountability in education, many school principals are looking for counselors who are able to implement a comprehensive counseling program that can show evidence of its effectiveness. The ASCA National Model® (2005) provides a framework in which school counselors can show that what they do makes a difference with students. The assistant director for ASCA offered the following observation:

> Increasingly, the ASCA National Model is recognized as the benchmark in the school counseling field by building-level and central office administrators as well as school boards. Because of this it is critical for those seeking positions as school counselors to have experience implementing a comprehensive school counseling program and to be able to articulate and demonstrate how an effective school counseling program contributes to student success in school. (J. Cook, personal communication, January 8, 2009)

It is therefore important that counselors-in-training examine themselves in terms of the competencies essential for designing, implementing, and evaluating the program aligned with the ASCA National Model. The School Counselor Competencies and the ASCA National Model go hand in hand. Therefore, as you complete your experiences, you may wish to use the School Counselor Competencies as your rubric for self-assessment. The question you should ask yourself is, "As I fulfilled my clinical responsibilities, to what degree did I demonstrate the counseling competencies in terms of knowledge, skill, and attitude?"

Self-Assessment of School Counselor Knowledge

The area of knowledge competencies will begin the discussion of assessing yourself as a professional school counselor. The ASCA expects school counselors to be steeped in the knowledge of how to design, implement, and evaluate a comprehensive school counseling program based upon the ASCA National Model. Knowledge of its various components and elements are essential and have, no doubt, been a significant part of your training program. Using your experiences and evaluations, you can better assess the degree to which you have the knowledge to build a comprehensive school counseling program.

Self-assessment should measure the degree to which your knowledge of theories of learning and human development has been acquired, and the foundation to determine how effectively students gain academic skills. Also, this knowledge will guide you in planning activities designed to close the achievement gap among some student populations and to ensure equity of access to opportunities. On a broader scale, you need an understanding of the history, trends, and professional issues of our educational systems to understand the culture and dynamics within schools.

TABLE 14.1   Self-Assessment of School Counseling Knowledge

School Counselor Knowledge	Self-Rating		
To what degree do you understand:	Low		High
The ASCA National Model and its four components	1	2 3 4	5
How to design a comprehensive school counseling program for all students	1	2 3 4	5
Beliefs and philosophy of school counseling programs	1	2 3 4	5
The role of school counseling in academic development of students	1	2 3 4	5
The role of school counseling in career development of students	1	2 3 4	5
The role of school counseling in personal and social development of students	1	2 3 4	5
How to design and implement a guidance curriculum	1	2 3 4	5
Counseling theories and techniques that work in schools	1	2 3 4	5
Principles of career planning and college admissions	1	2 3 4	5
Responsive services	1	2 3 4	5
Crisis counseling, including grief and bereavement	1	2 3 4	5
The continuum of mental health services	1	2 3 4	5
How to collaborate with key stakeholders	1	2 3 4	5
Legal, ethical, and professional issues in counseling and education	1	2 3 4	5
The foundation and trends of American educational systems	1	2 3 4	5
Student standards and competencies	1	2 3 4	5
Developmental issues affecting student success	1	2 3 4	5
How to close the achievement gap among students	1	2 3 4	5
Principles of classroom management	1	2 3 4	5
Principles of working with diverse populations	1	2 3 4	5
Leadership principles and theories	1	2 3 4	5
Learning theories	1	2 3 4	5
Human development theories	1	2 3 4	5
Organization theory as applied to school	1	2 3 4	5
How to make effective presentations	1	2 3 4	5
Time management	1	2 3 4	5
Data-driven decision making	1	2 3 4	5
Current and emerging technologies	1	2 3 4	5
Basic concept of results-based school counseling	1	2 3 4	5
Basic research and statistical concepts	1	2 3 4	5
Use of data to evaluate program effectiveness	1	2 3 4	5
Program audits and results reports	1	2 3 4	5

Using your experiences as a foundation, you can reflect upon your knowledge of counseling theories and crisis counseling, and assess your understanding of how to respond to student needs in terms of their academic development, career development, and personal/social development. Table 14.1 provides an effective tool that you can use to begin your self-assessment of the knowledge needed to implement a school counseling program.

ACTIVITY 14.4

Complete the self-assessment found in Table 14.1. Determine the areas where you have a solid working knowledge and the areas where you will need to focus future professional development. Later in this chapter, we will discuss how you can use this tool to prepare yourself for job searching.

Self-Assessment of School Counselor Skills

Your abilities and skills as a school counselor are the next areas to examine. Again, the ASCA School Counselor Competencies were used to design the self-assessment tool seen in Table 14.2.

TABLE 14.2   Self-Assessment of School Counseling Abilities and Skills

School Counselor Abilities and Skills	Self-Rating				
The degree to which you have the abilities and skills to:	Low				High
Plan, organize, and implement a school counseling program aligned with the ASCA National Model	1	2	3	4	5
Serve as a leader in the school and community to promote and support student success	1	2	3	4	5
Advocate for student success	1	2	3	4	5
Collaborate with parents, teachers, administrators, community leaders, and others to promote and support student success	1	2	3	4	5
Act as a systems change agent to create an environment promoting and supporting student success	1	2	3	4	5
Develop beliefs and philosophy of the school counseling program that align with current school improvement and student success initiatives at the school, district, and state level	1	2	3	4	5
Develop a school counseling mission statement aligning with the school, district, and state mission	1	2	3	4	5
Use student standards to drive the implementation of a comprehensive school counseling program	1	2	3	4	5
Apply ethical standards and principles to the school counseling profession and adheres to the legal aspects of the role of the school counselor	1	2	3	4	5
Implement a school guidance curriculum	1	2	3	4	5
Facilitate individual student planning	1	2	3	4	5
Provide responsive services	1	2	3	4	5
Implement system support activities for the comprehensive school counseling program	1	2	3	4	5
Negotiate with administrator to define the management system for the comprehensive school counseling program	1	2	3	4	5
Establish and convene an advisory council for a comprehensive school counseling program	1	2	3	4	5
Collect, analyze, and interpret relevant data, including process, perception, and results data, to monitor and improve student behavior and achievement	1	2	3	4	5
Organize and manage time to implement an effective school counseling program	1	2	3	4	5
Develop calendars to ensure the effective implementation of the school counseling program	1	2	3	4	5
Design and implement action plans aligning with school and school counseling program goals	1	2	3	4	5
Use data from results reports to evaluate program effectiveness and to determine program needs	1	2	3	4	5
Understand and advocate for appropriate school counselor performance appraisal	1	2	3	4	5
Conduct a program audit	1	2	3	4	5

ACTIVITY 14.5

Looking over each item in Table 14.2, reflect upon your training experiences. Think about the degree to which you have the skills to plan, organize, and implement a school counseling program that is aligned with the ASCA National Model. Consider your level of competencies in working with significant people within your role as a school counselor, assess your skills to support student success in a variety of ways, and your ability to lead and manage a school counseling program. Reflect upon your skill in working with administrators, teachers, parents, and others to implement various school counseling activities, and rate your abilities to respond to student needs, to facilitate individual student planning, and to implement a guidance curriculum. After you have completed the assessment, review your responses and talk to a peer or your supervisor about your current strengths and weaknesses. Consider steps you can take to make improvements.

Self-Assessment of School Counselor Attitudes and Values

The most important self-assessment is to reflect upon the attitudes you have and the values you hold. Basic understanding of human behavior indicates that beliefs and values drive thinking, feeling, and doing. If you believe that students can learn and succeed, then you will work hard to remove systemic barriers that impede learning. If you value equal opportunity for all students, then you will advocate for fair treatment and for equal access to opportunities for each student.

Professional school counselors must understand themselves first and foremost. With self-awareness, school counselors can be more authentic and can function more effectively, because students respond best to open and honest counselors. In addition, teachers respect colleagues whom they understand and can trust, and administrators are more accepting of ideas from counselors when they sense those ideas are genuine. Table 14.3 is an opportunity for you to assess your attitudes and

ACTIVITY 14.6

As you prepare to complete the self-assessment of school counselor attitudes and values in Table 14.3, reflect upon your clinical experiences. Think about how deeply you believe that all students should have access to your school counseling program, and consider how much you believe in working with others to implement your counseling program. Give some thought as to how much you believe that counselors should use data to measure the effectiveness of their programs, and the degree to which you believe the counseling program should be integrated into the school's academic program. Upon completing this self-assessment, you will have an improved profile of your competencies as a professional school counselor. With this information, develop a self-improvement plan that includes both long-term and short-term goals that reflect the degree to which you need to acquire certain competencies. For example, suppose you expect to be employed as an elementary school counselor and you consider that you need more experience in classroom management. If so, then this is a high priority and you will need short-term goals to improve in this area soon. Completing this self-assessment will also give some points to consider when preparing to apply and interview for a counseling position. Interviewees will certainly wish to highlight their strong points and to acknowledge a plan to address relative weaknesses. For example, in completing an application or during an interview, prospective employees are often asked what they consider to be their strengths for the job and what they believe are weaknesses. The self-assessment provides an informed position from which you can confidently respond.

TABLE 14.3   Self-Assessment of School Counselor Attitudes and Values

School Counselor Attitudes and Values	Self-Rating		
The degree to which you believe:	Low		High
Every student can learn and succeed	1 2 3 4 5		
Every student should have access to and opportunity for a high-quality education	1 2 3 4 5		
Every student should graduate from high school and be prepared for employment or college	1 2 3 4 5		
Every student should have access to a school counseling program	1 2 3 4 5		
Effective school counseling is a collaborative process	1 2 3 4 5		
School counselors can and should be leaders in the school and district	1 2 3 4 5		
The effectiveness of school counseling programs should be measurable using process, perception, and results data	1 2 3 4 5		
School counseling is an organized program for every student and not a series of services provided only to students in need	1 2 3 4 5		
School counseling programs should be an integral component of student success and the overall mission of schools and school districts	1 2 3 4 5		
School counseling programs promote and support academic achievement, personal and social development, and career planning for every student	1 2 3 4 5		
School counselors operate within a framework of school and district policies, state laws and regulations, and professional ethics standards	1 2 3 4 5		
School counseling is one component in the continuum of care that should be available to all students	1 2 3 4 5		
School counselors coordinate and facilitate counseling and other services to ensure all students receive the care they need, even though school counselors may not personally provide the care themselves	1 2 3 4 5		
School counselors engage in developmental counseling and short-term responsive counseling	1 2 3 4 5		
School counselors should refer students to district or community resources to meet more extensive needs such as long-term therapy or diagnoses of disorders	1 2 3 4 5		
A school counseling program and guidance department must be managed like other programs and departments in a school	1 2 3 4 5		
One of the critical responsibilities of a school counselor is to plan, organize, implement, and evaluate a school counseling program	1 2 3 4 5		
Management of a school counseling program must be done in collaboration with administrators	1 2 3 4 5		
School counseling programs should achieve demonstrable results	1 2 3 4 5		
School counselors should be accountable for the results of the school counseling program	1 2 3 4 5		
School counselors should use quantitative and qualitative data to evaluate their school counseling program and to demonstrate program results	1 2 3 4 5		
The results of the school counseling program should be analyzed and presented in the context of the overall school and district performance	1 2 3 4 5		

values that the ASCA has identified in its School Counselor Competencies as essential to implement the ASCA National Model.

Application Process

Searching for a job as a professional school counselor can be a daunting process. The following are a few tips to assist you with this journey.

Searching and Applying for Job Openings

- *Use technology to accelerate the search.* As the old commercial said, "Let your fingers do the walking." Use the Internet to research all of the school systems where you wish to apply. Go to the human resources link at their Web sites and complete the online application. You will find that almost all school systems now prefer applicants to submit electronic applications. Even though surrounding area school systems may not currently have a school counseling position posted, you should complete an application for each of your desired locations anyway. You will soon learn that school principals know of their staff vacancies long before they are announced and generally begin a search to fill the opening long before the position is officially posted. Therefore, it is better to have your application on file for principals to review as soon as they begin their search.
- *Proofread online applications.* A word of caution: It would be prudent for you to complete a hard copy of the application before you enter it online. Before you hit the "submit" key, you should make a copy of your online application and proofread it. Proper grammar and spelling are essential.
- *Attend monthly meetings of the local counselor association.* You should attend these meetings, especially during your clinical experiences. It is here that you will develop your professional network and hear of potential job openings. This will give you advance notice to begin developing your strategy for applying. You can "pick the brains" of your new colleagues to assess the counseling needs of the schools where vacancies will be. You can begin to shape your application and start to prepare for the interview for those schools.
- *Request letters of recommendation.* Ask professors who know the quality of your work best, especially internship and practicum professors, as well as your school site supervisors to write a recommendation. Give them something in writing that describes some points about yourself and some activities you conducted well at your sites. Express your passion for school counseling, but do not use too much hyperbole. You may also provide them with a list of your strengths and skills (see your self-assessment results) for them to use.
- *Prepare a portfolio.* Your professional portfolio could contain examples of your class work that is applicable to developing a school counseling program. For example, you could include a career guidance lesson plan you wrote for one of your classes. Your practicum and internship will also provide excellent opportunities to add to your portfolio. Include counseling activities, group guidance lesson plans, pictures of students, notes from people you helped, and the like. Make it well organized and visually attractive.
- *Develop a strong résumé.* Prepare a one- or two-page résumé that is concise, organized, and professional. It must present you as the outstanding candidate that you are. See Figure 14.1 for an example. E-mail it to principals who have or will have counselor positions available. You would be surprised by how many look at them.
- *Have others review your materials.* Ask your classmates, professors, site supervisors, and others to review your résumé and portfolio. They may have some great suggestions to add or other materials that will enhance your image.

ACTIVITY 14.7

Prepare or revise your résumé. Give it to three people and request written feedback. Make revisions based on this feedback. Be prepared to continue to update and revise your résumé on an ongoing basis.

William Robert Woods
46 Volunteer St.
Big Orange, TN 37830
(865) 326-3333
woodswr@utk.edu

Career Goal:
To develop a comprehensive school counseling program aligned with ASCA National Model®.

Education
The University of Tennessee-Knoxville
MS in School Counseling (2009)
GPA (4.0 Scale): 3.95
BS in Psychology (2007)
GPA (4.0 Scale): 3.825
Dean's List, Phi Beta Kappa

Professional Association Membership
American School Counselor Association
Tennessee School Counselor Association
Smoky Mountain Counseling Association

Experiences
School Counseling Practicum at Modesto Middle School, Modesto, CA
- 60 hours of providing individual counseling
- 20 hours of conducting group counseling
- 10 hours of teaching classroom guidance lessons
- 15 hours of supervision

School Counseling Internship at Excel Elementary School and at Above Average High School, Oak Ridge, TN 37830
- Completed over 600 hours
- Counseled students individually and in small groups
- Consulted with teachers and parents
- Collaborated in IEP & RTI meetings and parent–teacher conferences
- Taught classroom guidance lessons

Volunteer at GREAT KIDS Summer Program, High Achievers School, Oak Ridge, TN
- Worked with special needs students in small group as teacher assistant

Accomplishments
- Created a career information webpage for middle school students
- Presented research paper at Smoky Mountain Counseling Association conference, titled "Effective Use of Peer Counselors in High School"

Skills
- Computer Skills: Proficient in word processing and data management, multimedia production, webpage development
- Foreign Language Skills: Spanish

FIGURE 14.1   Sample résumé.

Preparing for an Interview

Once you have received an appointment for an interview, you want to be overprepared. Visit that school's Web site and thoroughly research it. Also, visit Web sites of the school district and the state Department of Education. Analyze the school's testing results and its No Child Left Behind status. Pay particular attention to the disaggregated data of subgroups. Ask yourself, "What can I do as a school counselor to support the academic development of *all* students in this school? What special challenges does this student population have that I as a school counselor can address?" Note any special successes this school announces on its home page. Take time to visit Web sites of teachers that are linked from the school's home page. What feelings about the school climate do you glean from these home pages, its staff and students? This information can provide you with possible issues within this school that may indicate questions that you could be asked during the interview. It could also indicate questions that you wish to raise to your interviewer.

A drop-in visit to your interview school may be a turnoff to the busy principal and staff; however, it could be beneficial for you to drive around the community the school serves. If you get a chance to talk with parents or students, you might gather information that you may be able to use during your interview (perception data). For example, what are some needs of this school's student population? What are some strengths of this teaching staff? How does (or could) the counselor contribute?

With the data you have collected about this school, you are now ready to prepare for your interview. Think about the questions that may be asked and consider your responses. Table 14.4 includes actual questions asked during a school counselor interview.

The interview process has been such an important part of the transition from training to employment that suggestions have been made to counselor educators to add this component to their training programs (Nichter & Nelson, 2006). Administrators who want a counseling program that is aligned with the ASCA National Model are seeking school counselors who can deliver such a program and are receiving suggestions on interview questions to ask (Meyers, 2006). They can visit the ASCA Web site where they will find a link tab especially for "Administrators" and a link called "Interviewing School Counselors." As a counselor applicant you may wish to review these questions as well.

TABLE 14.4   School Counselor Interview Questions

1. Tell us about yourself—what experiences have prepared you for the position of professional school counselor?
2. Explain the national standards in school counseling and how you would use them to plan your counseling program.
3. Talk about how you would develop our classroom guidance program.
4. How will you establish relationships with outside school resources?
5. Tell us about a small group counseling series you have conducted.
6. Our population is unique—what strengths do you have to work with our students and their families?
7. We have kindergartners who cry every day for weeks into the school year. How would you help beginning kindergartners and parents adjust to school?
8. Tell us how you would help a teacher who is highly frustrated and feeling overwhelmed with the behavior of a student.
9. What are some of the best practices in school counseling you have come across?
10. How can you help us analyze and interpret test data to guide our instruction and curriculum decisions?
11. As a school counselor, how would you facilitate parent involvement in our school and in our classrooms?
12. How would you use technology as part of your counseling program?
13. What do you love about school counseling?
14. How would you show that what you are doing is effective?
15. Do you have any questions for us?

ACTIVITY 14.8

After you have considered other questions that may be asked and you have considered your responses, role-play an interview with your peers. They may have other questions and suggestions on how to respond. While practice may not make you "perfect," in this instance practice will certainly help you fill gaps and build your confidence.

A final consideration before you go to your interview is to find out your status in obtaining your credentials as a professional school counselor. The principal will likely ask when you will obtain your license. If you need this information, ask your faculty advisor. You may be a bit nervous, but once you are in the interview and you have responded to the first question, you will grow confident because of your methodical preparation.

The Interview

The following are some tips on conducting yourself during the interview. By now you are fully prepared, and you want to make an outstanding impression that will remain with interview committee members long after you have departed the meeting.

- *Dress appropriately.* Business professional is considered clothing du jour.
- *Arrive early for your interview.* You might have an opportunity to chat with staff members before you go into the interview room.
- *Have several copies of your résumé printed on quality paper.* An intern who interviewed for a job made a good impression when she was able to distribute a copy of her résumé to each committee member after they realized that they did not have one (L. Marlar, personal communication, December 19, 2008).
- *Bring an attractive portfolio.* Have it available to show illustrations of your work during your training. For example, in response to a question, you might mention that you have an example in your portfolio of something similar you did during your practicum and internship. Or, you may also provide a link to your electronic portfolio.
- *Remember to use good nonverbal skills.* Lean forward slightly and maintain good eye contact with each committee member when answering each question. Do not just focus on one person or the committee member asking the question. This shows confidence.
- *Speak clearly and confidently.* Use a strong voice that reflects your assurance in what you say. Talk at your normal pace to show comfort and command of the comprehensive school counseling program.
- *Answer the questions directly and succinctly.* Principals like interviewees to keep their answers to the point. However, you want to ensure that you demonstrate sufficient knowledge and enthusiasm for school counseling.
- *Relax and believe in yourself.* Rely upon your training in human relationships and your preparation. You will do well.

Professional Credentials

Professional credentials are required at the state and district level to be employed to practice school counseling. They are also a way of promoting professional identity and of demonstrating a higher level of counseling competency. Three areas of professional identity are presented in this chapter: (1) the basic requirements for employment, (2) ways to continue professional development, and (3) paths to obtain national credentials.

Qualifications Vary by State

Requirements for credentialing professional school counselors differ from state to state. Some states issue a license to practice school counseling, while other states issue a certificate. In addition, states change their criteria for issuing credentials from time to time. You likely already know the qualifications to practice as a school counselor in the state in which you are receiving your training, but if you wish to apply for a school counseling position in another state, you will need to know the requirements in that state as well. Some states have a reciprocity agreement with neighboring states to allow a counselor with credentials in one state to practice in another state. Another resource is the ASCA home page (www.schoolcounselor.org) where you can search at the "State Certification Requirements" link or call the ASCA at 1-800-306-4722 if you need further assistance. A state-by-state description of requirements and a link to the Department of Education of each state will have more specific information.

The Praxis II

Most states require passing the Praxis II® for School Guidance and Counseling in order to earn licensure or certification. The Praxis Series™ Exams are developed and administered by the Educational Testing Service (ETS). The Praxis II has 120 multiple-choice questions that cover content such as counseling and guidance, consulting, coordinating, and professional issues. Forty of the 120 will be questions in which you will be asked to select the best counselor response to recordings of client statements. Ask your faculty advisor or contact your state Department of Education to determine which tests are required and what is considered a passing score. To register for the Praxis Series, go to its Web site at www.ets.org/praxis/, or call ETS at 1-800-772-9476 or 1-609-771-7395. You can purchase study guides from ETS to help you prepare for the exams.

Continuing Education Requirements

Once you obtain your state certificate or license, you will be required to renew it periodically. Each state has a specific time frame in which school counselors and teachers must apply for renewal of their credentials. For example, California issues a certificate that must be renewed every 5 years, while some states like Tennessee require its school counselors to renew their license every 10 years.

To renew state credentials, you must document the successful completion of a given amount of continuing education activities. This continuing education requirement could be called continuing education units (CEUs), professional development, in-service education, professional growth activities, or accredited institution credits. Ongoing professional training may be in-service programs hosted by your school district or it could include professional conferences held by your local, state, or national counseling association. The amount and type of continuing education you must complete within the given period varies from state to state. Check with your state department of education or your school district's human resources director for the specific requirements of recredentialing. On its Web site, the ASCA has a general overview of each state's requirements and contact information.

National Credentials

Once you have fulfilled the requirements for certification at the state level, you may wish to seek additional credentials. There are two organizations at the national level where you can obtain additional credentials: the National Board of Certified Counselors, Inc., and the National Board of Professional Teaching Standards®. The benefits of national certification are threefold: By participating in the certification process you will be acknowledged for your competencies and accomplishments as a nationally certificated counselor, you will be elevating your professional identity which could be important to your building principal and your community stakeholders, and you may receive financial incentives from your state and local school board.

National Certified School Counselor

The National Board for Certified Counselors, Inc. (NBCC), was founded in 1982 to develop an examination of counseling competencies for practitioners to obtain national certification. In the late 1980s, working with the American School Counselor Association and the American Counseling Association, the NBCC developed specialty credentials for school counselors called the National Certified School Counselor (NCSC). In 1991, the first school counselor was awarded the NCSC; by March 2009 more than 2,000 counselors had received their NCSC credentials.

The application process involves documenting master's-level training, 3 years of postgraduate counseling supervision and experience as a school counselor in a pre-K–12 setting, and obtaining a passing score on the National Certified School Counselor Examination (NCSCE). The NCSCE format includes seven simulated counseling cases and 40 multiple-choice questions. The exam covers the following content areas: school counseling program delivery, assessment and career development, program administration and professional development, counseling process, concepts and applications, and family–school involvements. Although there is not a study guide for the NCSCE, you can receive more information about the NCSC application process and the NCSCE test by visiting the NBCC Web site at www.nbcc.org/.

National Certified Counselor (NCC) is the basic certification for all NBCC specialty areas, such as the NCSC. NBCC provides school counselors with the opportunity to earn two credentials with a single exam and application process. For counselors who do not hold NCC credentials, NBCC offers a combination NCC/NCSC application. By completing this combined process for the NCSC, counselors cover two credentials: NCC and NCSC. Counselors who already hold NCC credentials can apply for NCSC certification (P. Leary, personal communication, March 13, 2009).

These certifications are issued for a period of 5 years, during which you must complete 100 clock hours of counseling-related continuing education, 25 of which must be in the area of school counseling. Check the NCC Web site for current costs of exams and annual maintenance fees.

As of 2009, five states (Mississippi, Louisiana, Nevada, West Virginia, and Delaware) provide financial incentives to NCSC-certified counselors. In addition, some local school districts, primarily in Georgia and Indiana, award salary supplements to school counselors with NCSC certification. Massachusetts honors NCC credentials for school counselors upgrading from initial to professional school counselor licensure credentials (P. Leary, personal communication, December 30, 2008). For more information about NCC/NCSC advantages and the application process, visit the NBCC Web site (http://www.nbcc.org/) or call 1-336-547-0607.

National Board for Professional Teaching Standards

Founded in 1987, the National Board for Professional Teaching Standards (NBPTS) is dedicated to advancing quality instruction by recognizing teachers, school counselors, and others who distinguish themselves through accomplishing certain performance standards. There are 11 standards in which school counselors must show evidence of meeting. They are school counseling programs; school counseling and student competencies; human growth and development; counseling theories and techniques; equity, fairness, and diversity; school climate; collaboration with family and community; informational resources and technology; student assessment; leadership, advocacy, and professional identity; and reflective practice. These are very similar to the School Counselor Competencies as identified by the ASCA.

In 1993, the first teacher earned National Board Certified Teacher® status and, in 2004, a school counselor was awarded national credentials from NBPTS. As of December 2007, there were 1,224 accomplished school counselors with NBPTS certification.

Applicants for NBPTS must hold a state school counselor certificate and have practiced school counseling for 3 years. Interestingly, they do not need to have a master's degree. The application process for NBPTS involves a performance-based assessment with two key components: a portfolio of counseling practice and an examination of counseling knowledge. The portfolio includes student work, video recordings, and other counseling examples. An illustration of a required portfolio entry reads: "You will video record a whole class engaged in a career development lesson. You will complete a written commentary that describes the lesson and student reactions as they relate to the lesson and that analyzes and reflects on the lesson" (National Board for Professional Teaching Standards, 2008, p. 7).

NBPTS certification for accomplished school counselors is for a 10-year period. Check the NBPTS Web site (www.nbpts.org) for current application and recertification fees. There is no annual fee to maintain the certification, but the Profile of Professional Growth must be completed within the 10-year period. The Profile of Professional Growth documents the three areas of continuing education that accomplished school counselors have completed. The recertification process involves a video recording of performance.

All 50 states offer some financial incentives to offset the application costs involved in the NBPTS certification process; however, those funds are limited. Each state has specific guidelines and deadlines, so counselors seeking to request these funds to help with the cost of NBPTS certification should contact their respective state Department of Education as soon as possible. Approximately 34 states provide some form of salary supplements to NBPTS-certified school counselors. An increasing number of local school districts are electing to provide increased pay to accomplished school counselors certified by NBPTS. You should check with your local human resource director and your state's Department of Education for details before you begin the application process. For more information about the application process and possible financial support available to assist with the application costs, visit the NBPTS Web site at (www.nbpts.org) or call 1-800-228-3224.

Comparison of NCC/NCSC and NBPTS

Both the NCC and the NBPTS offer opportunities for school counselors to grow professionally and to be acknowledged by demonstrating competencies beyond state credentialing requirements. Both afford school counselors a higher level of professionalism when they earn national credentials, and both require additional assessment of knowledge and skill in implementing comprehensive school counseling programs (Milsom & Akos, 2007).

Each approach has advantages and limitations as you can see in Table 14.5. Should you prepare yourself to earn national certification? If so, which path to national certification should you choose? Both require 3 years of experience before one can obtain national certification, which gives

TABLE 14.5   NCC/NCSC versus NBPTS

	NCC/NCSC	NBPTS
Educational requirement	MS	BS with state license
Supervision experience requirement	100 hours over 3 years	3 years
Written examination	Yes	Yes
Portfolio of work	No	Yes
Period of certification	5 years	10 years
Required continuing education	100 clock hours	Complete Profile of Professional Growth
Salary supplements	5 states	34 states
Number school counselors certified at time of publication	2,244	1,514

a beginning counselor ample time to prepare for the rigors of an evaluation based upon national standards. The NBPTS assessment is heavily weighted in performance and written measures, whereas the NCC/NCSC is rooted in a multiple-choice examination. Although NBPTS is initially more expensive, limited financial assistance is available from some local districts, state Departments of Education, and national resources.

It is believed that pursuing either one or both certifications will make one a better school counselor (Milsom & Akos, 2007). Nationally certified counselors are perceived as more professional and competent, and they are likely to be more respected by their principals. This typically means more support for their counseling programs. The bottom line is that a growing number of states and local school districts are providing additional compensation to nationally certified teachers and counselors.

Membership in Professional Organizations

As you complete your final preparations to become a professional school counselor, it would be prudent for you to consider membership in professional organizations. Associating with other counselors will help you to maintain your enthusiasm and your passion for your work, and it will offer you opportunities to engage in professional activities and resources specific to the field (Bauman, 2008).

The American School Counselor Association (ASCA) is the American Counseling Association (ACA) counselor division that supports and advocates for school counselors; however, only one in nine school counselors belong to ASCA (Hatch, 2008). This is unfortunate because many school counselors are missing out on the personal and professional growth activities that the ASCA promotes through its many workshops and conferences, and the tremendous resources available to members only at its Web site (www.schoolcounselor.org). The following links contain professional materials and information members can access at the ASCA Web site:

- *ASCA Resource Center* contains links, publications, sample articles, sample documents, and journal articles on almost 50 topics ranging from abuse to war/deployment.
- *ASCA Legal & Ethical* includes ASCA's Ethical Standards for School Counselors, journal archives on legal and ethical issues, and a forum where members can submit ethical questions.
- *Publications* enables members to search the archives of ASCA publications such as *Professional School Counseling, ASCA School Counselor,* and *ASCA Aspects.*
- *Professional Development* provides a comprehensive listing of state conferences, site-based training, upcoming conferences, and training opportunities on the ASCA National Model.
- *Online Store* offers professional books and materials at discounted prices to members.
- *ASCA National Model* gives detailed information about the four quadrants of the model and how to become involved in the Ramp Program.
- *ASCA Scene* is a social networking site that gives school counselors a method to connect and to communicate using blogs, discussion forms, and the like. This is an excellent service for soliciting suggestions to issues and concerns school counselors typically face.
- *ASCAway* is a podcast service providing members with information about school counseling issues, trends, and interviews. You can hear relevant information presented in a timely and portable manner.
- *Press: Position Statements* is a popular link that provides ASCA positions on a variety of issues important to professional school counselors. You receive the benefit of knowledge and expertise from others by reviewing these position statements. This link is open to the public.

The ACA is the umbrella organization dedicated to promoting counseling as a profession. Its mission is more global and its scope is broader than the ASCA, but the ACA still provides a very useful service to school counselors. There are additional resources the ACA provides that are of mutual interest to school counselors that can be accessed on the ACA Web site (www.counseling.org):

- *Resources: Ethics* provides ethics and professional standards services and promotes ACA online learning opportunities to receive continuing professional education.
- *Publications* allows ACA members to search articles among its publications. This tool is valuable when a counselor needs to find critical information in a timely manner.
- *Counseling Corner* provides special-interest documents on mental health issues that school counselors may find useful to share with teachers, parents, and others who are challenged.

As education reformers rapidly revise the educational landscape on which school counselors must tread, it is important to be astute for proposed changes. The combined numbers of school counselors and other counseling professionals can have an impact on state laws and regulations that affect our counseling practice and professional image. It would be important for beginning school counselors to join forces with others to provide new approaches and fresh energy to association work. Collaboration with counseling colleagues can be highly rewarding work for new school counselors who wish to use their leadership and advocacy skills to make a difference on a larger scale.

Conclusion

This chapter began with a few suggestions on how to conclude your counseling and collaborating work at your clinical school sites in a manner that is both personal and professional. Taking a little extra time to plan positive closure activities with students and staff will not only help establish effective future behavior patterns, it will enhance your professional reputation as well.

As you prepare to leave your counselor training program and begin the transition into the world of a professional school counselor, you will want to improve your emerging knowledge and skills. Use the self-assessments provided in this chapter to annually monitor your professional development in order to focus on your career goals and provide reassurance in what you do.

Be mindful of your identity as a professional school counselor. You possess unique knowledge and skills that are greatly needed in schools today. The vision you have for developing a comprehensive school counseling program requires the support of significant others in your school, community, and state, but you will want to follow the advice of the Chinese philosopher Lao-tzu who wisely stated, "The journey of a thousand miles begins beneath your feet." Build your school's counseling program component by component, and let data guide your journey.

This is the best time in history to be a well-trained and prepared school counselor. Whether you are hired in an elementary school, a middle school, or a high school, challenging and rewarding work awaits you there. What better calling can there be than to have a dream to build a comprehensive school counseling program and to have the abilities to design and deliver it for our nation's future generation?

Web Sites

- This article from *U.S. News and World Report* lists nine ways to ruin a job interview: http://www.usnews.com/blogs/outside-voices-careers/2008/12/22/9-ways-to-ruin-a-job-interview.html
- Microsoft Office Online provides various templates that you can use to build your résumé: http://office.microsoft.com/en-us/templates/CT101448941033.aspx

References

American School Counselor Association (ASCA). (2005). *ASCA national model: A framework for school counseling programs.* Alexandria, VA: Author.

American School Counselor Association (ASCA). (2008). School counselor competencies. *ASCA School Counselor, 45*(4), 64–73.

Bauman, B. (2008). To join or not to join: School counselors as a case study in professional membership. *Journal of Counseling & Development, 86,* 164–177.

Hatch, T. (2008). School counselor beliefs about ASCA national model school counseling program components using the SCPCS. *Professional School Counseling, 12,* 34–42.

Lambie, G. E., & Williamson, L. L. (2004). The challenge to change from guidance counseling to professional school counseling: A historical proposition. *Professional School Counseling, 8,* 124–131.

Meyers, P. (2006). Finding the perfect match. *ASCA School Counselor, 44*(1), 31–32.

Milsom, A., & Akos, P. (2007). National certification: Evidence of a professional school counselor? *Professional School Counseling, 10,* 346–351.

National Board for Professional Teaching Standards. (2008). *Scoring guide: School counseling/ early childhood through young adult.* Retrieved December 21, 2008, from http://www.nbpts. org/for_candidates/certificate_areas1?ID=20&x=53&y=11

Nichter, M., & Nelson, J. (2006). Educating administrators. *ASCA School Counselor, 44*(2), 15–20.

Index

Absences/tardiness, 48–49
Action plans, 116–117
Administrators, school
    closure with when leaving practicums/
        internships, 208, 209
    relationship building with, 21
Adolescent egocentrism, 196
Alcohol abuse, 196, 198
American Counseling Association
    Code of Ethics, 52. *See also* Ethics
    ethical decision-making models, 148–151
American School Counselor Association
    Ethical Standards, 149, 151, 153–154, 156. *See
        also* Ethics
    goals of, 4
    leadership, 209–210
    National Model. *See* ASCA National Model
    role in policy shaping, 3
Application process for school counselors, 214–215
Art therapy, 39–40
ASCA National Model, 54
    Accountability System component, 82, 112,
        133–134
    benefits of, 80, 81, 83, 93
    comprehensive school counseling (CDSC)
        program. *See* Comprehensive school
        counseling (CDSC) program
    Delivery System component, 82, 91, 119, 131
    Foundation component, 82, 95–96, 104, 105
    historical overview, 79–80
    Management System component, 82, 107, 117
    National Standards, relationship to, 79, 81
    performance standards, 83–84
    personal values, 96, 98
    philosophy of school counseling, 98–100
    professional development, 129–1230
    professional values, 96, 98
    public relations aspect, 115–116
    standards and competencies, 100, 101–104*t*, 214
Assessment instruments, 143
Assessment techniques (students)
    experimental action research, 139
    MEASURE program, 140
    pretest-posttest assessment, 135
    retrospective assessment, 137–138
    surveys, 136–137
Assessment techniques (supervisees)
    peer assessment, 140–141
    portfolio, 142
    self-assessment, 141
    student assessment, 141

Asthma, students with, 192
At-risk students, 81–82, 199
Attention-deficit hyperactivity disorder, 192–193
Autism, students with, 192

Biological development issues
    ADHD, 192–193
    asthma, 192
    autism, 192
    obesity, childhood, 191–192
    overview, 191
    puberty, 195–196
    stress, 195
Bullying, 16

Children of alcoholics, 37
Choice therapy, 33–34
Classroom management, 120, 121–122
Clinical experience, 4
Cognitive development, 193–194, 196
Cognitive therapy (CT), 35–36
Cognitive-behavioral counseling, overview, 35–36
Communication
    prompt, 18
    stakeholders, with, 18–19
    technology, via. *See* Technology
Community agencies, 28
Comprehensive school counseling (CDSC) program
    prototype, 80
    standards and competencies, 100, 101–104*t*
    summary, 81
Conceptualization skills, 66
Confidentiality, 151
Consent forms, 10
Consultations, 130–131
Continuing education requirements, 219
Cornell method of note taking, 123
Council for the Accreditation and Related
        Educational Programs (CACREP)
    internship accreditation, 4
    practicum accreditation, 4
    role of, 4
Counselor identity, 3–4
Counselors, school
    attitude, positive, 8
    communication. *See* Communication
    counseling professionals, interacting with, 26
    payment for trainees, 8
    responsibilities, division of, 17–18

responsibilities, negotiating, 18
school personnel, interacting with, 26–28
teaching experience *versus* no teaching experience, 20
Creative counseling approaches. *See* specific therapies
Credentials, professional
　continuing education requirements, 219
　national credentials, 219–220
　overview, 218
　PRAXIS II, 219
　state variations, 219
Crisis counseling, 127–128
Culture, school. *See* School culture
Custodians, school, 27

Depression, 196, 198
Development theories
　biopsychosocial framework, 190
　learning theory, 185
　overview, 180
　psychodynamic theory, 180
　systems theories, 188–189
Developmental issues, student
　biological development of children. *See* Biological development issues
　cognitive development, 193–194, 196
　cognitive theories, 187, 188
　continuity *versus* discontinuity, 179–180
　development theories. *See* Development theories
　identity, development of, 199–200
　independence, establishing, 199
　moral development, 189, 190
　nature *versus* nurture debate, 179
　normative influences, 180
　parent/guardian influences, 186–187
　psychosocial development, 194–195, 199–200
　social influences, 186–187
　universal *versus* context-specific development, 180
Developmental models of supervision, 61
　autonomy, 63, 64
　conflict, 63
　integration, 64–65
　motivation, 62, 64
　other-awareness, 62, 63, 64
　overview, 62
　self-awareness, 62, 63, 64
Discipline, school counselor's role in, 16
Discrimination model of supervision, 66
Diversity. *See* Multiculturalism
Drug abuse, 196, 198

Ellis, Albert, 35
Enumerative data. *See* Process data
Epston, David, 37
Erikson, Erik, 180, 181*t*

Erikson, Milton, 36
Ethical decision-making models
　actions, potential, 150
　applying ASCA ethical standards, 149
　consequences of actions, measuring, 150
　identifying the problem, 149
　implementing actions, 150–151
　measuring the problem, 149
Ethics
　ASCA Standards, 149
　autonomy, 147
　beneficence, 148
　colleagues, responsibilities to, 154
　confidentiality. *See* Confidentiality
　decision making. *See* Ethical decision-making models
　dual relationships, avoiding, 72–73, 151
　fidelity, 148
　justice, 147–148
　nonmaleficence, 148
　principles, 147–148
　privacy. *See* Privacy
　profession, responsibilities to, 156
　school, responsibilities to, 154, 156
　self, responsibilities to, 156
　sexual relationships in supervision, 73
　students, responsibilities to, 151, 153–154
　veracity, 148
Evaluations, 69. *See also* Assessment techniques (supervisees)
Experimental action research, 139

Federal Education Rights and Privacy Act (FERPA), 9

Gay students. *See* LGBTQ students
Gifted students, 168–172
Glasser, William, 33–34
Group advisement, 67
Group counseling, 206, 207
Guidance curriculum
　advisement, 126
　appraisal, individual student, 125
　classroom management, 120, 121–122
　lesson plan development, 119–120
　overview, 119
　placement/follow-up, 126
　study skills, 123–124
　test questions, 124

Health Insurance Portability and Accountability Act (HIPAA), 9

Identity confusion, 199
Individualized Education Plan (IEP), 134, 193

Individuals with Disabilities Act (IDEA), 125, 167–168
Integrated models of supervision. *See* Social role models of supervision
Internship
    class size, 6
    closure with administrators, 208, 209
    closure with colleagues, 208
    closure with students, 205, 206
    contract sample, 55*f*
    practicum, *versus,* 4
    purpose of, 52
Intervention skills, 66
Interviewing for a school counseling job, 217
Invincibility fable, 196
IQ testing, 193

Kohlberg, Lawrence, 189, 190

Learning theory, 185
Lesbian students. *See* LGBTQ students
LGBTQ students
    legal issues related to, 173–174
    overview, 172–173
    terminology in the community, 174*t*
Likert scale, 134

Management agreements, 110
MEASURE program, 140
Memory aids, 123
Mission statements, 100
Moral reasoning, development of, 189, 190
Multiculturalism
    competence in handling, assessment of, 161–162
    cultures, 165, 167
    ethnicities, 165, 167
    gifted students. *See* Gifted students
    LGBT/queer students. *See* LGBTQ students
    overview, 161
    person-centered counseling, use of, 33
    School Counselor Multicultural Competence Checklist, 163–164*t*
    school profiles, 165
    special needs students. *See* Special needs students
    supervisor-supervisee relationship, 70
Music, use in counseling, 41

Narrative therapy, overview, 37–38
National Association for Gifted Children, 169–170
National Board of Certified Counselors, Inc., 219, 220
National Board of Professional Teaching Standards, 219, 220–221
Nature *versus* nurture debate, 179

Needs assessment, 114
No Child Left Behind (NCLB)
    counselors, implications for, 16–17
Nurses, school, 26–27

Obesity, childhood, 191–192
Offices, school counselor, 107, 108
Organizational charts, school, 108, 110

Parallel process, 71
Parents/guardians
    relationship building with, 24–25
    responsibilities to, 153–154
Peer facilitation programs, 128–129
Perception data, 112
Person-centered counseling
    multicultural settings, use in, 33
    overview, 32–33
Personal fable, 196
Piaget, Jean, 187, 188*t,* 189
Play therapy, 40–41
Practicum
    closure with administrators, 208, 209
    closure with colleagues, 208
    closure with students, 205, 206
    internship, *versus,* 4
    purpose of, 8, 52
    supervision aspects of, 6
PRAXIS II, 219
Premack principle, 121
Privacy issues, 9
Process data, 112
Professional disclosure statements, 10, 50–51
Professional dress, 47–48
Professional organizations, 222–223
Profile, school, 165
Program supervisor, 6
Psychodynamic theory, 180
Psychologists, school, 27
Psychosocial development, 194–195, 199–200

Rational emotive behavior therapy (REBT), 35
Reality therapy, 33–34
Rebellion, adolescent, 199
Reframing technique, 24–25
Results data, 114
Resume, sample, 216*f*
Rogers, Carl, 32

Safe school initiatives, 16. *See also* Security
Safety plan, personal, 56
School board
    policies, 21
    relationship building, 20–21
School counselor supervision model (SCSM), 67

School counselors
    importance of, 81–82
    management agreements for, 110
    professional development, 129–130
    teamwork, 130–131
School culture
    defining, 15
    discipline. *See* Discipline
    healthy, indicators of, 15
    overview, 15–16
    responsibilities, division of, 17–18
    safe school initiatives, 16
School environment (physical), 197–198
School improvement plans, 17
School nurses, 26–27
School policies, 49
School profile, 165
School social workers, 26
Security
    high-crime-area schools, 56
    personal safety plan, 56
    resource officers, 27–28
Self-assessment, 141
    overview, 209–210
    school counselor knowledge, of, 210, 211
    school counselor skills, of, 212
    school counselor values, of, 213–214
Sexual activity among teens, 196, 198
Sexual relationships in supervision, 73
Site supervisor, 6
    initial contact with, 47–48
Small group counseling, 127
Social comparison, 194–195
Social role boundaries, 73
Social role models of supervision, 61–62, 66
    discrimination model, 66
    overview, 65
Solution-focused brief counseling, 36–37
Special needs students
    class sizes, 19
    computer use by, 58–59
    counselors' roles with, 19
    historical treatment of, 167
    IDEA accommodations, 125, 167–168
Stress, 56–57, 195–196
Students
    assessment techniques. *See* Assessment
        techniques (students)
    relationship building with, 23–24
    responsibilities to, 151, 153–154
Suicide, 196, 198–199
Supervisees. *See also* Supervisors
    absences/tardiness, 4849
    anxiety, 70–71
    professional dress, 47–48
    resistance behaviors, 71
    safety plan, personal, 56

Supervision
    contracts, 7
    definition, 6
    evaluations, 7–8
    goal setting, 53–54
    group, 8
    introductions to students, staff, and parents, 49, 51
    overview, 6–8
    resistance to, 71
    roles. *See* Supervision roles
    school counseling programs, accredited, 73
    school site, choosing, 10
    self-reflection regarding, 52
    supervisors, choosing. *See* Supervisors
    taping session. *See* Taping counseling sessions
Supervision roles
    developmental models of. *See* Developmental
        models of supervision
    overview, 61–62
    school counselor supervision model (SCSM), 67
    social role models of supervision. *See* Social role
        models of supervision
    training, 61
Supervisors. *See also* Supervisees; Supervision roles
    choosing, 11–12
    dual roles, avoiding, 72–73
    individual differences with supervisee, 69
    multiculturalism in relationship with supervisee, 70
    working alliance with supervisee, 69
Systems theories of development, 188–189

T-note system, 123
Taping counseling sessions
    confidentiality issues, 9
    equipment, 8–9
    privacy issues, 9
Teachers, relationship building with, 22–23
Technology
    communicating with parents via, 25
    computer use, 58–59
    taping counseling sessions. *See* Taping
        counseling sessions
Testing, counselors' roles in, 19
Time management for school counselors, 111, 113*t*
Transforming School Counseling Initiative, 98

Values, defining, 96
Vygotsky, Lev, 188

WDEP system, 34
White, Michael, 37

Zero-tolerance policies, 16

EDUCATIONAL RESOURCE CENTER
COLLEGE OF EDUCATION & HUMAN SERVICES
WRIGHT STATE UNIVERSITY